D0458708

05/12 ⑤

THE ESCAPE ARTISTS

How Obama's Team Fumbled the Recovery

NOAM SCHEIBER

SIMON & SCHUSTER

NEW YORK   LONDON   TORONTO   SYDNEY   NEW DELHI

Simon & Schuster
1230 Avenue of the Americas
New York, NY 10020

First Simon & Schuster hardcover edition February 2012

SIMON & SCHUSTER and colophon are
registered trademarks of Simon & Schuster, Inc.

For information about special discounts for bulk purchases,
please contact Simon & Schuster Special Sales at
1-866-506-1949 or business@simonandschuster.com.

The Simon & Schuster Speakers Bureau can bring authors to your live event.
For more information or to book an event contact the Simon & Schuster Speakers
Bureau at 1-866-248-3049 or visit our website at www.simonspeakers.com.

Designed by Ruth Lee-Mui

Manufactured in the United States of America

10 9 8 7 6 5 4 3 2 1

Library of Congress Cataloging-in-Publication Data

Scheiber, Noam.
   The Escape Artists / Noam Scheiber.
      p.   cm.
   Includes bibliographical references and index.
   1. United States—Economic policy—2009–   2. United States—Politics and
government—2009–   I. Title.
   HC106.84.S34   2012
   330.973—dc23   2011045693

ISBN 978-1-4391-7240-7
ISBN 978-1-4391-7242-1 (ebook)

To Amy, Finoula, and my parents

CONTENTS

PROLOGUE

Shortly after four o'clock on the afternoon of Wednesday, April 13, 2011, U.S. Treasury Secretary Tim Geithner walked down the hall from his office toward a large conference room facing the building's interior. He was surrounded by a retinue of counselors and aides. When they arrived in the room—known around Treasury simply as "the large"—four people were seated at a long walnut table on the side near the door. Geithner and his entourage greeted them, then walked around to the far side and took their seats.

At first glance, Geithner gave the impression of the former Wall Street banker many Americans assumed him to be. He wore elegant suits and alpha-male ties. His spread collars suggested a Savile Row provenance. But, given a moment to focus, the eye noticed hints of something else. His shoes were a bit shabby. On his wrist he wore an old digital watch. The suit, upon closer inspection, was Brooks

Brothers—off the rack. It had only seemed nattier because he was well-proportioned and boyishly trim. Geithner wasn't an ex-banker after all. He was a lifelong bureaucrat.

This status gave him a measure of independence of which he was rightly proud. While friends and former co-workers moved seamlessly from government to business and back, Geithner had resisted the easy payday time and time again. "I never worked on Wall Street," he told a group of congressional Democrats in early 2009. "I've worked in public service my whole life." Where others might be cowed in the presence of bankers, knowing they might soon petition the lords of finance for a sinecure, Geithner could have fun at their expense. As an assistant secretary in the late 1990s, he had once met a delegation from Goldman Sachs to discuss an obscure business matter. "Well, this is a fucking ugly issue, isn't it?" he said, before anyone else had uttered a word. The Goldman men laughed nervously.

But if Geithner's actions were independent, his mind was perhaps less so. As a government official, Geithner cared deeply about the constituents he consulted with, be they Wall Street big shots, financial technocrats, or market pundits. They were the people with whom a successful bureaucrat must have credibility, and there were few thoughts more mortifying to Geithner than looking unsophisticated in their eyes. He labored over draft after draft of his speeches and parsed every word of his op-eds. Back in December 2008, while Geithner was preparing for his Senate confirmation hearing, an aide asked if his family would attend. "Money will not be daunted by that," he said, waving off the suggestion. "Money" was an allusion to Wall Street and the people whose judgments Wall Street respected. He was keen to make a good impression.

By contrast, Geithner was decidedly less taken with those whose views he considered naive. And this explained his impatience with the group he was meeting today. The four visitors hailed from Standard & Poor's, the credit rating agency. They had come to voice their concern about the U.S. budget deficit, which was darkening their mood about the creditworthiness of the United States.

It turned out that S&P and its ilk were a species that "money" held in exceedingly low regard. Long before the financial crisis of 2008, Wall Street had derided the rating agencies as hubs for intellectual mediocrities—the clock punchers that banks and hedge funds had passed over. Then, in the bubble years, the big banks' financial engineers became expert at duping the agencies into blessing their dodgy mortgage securities, mostly by burying the agencies' leaden-eyed analysts in self-justifying math.[1] After the securities turned toxic and the agencies were justly vilified, their pleas of ignorance sounded all too plausible. Many of the S&P analysts weren't even based in New York. One of the men tasked with rating the trillions of dollars in U.S. government debt worked from an office in . . . *Toronto.*

Now Geithner spoke to the credit raters with thinly concealed skepticism. A few days before the meeting, S&P had warned Treasury it intended to downgrade its "outlook" on U.S. bonds, the first step toward withdrawing the triple-A status that stamped the bonds as essentially riskless. Geithner made clear he wasn't begging S&P to change its mind. The feeling inside Treasury was that, if S&P moved ahead with this decision, the company would embarrass only itself and not the U.S. government. In this vein, Geithner simply informed the visitors that his country's economic performance had exceeded expectations on almost every measure S&P claimed to care about. As for the one where it lagged—the deficit—Geithner pointed out that the president had proposed cutting this by $4 trillion that very morning.

Truth be told, Geithner might have offered these comments a bit more humbly. While the economy had indeed outperformed S&P's most recent predictions, it was still far from healthy. Some 14 million Americans were out of work, and the unemployment rate hovered above 9 percent. Millions had seen their homes foreclosed on or were in danger of defaulting on their mortgages. This was no doubt the work of the worst financial crisis in eighty years. But it was also the result of throwing too few resources at the problem. The administration's $800 billion stimulus package, while critical, had been too small to lift the economy out of its rut. Struggling homeowners never got the help they needed to crawl out from under mounds of debt. At the moment Geithner spoke, the economy was close to stalling, with growth puttering along at a mere 1 percent. About the only part of the economy that resembled its former self was the financial sector, where the traders and bankers were approaching their precrisis-level bonuses.[2] There had been plenty of resources for them.

The combination of these factors had arguably produced the worst of all worlds for the Obama administration: a country that took one look at the languishing economy and another at the recovery on Wall Street and concluded that its government had put big banks ahead of ordinary workers and homeowners. And so, a populist backlash that had initially targeted Wall Street increasingly took aim at Obama.

Generously, the S&P officials didn't point any of this out. Instead, the de facto spokesman for the group, a mustachioed fellow named David Beers, confessed that the agency was mostly concerned about the prospects for bipartisan compromise. Beers and his colleagues didn't think Republicans would take seriously the president's plan for shrinking the deficit by raising taxes and scaling back programs like Medicare and Medicaid, whatever the theoretical overlap between the two parties.

At this, Geithner became somewhat dismissive. He asked how S&P could handicap a *political* debate in Washington. It was a rating agency, after all, not a polling firm. It's not your "comparative advantage," the secretary said. Then he gestured toward the Obama officials seated on either side of him—Jack Lew, the White House budget director; Neal Wolin, the deputy Treasury secretary; Bruce

Reed, the vice president's chief of staff—and explained that all of them had been top aides to Bill Clinton during the last stand-off between a Democratic president and a Republican Congress. "We said, 'This is the way it worked in the nineties,'" recalled one administration official. "'After a big election, when you have divided government, you fight a bit, then find a middle ground.'"[3] Another recalled arguing, "When both sides had firmly committed to a goal and the public was in support of it, it eventually had to happen."[4]

The message was unmistakable: *Trust us, we've done this before.* It was, in many ways, the message the Obama economic team had been conveying to skeptics and outsiders since its earliest days in office. Now the same sentiment underlay its decision to put aside the task of creating jobs for much of 2011 and seek a grand bargain with the GOP on the deficit.

But Beers wasn't biting. Perhaps it was because he didn't work in Washington. Perhaps it was that his grasp of congressional budgeting was weak. Or that his knowledge of public opinion was crude. Whatever the case, he couldn't suppress his disbelief that a major deficit deal would be forthcoming. "We think the differences are too big," he said. "You won't be able to do it." He proved to be the wise one in the room.

THE ESCAPE ARTISTS

1

THE REUNION

Austan Goolsbee was on a campaign swing through Montana when he got a call from Obama headquarters. It was September 18, 2008, three days after the investment bank Lehman Brothers had failed, thrusting the financial world into an advanced state of panic. Hank Paulson, the Treasury secretary, was preparing a $700 billion plan to buck up the surviving banks, and Team Obama wanted to talk it over the next morning—in Florida. "Okay, great, but I'm in Helena, Montana," said Goolsbee, a thirty-nine-year-old adviser who taught at the University of Chicago. "How am I going to get to Miami by 9 am?"

By that afternoon, Goolsbee was on a flight to Salt Lake City, where he caught a connection to Las Vegas. A young staffer had turned up a red-eye from Vegas to Miami, and soon Goolsbee found himself sprinting from one side of the airport to the other so as not to miss his only chance at crossing the country overnight. When he finally stepped off the third flight the following morning, his clothes had the starchy texture of caked-on sweat. Goolsbee did what he could to freshen up, having exhausted his supply of clean clothing: he shaved off his stubble and splashed some water on his face.

Goolsbee had been Obama's top economic adviser ever since the candidate first ran for U.S. Senate in 2004, but the relationship had been something of an accident. The campaign first contacted the Harvard economics department in search of policy advice. But it had gotten precisely nowhere—the Harvard faculty wasn't exactly in the business of advising obscure midwestern state senators. Finally, one professor suggested trying someone local and passed along Goolsbee's name.

Obama had been forced to make do all over again once he started running for president. His rival, Hillary Clinton, was only eight years removed from the White House and had a whole administration-in-waiting at her disposal. Obama had wanted to offer the job of chief economic adviser to a brand name like Alan Blinder, a Princeton professor whom Bill Clinton had appointed vice chairman of the Federal Reserve. But when the campaign solicited recommendations from knowledgeable policy wonks, it was advised that no one of Blinder's stature would accept.

So Obama was left to choose from the people who, for whatever reason, had been either cast out of the establishment or never admitted in the first place—a collection of obscure academics, contrarian gadflies, and past-their-prime bureaucrats. Goolsbee, who stayed on as his economic aide, was emblematic of the group. But he was hardly the only one. There were ex-Clintonites like Robert Reich, the onetime labor secretary who had been a liberal voice of dissent within the administration; and Dan Tarullo, a Georgetown law professor who'd served in the Clinton White House but was never at ease with its attentiveness to Wall Street. There were aging eminences

like Paul Volcker, the former Fed chairman revered for besting infla-
tion in the 1980s; and Bill Donaldson, who'd been squeezed out
of his job running George W. Bush's SEC for trying to tighten the
screws on hedge funds and mutual funds.

As a group, the Obama wonks were united more by their outsider status than any coherent set of views. Goolsbee was cut in
the mold of an engineer, constantly tweaking and tinkering to solve
workaday problems, not some grand ideologist or high priest of
social criticism. The epitome of a Goolsbee proposal was a scheme
he dubbed the "automatic tax return," in which the IRS would send
people a filled-out tax return that they could simply sign and mail
back.[1] Reich, by contrast, was an orthodox liberal known for his
treatises on the human costs of globalization.

Yet there was something about the grab-bag character of the
team that actually suited Obama. What began as a matter of necessity ended up playing to his nonideological style. Though Tarullo
and Volcker subscribed to different schools of financial regulation,
Obama had taken the best ideas from each and worked them into a
single, formidable speech.[2] One aide recalled that Obama was never
more annoyed than when sitting across from three experts who all
had the same views.

By September 2008, however, Obama had not one but two economic teams jostling for position within his campaign. And if the
first was a ragtag bunch of quirky outsiders, the second was composed of well-heeled insiders. Most had worked for former Clinton
Treasury secretary Robert Rubin at one point or another and largely
echoed his views on the importance of balanced budgets and free
trade. Perhaps even more than that, though, the bond the Rubinites
shared was self-assurance: the comfort of having performed well at
the highest altitude of government.

Around the same time Goolsbee was dusting himself off at the
airport in Miami, Rubin and Larry Summers, another former Trea-

sury secretary, were descending from the skies aboard a private jet that Rubin had procured. They sent one of the young campaign aides who greeted them to collect their luggage. To them, the appearance in Miami was a bit of an audition, but one in which the candidate was auditioning for the advisers as much as vice versa. Rubin liked Obama personally and thought he showed promise, but had doubted he was ready to be president. Earlier in the campaign, he'd commented to friends that Obama needed to put some meat on his policy positions.

Once they were all together in Miami, Obama and his brain trust spent more than an hour chewing over which portions of the financial system would need government backing and which could fend for themselves. It was here that the candidate struck Rubin and Summers as impressively fluent. After the meeting ended, they mused about how they would grade his financial know-how, and both were pleasantly surprised to find themselves in agreement: A or A-plus.[3] Obama had won over the establishment.

Six months earlier, in March 2008, Larry Summers had sat down at an unglamorous Italian restaurant on the west coast of Florida with several of his former colleagues, including Gene Sperling, who'd been Clinton's top White House economic adviser, and Lee Sachs, a former assistant Treasury secretary. The meal was part of an annual pilgrimage to the Nick Bollettierri Tennis Academy in Bradenton, Florida, that Summers and Sachs had inaugurated after leaving office in 2001.[4] On this occasion, the conversation turned naturally to the Democratic presidential primaries, where Obama was busy pressing his advantage against Hillary Clinton. Though not everyone in the group had actively supported Clinton, most were identified with her or her husband. Some worried that they'd be shut out of the new administration as a result.

By June, however, their prospects suddenly improved. From time to time during the previous few months, the Obama high command had fretted about the strength of its economic team. Goolsbee was a first-class intellect, no doubt. His chemistry with Obama was evident and his loyalty beyond question. But he was not the least bit expert in distilling economic know-how into the basic currency of a campaign—the daily run of talking points and policy pronouncements that respond to ever-changing events while passing muster with the knuckle-rappers in the media. Goolsbee was an economist. It was becoming increasingly clear that the campaign also needed an economic policy broker.

The person the Obamans eventually landed for the job was arguably the best in the business, a Harvard-trained, Washington-seasoned economist named Jason Furman. Furman had played a similar role in the presidential campaigns of John Kerry and Al Gore. By 2008 he was heading the Hamilton Project, the economic research and advocacy group created by Rubin and funded by a circle of Clinton-friendly financiers. After Obama effectively clinched the nomination in late May, Furman signed on to the campaign.

The timing was fortunate. Within six weeks, it was hard not to see that there was something deeply amiss in the markets. Supposedly staid, low-risk banks were crumbling—on July 11, the savings and loan institution IndyMac became the fourth largest bank to fail in U.S. history. By late summer the rest could borrow money only on exorbitant terms. Those who'd had the misfortune of making a subprime loan or buying a subprime mortgage security, a group that included just about every major firm on Wall Street, suddenly noticed an ugly hole where they'd parked it on their balance sheet. The turmoil was illustrated in early September by the spectacle of the George W. Bush administration taking over the two mortgage-munching behemoths, Fannie Mae and Freddie Mac. But then perhaps the only thing more disconcerting than watching the theologically pro-business Bushies nationalize a shareholder-owned company was watching them *not* do it. Less than two weeks later, they set off a global financial panic by letting Lehman Brothers collapse. It fell to Furman to calibrate the campaign's response to each grim turn of events.

Furman had been close to Rubin and Summers dating back to the Clinton White House, where he'd toiled as a junior economist. Before long, Obama and his senior adviser David Axelrod suggested that Furman press them into a more formal role. This in itself was hardly surprising. A presidential nominee will almost inevitably turn to party eminences in a crisis, if only to reassure an anxious public that he is receiving the wisest counsel. And those elders will almost always feel an obligation to assist him, whether or not they have a personal connection to the campaign.

The practical upshot of having Furman was more significant: Team Clinton was now in. Furman ensured that the two former Treasury secretaries would be incorporated directly into the campaign's nerve center, rather than languish as overqualified props. Goolsbee had been consulting with Summers every few weeks; not long after Furman joined Team Obama, he and Summers began speaking almost every day. Furman's deputy, Brian Deese, spoke with Rubin nearly as often.

The Furman connection also brought Summers and Rubin into close proximity with Obama himself, at least once the tremors in the financial system erupted. Every few days, Goolsbee and Furman would convene a conference call to discuss the latest jaw-dropping development and how the campaign might respond. Beyond Volcker, only Summers and Rubin had standing invitations to the call, and Summers soon enjoyed a kind of first-among-equals status. It was his job to frame the issue of the day for the candidate before the discussion began. More so than can be said of anyone else, the future president would see the crisis unfold through Larry Summers's eyes.

• • •

On Wednesday, November 12, just over a week after capturing the presidency, Barack Obama sat down for a meeting in his transition headquarters in downtown Chicago. It was only the second formal discussion of how the president-elect would fill his cabinet. But, with the economy collapsing, the banks between rounds of government bailouts, and the Dow Jones down 3,000 points since the summer, Obama hoped to settle on a Treasury secretary.

Most of the advisers in the room would have been familiar to any casual observer of the recent election: David Axelrod, the president-elect's political guru; Valerie Jarrett, his longtime friend–cum–campaign aide; Rahm Emanuel, his incoming chief of staff. Even those advisers less visible to the poll-consuming public, like his counselor and Senate aide Pete Rouse, were natural participants in a meeting of such consequence. But there was at least one person whose presence wasn't immediately comprehensible: a slightly balding, slightly thickening man with bags under his eyes and a voice as smooth as chamomile. His name was Michael Froman.

Anyone who'd heard of Mike Froman at this early date in the career of Barack Obama was no mere political junkie but a devoted student of Obamanology. Officially, Froman (not to be confused with Jason Furman) was the transition's personnel chief and one of twelve members of its advisory board. Unofficially, Froman was an influential liaison to Wall Street and a trusted consigliere of Obama's. The two men had known each other since law school at Harvard.

One of the crowning achievements of Froman's tour as Obama's human resources director was a lengthy memo suggesting candidates for every top economic job in the future administration. The memo identified two front-runners to lead the Treasury Department: Larry Summers and Tim Geithner, a onetime Summers lieutenant then serving as president of the Federal Reserve Bank of New York. If the president-elect wasn't satisfied with these options, Froman offered him two more: Jamie Dimon, CEO of the massive bank JP Morgan Chase; and Jon Corzine, the former U.S. senator and CEO of Goldman Sachs. The names were revealing, if hardly surprising: some parts Washington, some parts Wall Street, and, in the case of Corzine, some parts both. Which is to say, precisely who you'd expect to find on a list from Mike Froman.[5]

Froman had been a young aide to Rubin in the early nineties, when the former Wall Street icon served as Clinton's top White House economic adviser. After Rubin took the helm at Treasury in 1995, Froman joined him as a deputy assistant secretary and later became his chief of staff. In retrospect, Froman had all the hallmarks of a Rubin man, that combination of pragmatism, brains, and pedigree. He was always ready with the insight you'd been groping for, the fact that had eluded you. When the Russians teetered on default in 1998, Summers, then Rubin's deputy, asked his troops about the urtext of financial crises, Charles Kindleberger's *Manias, Panics, and Crashes*. "Has anyone here actually read this book?" the deputy secretary wondered. Froman was the only one who raised his hand.

By the time Froman and Obama were reacquainted in 2004, their paths had thoroughly diverged. Froman, who'd followed Rubin again when the Treasury secretary left for Citigroup in 1999, had remade himself into a financier. Obama was chasing higher office from the purgatory of the Illinois state legislature. Still, Froman knew a good investment when he saw one. He brought his old classmate to Citigroup to introduce him to Rubin. And, once Obama arrived in Washington, Froman organized an economics tutorial for him with Rubin, Summers, and several other Clinton Treasury alumni.

By 2007, Froman had thrown himself into the cause of Obama's presidential prospects. He canvassed the hedge fund world and vouched for the young senator across the Upper East Side. Obama, in turn, brought his former classmate into his inner circle, giving him a job with enormous influence over his future administration. In the process, Obama was making a highly consequential decision. By putting Mike Froman in charge of hiring, Obama was, in effect, choosing to staff his administration with insiders and establishmentarians.

Obama had always had a healthier respect for the establishment than the typical insurgent candidate. Early in the primaries, he'd leaned on his staff to procure white-shoe authorities on the subject matter du jour. "What he wants to know is that he's really talking to experts in the field," a staffer told one academic. "When you go see him, you know, make it clear that you're an expert."[6]

Unlike Bill Clinton, Obama wasn't socially needy. He didn't seem to care whether he had a friend in the world. But he craved intellectual affirmation. For example, he had a habit of prompting his aides to acknowledge his wisdom and foresight. "Whose idea was that?" he'd ask, when everyone knew it was the boss's. During one staff meeting in the summer of 2008, Obama used the refrain so many times Axelrod was moved to groan, "Can you imagine four more months of this?"

To an outsider, it might have seemed suspicious that Froman had listed his two former Clinton colleagues as the leading candidates for Treasury. In fact, there was a relatively benign explanation: with Wall Street practically folding up on itself, Obama had told his transition staff he didn't want mere market experience at the top of his economic team; he wanted public officials practiced in the art of stanching financial crises. As a practical matter, this winnowed the Treasury short list to the most inside of insiders—the handful of Clinton alumni who had defused the global financial panics of the 1990s.

Though Obama and his aides would still have to choose between Geithner and Summers, there were few policy differences between the two, and certainly no ideological rifts. In any case, Obama planned to offer both men jobs, and so the question was really who sat where. The basic path had effectively been chosen.

When Obama opened the floor to discussion at that early transition meeting on November 12, the considerations were almost entirely tactical and personal, not substantive. Emanuel and Axelrod weighed in for Summers. The former secretary was known to the markets and the public, they argued, and had been tested under the klieg lights. His presence would be reassuring from the get-go.[7]

John Podesta, the former Clinton chief of staff then serving as head of the transition, chimed in on Geithner's behalf. He believed Geithner and Obama would mesh better personally. Ironically for a former Clinton hand, he also worried about a glut of officials so easily identified with the former president, lest the man from Change produce an administration full of retreads. Jarrett favored Geithner for similar reasons. She'd also received e-mails and phone calls from Obama supporters unnerved by Summers's controversial Harvard presidency, which he'd resigned in 2006 under pressure from the faculty. Of particular concern was his suggestion, during a talk he'd given as president, that genetics might help explain the paucity of women in the top ranks of the science and engineering professions.[8]

Most important of all, Obama himself was unconvinced by the case for Summers. He didn't share Jarrett's concerns about the Harvard debacle. And there was no denying Summers's analytical brilliance. He'd been one of the youngest ever tenured professors at Harvard and later won the John Bates Clark Medal, awarded to the most outstanding American economist under forty and often a prelude to a Nobel Prize. But Obama was skeptical in other ways. Emanuel and Axelrod seemed to think the mere act of appointing a familiar face could help defuse the economic crisis. Yet if familiar faces were what the country wanted, Obama himself wouldn't be there. Experience mattered, but it was no substitute for poise and judgment.

Besides, he liked this Geithner fellow. The two men had first met at the W Hotel in New York toward the end of the campaign. For the better part of an hour, the politician and the technocrat had sat talking and generally becoming fans of each other. Geithner had lived in India, Africa, and Thailand as a child, and Obama in Indonesia. They spent the first fifteen minutes bonding over having grown up abroad. Geithner told the future president that living outside the United States "and looking at the impact of the United States on the world made me want to work in government," he later recalled.[9]

When Obama said, "I might need to ask you to come to Washington," Geithner's protest seemed both genuine and perfectly calibrated to impress. "Don't do that," he told Obama. "I promised my family I wouldn't move them again." He then unfurled a list of knocks against himself—his minuscule public profile, his perceived lack of gravitas—and urged Obama to pick Summers or Rubin. With his cosmopolitan upbringing and understated style, Geithner was like a flattering reflection of Obama himself.

To break the stalemate, Obama agreed to hold a final one-on-one interview with each candidate in Chicago on Sunday, November 10. But those conditions effectively tilted the job to Geithner, who held the advantage in personal rapport. Soon after, Obama called Emanuel and informed him of his decision. Later, the president-elect called Summers and offered him the job of director of the National Economic Council (NEC), the top White House economic aide. When Summers accepted a few days later, Obamaland was giddy at assembling an economic dream team.

Only the captain of the team grasped the backlash that lay ahead. To the extent anyone knew anything about Tim Geithner in the fall of 2008, it was that he was one of three people in the room when the Bush administration saved the country's biggest banks. The action was almost instantly unpopular, and Geithner had talked the future president through the implications during their first meeting at the W. "You will be tying yourself to a strategy I was intimately involved in," he said. "I will not walk away from it. You need to understand the cost you take in doing that." Obama told Geithner he understood.

Strangely, no one gave much thought to the fact that a team headed by Geithner and Summers would have a particular way of looking at the world, one that would imply a specific set of policy choices and political consequences. When one Democratic senator protested that the emerging team had been too sympathetic to Wall Street during the nineties—"cats don't change their stripes," the senator pleaded—Obama responded that he needed people he could count on in a crisis. Besides, he said, they *had* changed.[10]

2

THE BIG IDEAS PROJECT

Every president faces a conflict between the ideas that animated his designs on the Oval Office and the unforgiving crush of circumstances that greet him once he occupies it. Bill Clinton touted middle-class investments as a candidate, only to later conclude that the deficit was the biggest threat to the U.S. economy. George W. Bush promised a humbler presence on the world stage, then shifted course once the Twin Towers fell eight months into his term.

But for Barack Obama, the conflict was perhaps more acute than most. Obama had envisioned a presidency dedicated to lasting achievements: to health care for every American; to ending global warming; to solving the "problems that George Bush made far worse, but that had festered long before George Bush ever took office," as he liked to say on the campaign trail.[1] In so doing, Obama hoped to lay the foundation for long-term prosperity. And yet the crisis he inherited was the ultimate short-term emergency: a financial collapse and an economic abyss.

The tension had actually been building throughout the campaign. Even before Lehman Brothers failed, Obama could see that voters were anxious about their houses and their jobs. But he could never entirely grasp what a president was supposed to do about it. You could try to convince them you felt their pain with a bunch of showy gestures. But if you were being honest, you had to concede how little influence a president had over the week-to-week drift of statistics, how little he could affect next month's unemployment rate in a country of 150 million workers, or next quarter's gross domestic product reading in a $14 trillion economy. The best you could hope for was to get the fundamentals right, to influence the "long-term" direction. To suggest anything else was just pandering.

With Memorial Day looming back in the spring, the country had gotten amped up on gas prices. Hillary Clinton promised voters she'd give them a gas-tax holiday, to put some extra change in their pockets. John McCain had recently locked up the Republican nomination and started in on the gas-tax holiday, too. But it made no sense. The economists all said it wouldn't lower the price of gas. The money would flow right to the oil companies.

Obama told his political brass he wouldn't support it; Clinton and McCain could flog him all they wanted. By this point, the pros knew they couldn't budge him and so they didn't even try. "Axe [Axelrod] was the one. He said, 'First, you're right. Let's take the high road. Make an argument,'" recalled Pete Giangreco, a top Obama consultant. "The argument was: This is what Washington does. It comes up with a phony baloney way of fixing the problem."[2] In truth, it was a stunt in its own way, a stunt about not doing stunts. But the impulse was vintage Obama.

Once the financial crisis hit, the tension only grew. You could practically sense the irritation when reporters asked Obama how the crisis might change his priorities. The current problems were symptoms of a deeper rot, he'd protest, and it was the rot he intended to fix. Obama was scheduled to give a major health care speech three weeks after Lehman Brothers went down, but there was little appetite within the campaign or the media for a major push on the subject. It was Obama himself who insisted on sticking with health care rather than lunging for the topic of the moment. "Our big health care speech was the first to make the connection between these long-term problems and the economic issues," said a campaign aide. "[That] was all him."[3] Or, as Obama put it in his speech: "[T]he question isn't how we can afford to focus on health care, but how we can afford not to. Because in order to fix our economic crisis, and rebuild our middle class, we need to fix our health care system too."[4]

The irony, of course, was that the crisis would make him president. It was the crisis that drew out the contrast between the law review president who never broke a sweat and the ex-POW with his jaw clenched so tight it would take a tire jack to pry it open. A week and a half after Lehman, McCain abruptly announced he was suspending his campaign to help save the banking system. Team Obama was holed up in Tampa preparing for a presidential debate when the team members heard the news and quickly concluded that the race might be over. Obama himself was practically beaming. The campaign had spent the last three months conspicuously hinting that the old man was erratic. Now he'd finished the job for them with a single half-baked idea. "I believe we won the election in the ten days between the collapse of Lehman and the first debate," said one senior Obama campaign aide. "It created the sense that one guy was solid and had his feet on the ground, and the other guy was not."[5]

But even after winning the presidency, Obama was loath to accept that the economy was singularly important. During a conference call with several senior aides early in the transition, Geithner remarked to his new boss that "your signature accomplishment is going to be preventing a Great Depression." The incoming Treasury secretary was an unflappable man—this was his great virtue as a bureaucrat. Even so, Obama's response was slightly jarring. "That's not enough for me," said the president-elect. It suddenly dawned on Geithner that he and his colleagues were a sideshow rather than the main attraction. A magnificently pedigreed sideshow facing a preposterous challenge, but a sideshow nonetheless. "If you don't do that, nothing else is possible," Geithner protested. "Yeah," the president-elect repeated, "but that's not enough."

There was a strain of messianism in Barack Obama, a determination to change the course of history. And it was this determination that explained his reluctance to abandon his presidential vision. Recessions would come and go, even recessions as painful as this one. But the big achievements—like health care and climate change—were the accomplishments that posterity would recall. "I always admired the president's courage for recognizing that fifty years from now people would remember that all Americans had health care," Larry Summers later said in an interview. "And even if pursuing health care affected the pace of the recovery, which was unlikely in my view, people wouldn't remember how fast the recovery from this recession was."[6] It was a formulation Obama himself was fond of. "I am absolutely certain that generations from now, we will be able to look back and tell our children that this was the moment when we began to provide care for the sick," he said in St. Paul, Minnesota, the week he clinched the Democratic nomination. "[T]his was the moment when the rise of the oceans began to slow and our planet began to heal."[7]

Perhaps the messianism was inevitable. Given the speed of his rise, it would be hard not to suspect some metaphysical intervention. In February 2004, as a candidate for the U.S. Senate from Illinois, Obama was the sort of amateur the pros rolled their eyes at:

unproved and with a stench of desperation. The plan had been to husband his cash for a last-minute ad blitz in the primary. But to Obama's mind, the only thing the plan had produced was a gap between him and the front-runners.

One week before the scheduled ad salvo and he'd had enough. Enough of the late-night calls from worried friends, enough of the media irrelevance, enough of the punishing stasis. He flagged down his manager, a weathered Kentuckian named Jim Cauley, and pressed him to get going. "Why not just $100,000?" he pleaded. You could do that, Cauley twanged. But in a market the size of Chicago, you might as well take the money and burn it.[8]

Obama knew Cauley was right, but what else could he do? There was a time, after he'd won his state senate seat, when he'd been a comer: thirty-five years old, the first black president of the *Harvard Law Review*. Now he was a forty-something nobody who'd already lost one bid for higher office and was struggling to crack double digits on his second try.

Then something funny happened. It was a day or two after the spots finally ran and he was at his local supermarket. He noticed himself being watched. Hell, he could hardly inspect a box of cereal without attracting a well-wisher. "Man, those ads really worked," he told Cauley. The manager was pained yet again by the boss's naïveté. *Any fool can get recognized at the A&P*, he thought. *Let me know when we break through in Peoria.*[9] But it was a sign of things to come. Just as Obama was introducing himself to Illinoisans, the leading Democratic candidate was drowning in a domestic abuse scandal. Three weeks later, Obama was the nominee for U.S. Senate. He pulled down 53 percent of the vote—*53 percent*—in a seven-candidate field.

In the months that followed, Obama would give the keynote address at the Democratic National Convention and become an international celebrity. This gave him what one aide called a "bully pulpit" when he arrived in the Senate, and he intended to use it. Obama set up an internal think tank to cogitate on what the economy of the future should look like. To run it, he hired a policy expert named Karen Kornbluh, who'd made her name writing about families and income insecurity in an era of globalization. Kornbluh's mandate extended to just about every epochal challenge a U.S. senator could tackle, and many they couldn't: her first assignment was to reimagine the energy sector. Inside Obama's Senate office, they called her shop the "big ideas project."

Heading into the second year of his term, Obama and his staff had planned to focus on education, another one of the "structural" issues that instinctively appealed to him. Then he went home to Chicago over winter break and changed his mind. "Everyone in Illinois is talking about health care reform," he told his staff. "But when I go to Washington, no one is talking about it." This was a year after George W. Bush had dispatched John Kerry to win a second term. Obama found it absurd that Democrats assumed health care had died with the Kerry campaign when the country still hungered for reform.

And it wasn't just the uninsured. Health care costs had become a drag on the economy and would eventually bankrupt the government. There was no way to keep America competitive a generation from now without taking them on, too. Health care, it turned out, could be the biggest "big idea" of all.

When Obama launched his campaign for president the following year, he thought of it as the "big ideas project" writ large. "Let us be the generation that reshapes our economy to compete in the digital age," he said at his announcement speech. "Let's be the generation that ends poverty in America . . . that finally tackles our health care crisis . . . that finally frees America from the tyranny of oil."[10] Several months later, he told a crowd of Iowa Democrats, "I will lead the world to combat the common threats of the 21st century: Nuclear weapons and terrorism; climate change and poverty; genocide and disease." [11]

It was more than just the policies, though. The entire Obama campaign was shaded in messianic tones. Obama was selling the narrative of immaculate conception, a story about a man who'd turned up at the pinnacle of American politics without the taint of moral compromise the other candidates had spent their careers accumulating. "I'm not from central casting when it comes to presidents of the United States," was how Axelrod summed up his candidate's message. "I'm new, I'm relatively young. I haven't spent my life in Washington." [12] And a good thing for the rest of us. Because if you wanted to fix the problems the system had been engineered to ignore—heck, the system had practically caused them—you needed someone the system hadn't created. "[W]e have the chance to do more than just beat back this kind of politics in the short term," Obama told a crowd three days before the election. "We can end it once and for all." [13]

Better still, he somehow didn't make you gag on the righteousness. Just when Obama seemed ready to proclaim himself the son of God, he could let the air out a bit, make himself mortal, even clownish. It made you momentarily wonder if it was really you and not him who'd dreamed up the messianic stuff. A few weeks before the Iowa caucuses, a reporter asked his press aide how long their interview would last. Obama flashed an impish smile and interrupted: "Your time's already up. You just get to come in here and shake my hand." [14] The sly jokes about his alleged aura—that was vintage Obama, too.

And yet the messianism was unmistakable in the end. In fact, it was the off-the-cuff moments that made you certain of it. Any candidate might sound grandiose delivering a speech before thousands. If you really wanted to peer inside the engine, you had to sift through the unrehearsed riffs and find the unconscious tip-offs, and Obama provided them in spades.

Reporters would ask about his economic "narrative"—how would he sum up the plight of American workers? To the same question, Bill Clinton had said they were losing out to competitors in Europe and Japan, where governments invested more in their citizens. Not for Obama, this boilerplate. Instead, he'd resort to dialectical analysis: thesis, antithesis, synthesis. For almost fifty years in this country, the New Deal had reigned. Then "Ronald Reagan ushered in an era that reasserted the marketplace and freedom," he told the *New York Times*. Clinton and George W. Bush were each in his own way products of the Reagan era. It would fall to the next guy—to Obama—to reassert the role of government in the marketplace, albeit chastened and leaner. To achieve the final synthesis, in other words. He said, "What we need to bring about is the end of the era of unresponsive and inefficient government and short-term thinking in government so that the government is laying the groundwork, the framework, the foundation for the market to operate effectively." [15] Clinton had answered from the perspective of the American worker. Obama walked you through the stages of history.

Reagan was a particular obsession, the sort of transformational president Obama hoped to emulate, albeit with a different ideological tilt. In mid-January 2008, at the height of his pitched battle with Hillary, Obama offhandedly told a Nevada paper that "Ronald Reagan changed the trajectory of America in a way that, you know, Richard Nixon did not, and in a way that Bill Clinton did not. He put us on a fundamentally different path." [16] The press assumed it was just another subtle dig at the Clintons, who naturally took it in that spirit. [17] But it also happened to be another glimpse at the president he intended to be.

By the time of his conference call with Geithner during the

transition, Obama hadn't spent twenty-one months undergoing the inhuman endurance test of a presidential campaign just so he could clean up someone else's mess, however urgent the task. He'd run for president "to change the trajectory of America." He'd do what he needed to fix the economy, the country could rest assured. But he wasn't about to junk the rest of the agenda.

The question was: how? How could you defeat terrorism, bring health care to tens of millions, stop global warming, remake the educational system, eliminate poverty, fight genocide, and end a war (another campaign promise), all while stopping an economic free fall? The answer required a certain kind of pragmatism. You'd have to settle for imperfection, take an expedient path or two, forge alliances with people you might not normally climb into bed with.

Such pragmatism wasn't alien to Barack Obama, of course. For all the grand ambitions, he'd never been some starry-eyed dreamer. From the earliest days, he'd decided that if you were going to do big things, sometimes you had to give history or destiny or whatever it was a little shove. Alice Palmer could have told you that. She once owned a state senate seat that Obama wanted. In fact, there was a time, back in 1995, when Alice Palmer wanted him to have her seat, too. Then Palmer lost a congressional primary and decided she wanted to keep it. Damned if the Harvard man didn't tell her to get lost. He challenged her ballot petitions in court in case she missed the point. A judge tossed out half her signatures, keeping her out of the race.

Eight years later, Obama was running for U.S. Senate, and an African-American woman named Joyce Washington joined him in the Democratic primary. Washington was coming off a strong showing for lieutenant governor, and Obama's campaign pros worried that she'd siphon off his black supporters. They started the routine all over again: The lawyers pulled her ballot petitions and flagged

the dodgy signatures. This went on for days and cost tens of thousands of dollars—no small sum back then—but it looked as if they'd
be able to get Washington tossed. It was only when some genius on
the campaign realized that two times is a trend so far as the press
is concerned that they dropped the idea. Who wanted to be the guy
who bumps black ladies off the ballot?[18]

Of course, rivals were one thing—lots of people could get up for
kneecapping the competition. But Obama was just as unsentimental
when scoping out allies. In 2003, William Daley, the brother of Chicago mayor Richard Daley, helped convince the Illinois legislature to
heap a major concession on SBC, the telecom giant that employed
him. Obama had stood with the reformers who cursed the Daley
machine throughout his state senate days. He considered Bill Daley
a fixer with a fancy title. "Ramrodding bills through because you've
got the clout to do so—rather than because you've got arguments on
your side—is not a good way to do the people's business," Obama
said of Daley's handiwork.[19] But it didn't stop him from arranging
Bill Daley's endorsement in his 2004 Senate campaign, or from en-
dorsing Richard Daley for reelection in 2007. (He would later make
Bill Daley his White House chief of staff.)

By the time he ran for president, Obama had no trouble making
cold calculations. He straight-armed his longtime pastor, Jeremiah
Wright, when the pastor became a liability, and reversed his long-
standing support for the public campaign finance system so he could
bury McCain in television ads. But the clearest examples came after
the election, as he organized his administration.

There was, for one thing, Obama's decision to make Hillary
Clinton secretary of state, a strange bedfellow pick if there ever was
one. The pundits assumed he was sidelining a former (and perhaps
future) challenger. But it soon became clear that the calculation was
brutally pragmatic in another way: Obama was picking people to
whom he could delegate key swaths of his presidency, the only way

to make all the ambitions add up. In Clinton, he had someone whose international celebrity nearly equaled his own, a huge plus given how little time he'd have for tending to foreign leaders, to say nothing of traveling abroad.[20]

Obama went on to name Tom Daschle, the former Senate majority leader, as his health care czar (Daschle would later decline the post over tax improprieties), and Carol Browner, the former head of Clinton's Environmental Protection Agency, as his climate and energy czar, so that these two priorities had stewards of similar stature. He left Robert Gates in place as secretary of defense, and installed Geithner and Summers to run his economic team.

"One of the things that made him quite extraordinary as a manager is that he really does delegate," said Ted Kaufman, a Joe Biden lieutenant who observed Obama at close range as a top transition official. "He finds a good person—he's good at sizing people up—and he delegates." Kaufman explained that Obama "believes in management by exception," the idea that, in a company with five divisions, the CEO should focus on the one that's underperforming, not the four that are passing muster.[21]

The beauty of all this delegation was that it would allow the administration to range across a breathtaking list of tasks in a way that no micromanaging president ever could. The downside was that it ceded enormous authority to subordinates. And if there did turn out to be a problem in one of Obama's numerous divisions, the damage might be done before he could step in to correct it.

3

"PEOPLE WILL THINK WE DON'T GET IT"
—LARRY SUMMERS

In early December 2008, Christina Romer sat in a meeting at Obama's transition headquarters in Washington feeling distracted and overwhelmed. This was not unusual in those days for the incoming White House economist. Ever since she'd arrived in DC the Monday after Thanksgiving to head the president's in-house economic think tank, the Council of Economic Advisers (CEA), Romer had struggled with the grueling demands of her new life.

There was, for one thing, the relentless piling-on of meetings. Romer had come from academia, from Berkeley, where you might sit down with other faculty members twice a month or attend a weekly seminar, but other than that they left you alone to think your thoughts and teach your classes. Now she was squeezing in half a dozen meetings between the time she showed up in the morning and the time she left at night.

Just the economic principals alone—Romer, Summers, Geithner, and Peter Orszag, soon to be the president's budget director—would array themselves around a table three times a day. Then there were all the other issues demanding their own regular gatherings. Tom Daschle convened a standing health reform meeting. Carol Browner held regular meetings on climate change. If a topic had merited so much as a paragraph on the Obama campaign Web site, chances were someone was having a meeting about it somewhere during the transition.

Romer had few illusions going into her job. She fully expected a bruising adjustment to the metabolism of Washington policy making, all the more so during a crisis. Not only had she never served in government—a fact that distinguished her from most of the president's wonks—but she'd hardly so much as counseled a candidate for public office. After she'd first contacted the Obama campaign in early 2008, months went by before she received a response. When she finally got one, it wasn't an invitation to weigh in on interest rates or unemployment, but a query about whether the campaign could list her as an adviser for a feature in *The Economist*. Thereafter, her interaction with the campaign was so minimal she nearly deleted the e-mail inviting her to interview for a White House job. She hadn't recognized Mike Froman's name.

Still, Romer hadn't quite expected *this*. She may have never sat in a budget meeting before, but as one of the country's premier macroeconomists, Romer assumed she knew the rudiments of government accounting. Then her colleagues started tossing out terms like "FMAP" (federal matching funds for Medicaid) and "PEP" and "Pease" (limits on tax deductions for the affluent) and she realized how much there was to learn.

The lingo may have been obscure, but at least it was concrete; you could nail it down if you had to. The protocol you could only

guess at. Romer once gave the president-elect an obscure unemployment figure off the top of her head, only to watch in horror as he
later repeated it, unchecked, to a roomful of reporters. (Fortunately
it was correct.) There seemed to be all sorts of unwritten rules about
what you said and to whom; about when your presence was essential and when it wasn't. Romer had been killing herself to attend
every climate conclave, every education powwow, every health care
mind-meld on the docket. Then one day Orszag took her aside and
explained that she needn't strive for perfect attendance. The CEA
chairman had the luxury of picking and choosing. How was a person supposed to know?

On this particular day, Romer found herself in a meeting about
the country's failing banks, and she was more preoccupied than
usual. It wasn't just the bleakness of the subject matter. In fact, bleak
was something she already knew disconcertingly well. The CEA
oversaw all the internal number crunching that went on in the White
House, while the National Economic Council, which Larry Summers
headed, was responsible for taking the numbers and translating them
into policy.[1] The first assignment Summers had given Romer when
she turned up at transition headquarters was to predict the future
of the recession-battered economy. "We're really going to need a
forecast," Summers said, slouching into a chair beside her desk. "It's
something the CEA does. Why don't you get on the phone and try to
figure this out."

So Romer spent the next few weeks sizing up the blow to the
economy. Not yet having access to the most sophisticated data-
sifting apparatus ever invented, that being the U.S. government,
she hit up the brand names of the forecasting profession for whatever figures they could spare. She called the famed consulting firm
Macroeconomic Advisers, and Mark Zandi, the ubiquitous econo-
pundit. The Fed forked over its data, too. The numbers were similar

regardless of the source: the hole was as deep as any the economy had seen in decades.

Still, the precise source of Romer's anxiety at the early December meeting wasn't the recession per se but the stimulus—the mix of tax cuts and government spending Obama would use to limit the economic damage. The stimulus was the single most important step the administration could take to protect jobs: it would boost GDP, and higher GDP growth meant lower unemployment. This was as close to an iron law as the economics profession had produced.

Romer's fellow economic aides had loosely settled on a price tag of $500 billion to $600 billion for the stimulus. But when she ran a simulation to test the healing powers of a stimulus that size, unemployment soared past 8 percent, far above the roughly 5 percent economists consider healthy. Even a stimulus package of $800 billion to $900 billion barely kept unemployment from crossing the 8 percent threshold; it would take two anguished years just to drive it back below 7.[2]

According to a draft of an internal memo Romer prepared a few days later, you had to go all the way up to an eye-popping $1.8 trillion to fill the entire hole in the economy—the "output gap," in economist-speak. "An ambitious goal would be to eliminate the output gap by 2011–Q1 [the first quarter of 2011], returning the economy to full employment by that date," Romer wrote. "To achieve that magnitude of effective stimulus using a feasible combination of spending, taxes and transfers to states and localities would require a package costing about $1.8 trillion over two years."[3]

If anyone had asked her directly, Romer would have said the figure of $500 billion to $600 billion fell far short. But people hadn't asked yet, and she'd begun to despair that they ever would. On top of all the other stresses, Romer's colleagues were all former Clinton hands, and she was aware that she didn't quite fit into the club. In the meantime, she couldn't stop worrying that the administration was making a historic mistake before it even took office. And so finally Romer spoke up in front of everyone around the table: Orszag, Geithner, Summers, and their top deputies. "I really think the stimulus needs to be bigger," she said, practically blurting out the words. "I think this needs to be at least $800 billion." She didn't dare say what she really thought the number should be.

The responses to Romer's plea ranged from a distinct lack of enthusiasm in Geithner's case to displeasure in Orszag's. From the outset, Orszag had been the member of the economic team most concerned about a large stimulus. He worried that, even though the spending was designed to be temporary, Washington would let it linger on in the federal budget for years afterward, potentially darkening the ten-year deficit picture that was his focus as budget director.

As a practical matter, Orszag also wondered what the extra infusion of cash would entail. There were limits to how much the government could spend—about $200 billion to $300 billion in a single year, he believed—since there were only so many roads, bridges, and dams that were planned and permitted and ready to be built. In fact, the transition team had mostly exhausted that list of projects already. Were Obama to try to spend more, either he'd have to push the spending further and further into the future, until after the economy had probably recovered, or he'd have to cut taxes by a breathtaking amount, which could generate political resistance among Democrats who eyed tax cuts warily. There was a third option, a large dollop of aid to struggling state governments. But the politics of this were even less favorable, since members of Congress complain constantly about bailing out spendthrift states.

Geithner's views, on the other hand, were more complicated. Like Romer, he favored a large stimulus. But, to him, the stimulus was of secondary importance to saving the financial system. "There's more fiscal stimulus in TARP [the bank bailout] than there is in fiscal stimulus," Geithner would say, by which he meant that the financial rescue and not the stimulus would drive the recovery. If the banks were healthy, they would lend, and lending would help consumers spend and corporations invest. If the banks went under, credit would dry up and the economy would stall. In Geithner's mind, the point of the stimulus wasn't to fix the economy; the point was to prop up the economy until such time as you could revive the banks. For that matter, a stimulus wasn't even genuine economic nourishment. It was a "sugar high," as he would tell colleagues who later pleaded for more. It would provide a short-term boost, but the effect would soon fade.

Viewed in this light, the stimulus was important, but only up to a point. Beyond that point, spending another couple of hundred billion dollars was of limited use, since it wasn't a solution in its own right. If you could temporarily prop up the economy with $500 billion instead of $900 billion, you might very well want to do that. The less junk food the better.

There was, however, a hitch: even if Geithner was right and the banks really were the key to the recovery, the stimulus would have an awful lot to do with what happened in the meantime—with how high unemployment rose in the next two years, and how much cash people had in their pockets to spend. In that case, the difference between $500 billion and $900 billion could be quite significant. It might be the difference between a country that was willing to give its political leaders the space they needed to work through the crisis and a country that craved nothing so much as to string them up.

Perhaps more than any other Treasury alumnus, Geithner had been shaped by the 1990s. At the start of that decade, he was a junior civil servant. By the end, he was undersecretary of the world's most powerful financial bureaucracy. He'd received his first big promotion, to deputy assistant secretary, in March 1994, not long before Rubin arrived in the building and Mexico neared collapse. And he'd been in the room with Rubin and Summers for more or less every important conversation until the global financial fever finally broke in 1998.

In the years before and after that terrifying interregnum, Rubin and his closest aides were mostly famous for what they wanted to achieve: balanced budgets, freer markets, rising private investment. But while responding to the financial traumas that afflicted Mexico, Thailand, Indonesia, South Korea, and Russia, the Rubinites were known for a view not so much of what governments should do as of how they should do it. And that "how" could be neatly summarized with two evocative words: overwhelming force.

As with most prescriptions for action in a crisis, the approach lent itself to martial metaphors, and the Rubinites embraced them easily. Summers spoke of a "Powell Doctrine" of finance, which, like General Colin Powell's original formulation, would be an antidote to the creeping gradualism of halfhearted interventions.[4] Experience had taught Rubin and Summers and Geithner that the cheapest way to end a crisis was quickly and decisively. When markets overreact, they'd say, policy should, too.[5] As a practical matter, this meant spending however many billions it took to halt that first frenzied bank run, that first thunderous stampede of investors. The alternative was to pay ten or twenty times as much many months later, by which point the chances of success would have plummeted. General Powell was determined to avoid another Vietnam; Professor Summers derided any proposal he could fairly describe as a "Vietnam option."[6]

So "overwhelming force" became the Rubinites' mantra, even long after the nineties ended. They spent the next decade deploying it in books and speeches[7] and hushed conversations with grim-faced world leaders. Rubin invoked the phrase in his memoirs; Geithner in his pronouncements as New York Fed president. Once Obama brought them back into public view, the Rubinites uttered it like a ritual incantation, or maybe a Germanic salutation. In the post-Lehman world, no middling sums would do. What was needed was *overwhelmingforce!* The word bespoke sobriety and experience, a kind of battle-hardened wisdom. It epitomized what, in their minds, set them apart from counterparts in other eras and other countries. During the frantic May 2010 weekend when Europe faced down financial oblivion, Geithner politely asked what sort of bailout Brussels had in mind. Fifty billion was the reply. "If you announce 50 billion there's going to be a run on Europe," Geithner told them. "Why don't you do 500?"

Perhaps as much as any other episode, it was South Korea that had forged this view. If you were a banker in the mid-nineties with a big idea, chances were that the big idea was Korea. You couldn't go wrong in those days with the Koreans, those people who'd transformed their hut-riddled peninsula into a modern economic power in a few decades' time—who, for good measure, had refashioned their tin-pot dictatorship into a democracy.[8] The local banks might be a little inbred, the financial system a little opaque. And it was hard to believe those plodding industrial conglomerates—the *chaebols*, they called them—were the most efficient way to organize an economy. (The advantage of having a single company manufacture cars and build ships while running department stores and brokerage firms[9] wasn't immediately clear.) Still, the chance to get in on Korea in the early nineties was like a chance to get in on Japan in the 1970s, and who wouldn't want that?

For their part, the Koreans were happy to have the capital. They'd financed those decades of growth through inhuman discipline—scrimping and saving so that factories could be built and foreign markets conquered. Now the world's financiers were lining up to give them credit, many from the same countries whose lunch the Koreans were eating. The Koreans didn't entirely understand this

Western-style capitalism. They were frankly a little bemused by it. In their system, bankers funneled money to *Korean* companies (often at the urging of government bureaucrats who had gotten the bankers their jobs).[10] They didn't go looking for ways to help rivals. But if the Americans and Europeans (and Japanese) wanted to boost their industrial fortunes, the Koreans weren't going to talk them out of it.

All of which had been going on for half a decade when the doubts crept in. The Koreans were master exporters; that much was obvious. But the *chaebols* were getting so big and bloated you had to wonder who would buy all those cars and stereos and semiconductors.[11] And if you couldn't answer that question, then you had a hard time answering the next one: Having borrowed the money to build all those cars and stereos and semiconductors, how on earth would the Koreans pay it back?[12] The lenders began calling in loans.

Then, in the summer of 1997, the Thai real estate market collapsed. All of a sudden Korea's lenders could look at the beating investors were taking in Thailand and imagine how their own disaster might play out. In mid-October, Taiwan, one of Korea's biggest economic rivals, devalued its currency, and Korea's lenders went into conniptions. The loans to the Koreans were denominated mostly in dollars. If the Koreans allowed their own currency to weaken in response, they would instantly owe their lenders many, many more dollars. The odds of repayment would be even slimmer.[13]

Soon it became clear that the Koreans had only so many dollars to give them. The lenders called in their loans faster. An old-fashioned bank run broke out.

In Washington, the Clinton Treasury Department went into high alert. Frantic calls ensued, late-night meetings were convened, Bloomberg terminals were anxiously monitored. It was bad enough that Korea was the world's eleventh largest economy. So many foreign banks had lent so much money that a default could pound the global financial system into a vaguely premodern state. Worse, there was also the matter of geopolitics. Every few hours someone from the White House or State would call with a story about how the Communists in Pyongyang were primed to overrun South Korea the minute its economy gave out. If ever there was a case for overwhelming force, this was it.[14]

After some internal hand-wringing, the Rubinites hauled in the International Monetary Fund (IMF) and World Bank and informed them they'd be bailing out Korea to the tune of $55 billion. As a good faith gesture, Treasury topped off the package with $5 billion of its own (the Japanese were in for $10 billion).[15] In return, Washington asked the Koreans to ratchet up interest rates to an excruciating 25 percent, the better to keep foreign investors interested.[16] The Koreans would also have to start disentangling their government from the banks and the banks from the *chaebols*, the investors having decided that this inbreeding had caused the problem in the first place.[17] Many companies would be shut down.

From the perspective of the Koreans, these prescriptions were about as appealing as a program of mass unemployment, which, as it happens, was the upshot. Over one million Koreans lost their jobs in 1998—the equivalent of 6 million Americans—and the Korean unemployment rate would spiral from 2.5 percent to nearly 7 percent.[18] By contrast, foreign banks had to bear only mild discomfort. They were told to keep their capital in the country as a condition for the bailout money to flow.

One might wonder why the pain had landed almost entirely on the Korean worker and hardly at all on foreign banks and investors who, after all, had so eagerly pumped credit into the country. The answer was that the Rubinites calculated that saving the global financial system was far and away their most urgent priority. That meant easing the anxieties of foreigners so they didn't flee in a panic. "There was concern about a political backlash [in Korea], causing a worse recession," Rubin would later say of the rescue. "But you have to weigh the risks probabilistically. We decided the risk of a financial market meltdown was greater than the risk of a political backlash." [19] It was hard to argue with the results. The world held together. By mid-1999, the Korean GDP had recovered to its pre-crisis level. The prescription appeared to work.

The Rubinites had faced a choice, in other words: you could worry more about financial markets, or you could worry more about ordinary Koreans. And the one they'd made was eminently defensible. The risk of slighting markets was the possible end of civilization. The risk of slighting workers was a few percentage points of unemployment. A financial catastrophe they could feel in their guts; the specter of it haunted their dreams. But unemployment spiked every few years for one reason or another; it was hard to get too exercised about it.

The Rubinites had no interest in punishment. To the contrary, they believed—correctly, it turns out—that the Koreans would ultimately benefit. Certainly, had the bailout not worked, the Koreans would have suffered more than most. But at the moment you were deciding how to deploy your resources, the target had to be the global financial system, not the Korean worker per se. You wouldn't make the bailout 20 percent less effective to make life 20 percent better for the average Korean; it just wasn't a rational bet. Had you put the choice before every person on the planet at the peak of the crisis, probably only the Koreans would have objected in significant numbers.

Of course, there were limits to the historical analogies. Geithner and the other veterans of the 1990s understood that they'd have to face the U.S. crisis on its own terms. For example, the export-oriented Koreans could take their lumps at home and still recover with strong sales abroad. But U.S. firms were often strapped, papooselike, to their own domestic market. When the American consumer gave out in late 2008, there wasn't much to cushion the fall.

It was for these reasons that Geithner was more sympathetic to a stimulus this time around, more concerned about the short-term fate of workers than he had been in Korea. But, in the end, the legacy of Korea and the other Asian hot spots had been to impress upon him the importance of stopping the financial crisis at all costs; the immediate fate of workers was subsidiary.

The problem was that when you crossed out "Korean unemployment" and wrote in "U.S. unemployment" the difference between 6 or 8 or 10 percent wasn't chump change alongside the greater good of global financial peace. It could be the difference between whether your boss, the president, survived or was tossed out on his ear. Between whether his broader agenda succeeded or failed. When it was your country, it was your job to feel the pain of workers as acutely as you felt the terror of financial calamity. And if you couldn't—if, say, your success at averting disaster in other countries had conditioned you not to—well, sooner or later, that might be your downfall.

Christy Romer's view was as close to the opposite of Geithner's as mainstream economics would support. Shortly after Lehman Brothers collapsed in 2008, the Berkeley economics department held a faculty meeting for no other reason than to mull over the fallout. When the subject of TARP, the $700 billion bank bailout that George W. Bush's Teasury Department had initiated, provoked a debate among some of the country's leading economists, Romer interjected: "I don't see why we should plow $700 billion into the financial system. Why don't we just do a really big stimulus?" Romer was fond of telling Geithner that a traditional stimulus—tax cuts and government spending—wasn't just the best therapy for the broader economy. It was actually more effective than bailouts at healing the banks themselves. Boosting growth would lower unemployment and put borrowers in a better position to repay.

Romer was as much the product of her experiences as Geithner. After World War II, Romer's father, Clifford Duckworth, had used the GI Bill to become the first in his family to attend college. He'd earned himself an engineering degree and was working at the ammunition maker Olin Industries in East Alton, Illinois, when she and her brother were born. Aside from being hospitable to a young child on a bike, East Alton had little to recommend it. It was a small factory town, drab and dreary. "East Awful," her mother called it.

By the time his daughter reached high school, Duckworth had been transferred to Canton, Ohio—a step up from East Alton, but still tough to mistake for a hotbed of cosmopolitanism. Manufacturing was the city's lifeblood, and Romer's high school catered to the modest aspirations of its working-class students. The vocational curriculum loomed large: cosmetology, typing, auto repair. College prep courses were limited. Romer distinguished herself mainly outside the classroom, in drama and extemporaneous speaking.

For college, Romer ended up at William and Mary. She'd been accepted at Duke and Northwestern, but William and Mary was a public school, a bargain even if you came from out of state. The Duckworths were practical people. If you could get the same education for half the price, there was no sense distracting yourself with fancy names.

Clifford Duckworth had many progressive impulses, but he was still a product of his time and place. "Your brother's good in math, he'll be an engineer," he told his daughter. "You're good in English; you should major in something like that." Romer dutifully majored in political science intending to go to law school, then got hooked by a required course in economics. It turned out her mind had been built to handle a slide rule as easily as the Duckworth men. The field's quasi-scientific rigor appealed to her.

Romer's father was caught straddling two eras in more ways than one. A few years after she went off to college, he left Olin Industries to join a chemical manufacturer in Philadelphia for more pay and the promise of a promotion to plant manager. Duckworth had worked for Olin for twenty-five years. The company had shielded him from all manner of economic disruption. When the Vietnam War ended, making demand for ammunition its final casualty, the company shut down one plant but transferred him to another. But by 1983, the country was in the middle of a savage recession and the new company couldn't afford to be so magnanimous. The promised promotion never materialized. Now it was letting him go.

Romer was by this point a PhD student at MIT, just months from her wedding day. "I got sacked," her father called to say. Money had been set aside for the wedding, he told her. But somehow the reassurance made it harder to take—made her realize how important it was for him to think of himself as a provider, and how that was all gone now. That part of it seemed almost worse than the money. Before long, Duckworth took a job overseeing subway car renovation at the public transit authority in Philadelphia. It paid a lot less than being a plant manager and lacked the prestige of putting your engineering degree to work. But the chances you'd punch in one morning to find a pink slip on your desk were also pretty minimal. He stayed until retirement.

Romer believed in the power of stimulus over bank bailouts because she saw it in the data. When she studied the Great Depression, the subject on which she'd built her academic reputation, she noticed that the banks began to recover only toward the end of the 1930s, even though the worst of the bank runs had ended in 1933. What had come in between was four years of solid economic growth. (Franklin Roosevelt renounced the gold standard in 1933, stimulating the economy by allowing the money supply to expand.)[20] Clearly it wasn't enough to make sure the banks didn't go under. You had to help borrowers, too.

But, as with Geithner, Romer's views came from a part of the mind where intellect and experience bleed together. Like him, she was a product of those emotional blows that linger long after the fear or bitterness drains away. Geithner saw a financial crisis mostly in binary terms: if you somehow managed to avoid a free fall, everything else—slow growth, chronic unemployment—was just quibbling. Either the world survived or it didn't. "Everybody now has these cool ideas—why didn't we do it in this way, why didn't we do it bigger," Geithner would tell the *New York Times* in 2011. "All of that is marginal." He added, "[T]hat just misses the fundamental reality—it could have been so much worse." [21]

For Romer, though, success or failure depended on who you were. No one wanted to see the financial system collapse. But if you'd lost your job—your whole identity, really—then there wasn't much comfort in claims of victory. When Tim Geithner imagined the uses of overwhelming force, it was always to save *the system*. When Christy Romer imagined the uses of overwhelming force, it was to save human beings.

There was, of course, a final member of the economic team present at the December 2008 meeting where Romer insisted on a larger stimulus. And given his stature as an economic thinker and his relationship with Obama reaching back to the campaign, Larry Summers held the most important vote of all.

Like Geithner, Summers had been deeply influenced by the experiences of the nineties. He'd drawn similar lessons about the importance of saving the financial system during a crisis, though Japan and its twenty-year stagnation often loomed larger for him than the periodic flare-ups elsewhere in Asia. From the earliest days of the Obama administration, Summers spoke of Japan as the hair-raising example of how *not to* apply overwhelming force. Japan was to financial crisis mismanagement what the "Vietnam option" was to, well, American strategy in Vietnam. Among the first words out of Summers's mouth at a climactic March 2009 meeting when the president and his top aides debated the financial crisis were, "We don't want to have another Japan."

In Summers's mind, the biggest sin the Japanese had committed was to deny reality. The Japanese banks had begun wobbling in the early nineties, after the country's real estate and stock market bubbles burst. By 1997, Japan had entered a kind of post-Lehman phase, in which the major banks started keeling over into the government's arms. Even then, the Japanese remained convinced that the losses would be manageable, that the financial system could recover without radical treatment. It took another five years of stagnation before the Japanese government faced up to its banking mess.

Like Geithner, Summers believed in the application of overwhelming force to a country's financial sector. "He was definitely pushing for a more assertive financial rescue, willing to put a lot more money there," said a colleague.[22] But Summers was an altogether more agile thinker than Geithner. He'd had a formidable academic career before rising to prominence in government and was better able to transcend his direct experiences as an economic first responder and see a more complete picture of the economy. And when he considered the deterioration that Romer was picking up in her data, he became quite terrified. The two advisers had been commiserating about the situation since they arrived in Washington.

Summers worried about a succession of vicious circles descending on the real economy—on the workers and the factories—and triggering a depression. For example, the fear of unemployment could drive down consumer spending, slowing the economy and raising unemployment, and thus creating more fear and crimping spending even further.[23] He quickly recognized that it wouldn't do to apply overwhelming force to the banks alone. The real economy required the benefit of such firepower, too.

When Romer urged a bigger stimulus at the early December

meeting, Summers quickly seconded the notion: "I think you're right," he said. Once the meeting broke up, he told her they'd need to send Rahm Emanuel a private note making the case for $800 billion.

Not long after, word came back that Emanuel was open to recommending the higher number to the president-elect. Romer was thrilled. She believed the increase could be worth almost a million jobs. She was exhilarated by the way it had all been decided in a casual, five-minute exchange.

Summers's intervention was an important, even heroic, moment. And yet it was still vastly insufficient to the task at hand. Romer had determined that the stimulus would need to be at least $800 billion to be *minimally* effective. But according to the analysis she performed over the next few days, it would take something on the order of $1.8 trillion to heal the economy completely.[24]

In the meantime, Summers was pulling together a memo for the president-elect on the options for dealing with the teetering banks, the cash-poor automakers, and the country's tidal wave of foreclosures. Above all, the memo would lay out options for the stimulus. The document drew together the work of several colleagues, including Romer's description of how different doses of stimulus would affect the economy.

When Romer showed Summers her $1.8 trillion figure late in the week before the memo was due, he dismissed it as impractical. So Romer spent the next few days coming up with a reasonable compromise: roughly $1.2 trillion. In a revised document that she sent Summers over the weekend, she included this figure, along with two more limited options: about $600 billion and about $800 billion.

At first, Summers gave her every indication that all three figures would appear in the memo he was sending the president-elect. But with less than twenty-four hours before the memo needed to be in

Obama's hands, he informed her that he was striking the $1.2 trillion figure. The only two options would be $600 billion and $800 billion.[25]

Just as alarmingly to Romer, the document now included language she didn't agree with, language that undercut the case for a large stimulus. One new line claimed that the way to think of the stimulus was as an "insurance package against catastrophic failure"—that is, a measure to prevent the economy from shrinking a lot further, not nurse it back to health, as if the economy would do the rest of the work on its own. Another line pointed out that proposing too large a stimulus could panic investors in government bonds, who would worry about the deficit, and rattle financial markets. It was the kind of language that Orszag was fond of, and that both Summers and Romer rejected.

Why did Summers appear to be limiting the size of the stimulus after spending the previous week helping to increase it? The answer had less to do with economics than with politics. Simply put, Summers believed that a $1.2 trillion proposal, to say nothing of $1.8 trillion, would be dead on arrival in Congress because of the political resistance to such gob-stopping sums. And if Obama proposed $1.2 trillion but managed to obtain only $800 billion, he would appear to have failed. "He had a view that you don't ever want to be seen as losing," a colleague recalled.[26]

Moreover, since Emanuel and the other operatives were convinced that any stimulus approaching a trillion dollars was hopeless, Summers worried that urging more than this would stamp him as oblivious in their eyes. "One point two trillion dollars is nonplanetary," he told Romer, invoking a Summers-ism for "ludicrous." "People will think we don't get it."

Romer was uneasy with this. She felt that $1.2 trillion was itself a pragmatic middle ground. She also believed the president-elect should deeply grasp all the trade-offs he faced, and in this she was not alone. Even Orszag, who opposed the larger number, agreed in retrospect that the figure should have been included in Obama's memo. "I think there's a basic principle that if a senior member of the economic team wants something presented to the president, it should be presented—with the pros and cons," he said. "I do not think it's the role of the economic team to play politics." [27]

Still, Romer recognized how big a victory even $800 billion would be given the public's resistance to government spending—at least the *idea* of government spending—and its vague grasp of the situation. In any case, she was reluctant to second-guess Summers on political questions in light of his imposing government résumé. She protested, but dropped the matter when Summers held firm.

4

THE OPERATOR

Larry Summers, unlike the president he worked for, prided himself on being a Washington insider. Having served for eight years in the Clinton administration, he understood how White House aides perceived risk, how senators assessed their self-interest, how the media scored political conflict. He knew the incentives these actors responded to, the arguments they accepted and the arguments they dismissed. As a result, he knew how to wield power and influence those who had it.

For example, Summers had asked Romer to solicit the thoughts of some conservative academics—stars of the right like Martin Feld-stein of Harvard and John Taylor of Stanford—on how large the stimulus should be. When they responded that a figure approaching a trillion dollars was in order, Summers relayed their comments to Emanuel to urge a bigger stimulus. He knew the chief of staff feared for his right flank, and that validation from prominent Republican economists would set his mind at ease.

Even prior to the election, Summers had been offering Team Obama tactical advice that was often quite shrewd. A few days before the Bush administration allowed Lehman Brothers to fail, the Obama campaign prepared a statement supporting the no-bailout stance. Summers called Jason Furman in a frenzy and begged him not to release it. The Lehman bankruptcy would be a disaster, Summers told Furman. But even if it wasn't, the statement was a bad idea. If I'm wrong, he said, no one will care that Obama supported Bush's decision. "And if I'm right, and I'm confident I'm right, you're going to regard it as a momentous error to have praised an act of folly." The campaign mothballed the statement.

For a man who'd effectively talked himself out of the Harvard presidency with his impolitic pronouncements, Summers was oddly expert in the rhetorical norms of the capital. The day in late November that Obama unveiled his economic team, Summers and Romer shared a cab back to the airport in Chicago. Summers suggested some mock Q&A to prepare for the White House press corps. Dr. Romer, he inquired, affecting his best briefing-room inquisitorial style, could you comment on the exchange rate? Ever the teacher, Romer began to explain how the exchange rate is simply the price of one currency expressed in terms of another. "Wrong!" Summers interrupted. In official Washington, the correct answer went: "The exchange rate is the exclusive purview of the Treasury Department."

Summers was, it turned out, acutely sensitive to matters of Beltway protocol. He frequently instructed colleagues on what was and wasn't appropriate for discussion in front of the president.[1] When an aide once claimed the wrong seat in a sedan waiting to ferry them to a meeting, Summers piped up, "I don't want to correct you, but the senior man sits on this side."

Summers was keenly aware that, in Washington, geography signified status, and status meant power. About six months into the administration, he and Orszag were scheduled to join the vice president at a White House event. When Orszag arrived, a body man seated him next to Biden, only to return a few minutes later and ask him to move. Summers had insisted on taking the seat even though it was assigned to Orszag. "I'm really sorry. We had a seating chart. But Larry walked in and saw that you were sitting next to the vice president," the aide said. For Summers, protocol was expendable when it didn't serve him.

Like any bona fide Washington insider, Summers took more than a passing interest in political gamesmanship, the city's semiofficial pastime. During the presidential primaries, he would frequently check online betting sites to see how the smart money rated each candidate's prospects. So often did he cite *Politico*, the Web site that caters to Washington the way *Variety* caters to Hollywood, that the president's press secretary, Robert Gibbs, regularly provoked laughter at meetings by needling Summers for his addictive reading habits. (Gibbs would quip that he planned to go home and read the *Financial Times* so that he could wade just as far out of his depth.) Summers's obsessiveness extended to real-life politicos, with whom he was keen to share his tactical insights. At the end of a long day, Summers could often be seen trooping to David Axelrod's quarters abutting the Oval Office to offer unsolicited advice.

Early on, at least, Summers was at pains to defer to the judgments of the political hands, even when they bled into matters of economics. When Emanuel insisted that the stimulus include billions of dollars for high-speed rail, the economic team was nearly unanimous in opposing the idea, whose economic benefits were unlikely to exceed the cost. But Summers was reluctant to pan Emanuel's pet project, not wanting to alienate his powerful patron. "Larry wanted to be Rahm's best friend; that's where the power came from," said a White House colleague. Summers was "agonizing with himself over how far do we push this." When he did speak up at one point, Emanuel promptly blew off the criticism—"I don't care, it's good," he responded—and the chief economic adviser dropped the matter.[2] (Summers said that he later spoke to Emanuel about this privately.)

With his fellow eggheads, by contrast, Summers often had exceedingly little patience. He had been one of the top academic economists in the world by his late twenties, so his posture, as one colleague summed it up, was: "I was as good an academic economist as anybody. Now I know a zillion times more."[3] Summers complained that academics were often too invested in their own creativity to be of use to policy makers. He suggested they spend more time talking to investors and businesspeople than sketching theories on dry-erase boards. "You don't have to be original," he said. "You just have to be right." He reserved special disdain for ideas that looked elegant on paper but had little chance of working.

Never did Summers and the academics clash so violently as when the academics thumbed their nose at politics. When the CEA crafted a memo on the economic benefits of health care reform, Summers urged Romer to append one of the West Wing's pet talking points, the idea that reform could help American businesses compete with foreign companies. "I'm not going to put schlocky arguments in there," Romer protested, explaining that the point didn't hold up under scrutiny. "I'm not making a schlocky argument," Summers sniffed.[4] Summers "certainly superimposed on his thinking what he perceived to be politically plausible," explained one of his aides. "Christy relished the fact that she wouldn't ever impose the constraint of politics. Which was the source of most of their bickering."[5]

The memos Summers and his own staff prepared could contain peculiarly political jargon. A draft of the document he sent the president about the stimulus noted that a new employer tax credit would both "provide an incentive for hiring" and "message optics specifically around jobs"—a political operative's way of saying it would help the president show voters he was addressing unemployment. At times, Summers tacked back and forth so easily between the economic and the political that colleagues had trouble discerning where his heart really lay.

That Larry Summers would keep an ear to the ground is not surprising, since he spent much of his life trying to fit in. Though he'd inherited a breathtaking intellectual pedigree—each of his economist parents had Nobel-laureate brothers—socially he was born an outsider.

This was thanks in part to the anti-Semitism that persisted in the more affluent parts of the Northeast into the mid-twentieth century. Paul Samuelson, Nobel Prize–winning uncle number one, is widely believed to have missed out on a tenured Harvard professorship in 1947 because of his ethnicity, and the scar of the incident lingered for decades in the family consciousness. At a lunch discussion in New York in 2004, when he was the university's president, Summers reflected that "an uncle of mine lost the opportunity to be a professor at Harvard because he was Jewish." [6]

Nor was anti-Semitism a mere relic of Summers family lore. The Philadelphia suburbs where Larry Summers grew up in the 1960s and early 1970s—Merion, Narberth, Rosemont—were a world of de facto ethnic and religious segregation, replete with affluent WASP redoubts, working-class Catholic enclaves, and middle-class Jewish neighborhoods. Though the Summerses lived in a more integrated development, the groups sometimes mixed uneasily in the area's public schools. A Jewish kid who went to elementary school at the heavily Italian Belmont Hills walked home each afternoon steeled for a fight.

The Summers family had moved to Pennsylvania in 1961, when Larry was six years old. To ease young Larry's transition, his second-grade teacher pulled aside a well-liked student named Jim Weinrott and asked if he could look out for his new classmate. "He was very shy, that was my first impression," recalled the teacher, Anita Cohen. "I felt that it was important for Larry to have some friends. . . . Even at that age, Jim was a very compassionate person." [7]

Weinrott would be Summers's best friend and protector into adolescence. At Harriton High School, which they attended, a group of Italian jocks took sadistic pleasure in organizing an annual rite known as "The Turkey Hunt," in which they singled out a less athletic (often Jewish) classmate to chase around campus and generally traumatize for a day. Summers was sometimes a target of such bullying. "He had the posture of a sixty-year-old man at fifteen," said Mark Moskowitz, another childhood friend. "He was stooped, had a large head. He looked physically mature in a sort of aged way. . . . He took shit for that." [8] Weinrott would periodically insert himself between Summers and the jocks and plead with them to "give Larry a break."

Remarkably, the taunting rarely weighed on Summers, for the simple reason that he regarded the bullies' intelligence as primitive. He would respond to their hectoring by exposing the flaws in their logic, such as it was. "He was talking to people as if they can function on his rhetorical scale, and they're just interested in getting into a fight," Weinrott recalled. [9]

Though one might never guess it from his appearance, Summers was in fact socially ambitious. But the ambition took a particular form: he wanted to be liked by the people he regarded as worthy, by the elect and not the masses. This didn't necessarily mean the smartest kids in school; it meant the kinds of kids who seemed destined to influence the world.

As a practical matter, Summers had two social circles. The first was a group of physics lab nerds, who spent hours after school each day debating the nature of the universe. Many would go on to careers as research scientists. The second was a group of more socially deft but intellectually formidable kids who gave every indication of future success in law, business, and politics. Summers, with his sloped shoulders and his prowess for mathematical proofs, was at first glance a more obvious fit for the first group. But it was membership in the second that he actively cultivated.

The ambition came from Summers's mother, Anita. Whereas her husband, Bob, was the consummate academic, who could imagine no better life than the thoughtful solitude of the ivory tower, Anita Summers was deeply engaged with the world—a frequent attendee of local school board and Democratic Party meetings. She even belonged to a local group of feminist professionals that had formed in the late 1960s. One longtime Summers friend speculated that she might have been a senator had she been born a generation later.

Anita Summers saw that Weinrott was popular among the group of budding big shots and nurtured the friendship between him and her son. She asked Weinrott to stay for dinner almost once a week and invited him on trips to the family summer home in Cape Cod. (To pass the time en route, the family would engage in formal debates, complete with opening statements, rebuttals, and closing arguments.) The boys spent hours in the Summers basement playing Ping-Pong. In retrospect, Weinrott believed he'd been included partly to help Larry transcend his natural social circle. "I was a normal kid, had a lot of friends. I was in some way his passport to other friendships," he recalled.[10]

Summers's method of winning over the peers whose approval he craved was to wow them with his brainpower, efforts that were sometimes hard to distinguish from sheer arrogance. As a junior high school student, Summers told a friend he valued his time at $500 an hour, the equivalent of $3,400 today.

One favorite pastime was to seek out debates when he knew nothing about a subject in which his opponent was expert; somehow he would bludgeon his way to victory. There was, for example, the summer evening in 1973 when Larry and a high school classmate named Michael Finkelman spent hours sparring over whether the pianist Van Cliburn deserved to win the prestigious Tchaikovsky Competition in Moscow for his rendition of Rachmaninoff's Third Piano Concerto, widely regarded as the most difficult piano composition ever written. Finkelman, an accomplished musician who would become a leading expert on the English horn, said no, because the rendition lacked soul. Summers, who had never even heard of Cliburn before that day, said yes because the performance was technically flawless. Two of the classmates who observed the jousting felt Summers had fought to a draw.

But sometimes the audaciousness backfired. At one point in high school Summers decided there was no reason he shouldn't excel at chess, with his analytic mind and strategic bent. He taught himself the game and began mopping up the board against lesser opponents. Before long, he challenged Mark Moskowitz, a citywide junior champion who would later achieve renown as a political consultant. His friend was unintimidated. "Larry, I could beat you blindfolded," Moskowitz sneered. "That's impossible, not possible," Summers retorted. The two sat down to test the proposition. "I did of course, blindfolded," Moskowitz recalled. "That is him. You have it all figured out. But then there's life."

But beneath the bravado there was an almost poignant need to belong. Weinrott and Moskowitz, along with Arn Tellem, a future professional sports agent, and Richie Neff, who would become a prominent technology lawyer after attending Yale Law School, formed the core of Summers's more aspirational social circle. Every Saturday, the group would convene a game of football at a local junior high school; though nominally of the "touch" variety, it was contested so fiercely the players sometimes left the field bloodied.

If the chessboard was a field of play on which Summers might plausibly excel, the opposite could be said of the gridiron. "Larry was the slowest runner you'd ever seen," said Weinrott, adding, "Strength was not his strong suit." [11] And yet, more weekends than not, there was Summers, trundling up to the field, ready to take whatever physical and verbal punishment came his way.

Summers's need for social acceptance was often at odds with his contrarian instincts. The way he reconciled them was by seeking out groups of contrarians and glomming onto them. One natural home for the contrarian-minded undergraduate was college debate, and Summers threw himself into the activity as a student at MIT. Though the school's program was relatively weak and only intermittently coached, Summers was able to make himself into a top-flight debater. [12]

Even more than a competitive undertaking, debate was a social activity. The best debaters in the country saw one another week in and week out at the most prestigious tournaments. They socialized afterward at parties and paid homage to one another's rhetorical brilliance. They spent summer vacations living together at a handful of exclusive debate camps, which inculcated the craft in promising high schoolers. Many remained friends for decades, even though they'd attended college hundreds of miles apart. Summers was eager to break into this group. "My speculation is that one of the things he was trying to do was fit in," said Ted Belch, who ran a debate camp where Summers taught, of the reasons Summers took the job. "He sort of burst onto the successful college debate scene, didn't know a lot of people. . . . Larry was pretty shy." [13]

Around the same time, Summers fell in with a small minority of conservatives at MIT and Harvard who stood apart from their overwhelmingly liberal campuses. He'd come from a family of loyal Democrats—his uncle Paul Samuelson had even worked in the Kennedy administration. But now he was drifting in the opposite direction. Though it would be more than a stretch to say Summers was becoming a Goldwaterite—the word "ideologue" has never suited him—those who knew him at the time detected a growing rightward bent.

"He was quite conservative as a student," said Dallas Perkins, a Harvard Law student who served as Summers's college debate coach during his senior year. "His politics tended to be pretty right." Summers, Perkins recalled, was a hard-liner on crime, favoring lines like "We've got to crack down."[14] He also questioned whether welfare's costs, in terms of discouraging the poor from working, might outweigh its benefits. More broadly, Summers showed a bias toward free markets and limited government at home and a hawkish foreign policy.

This isn't entirely surprising given Summers's intellectual influences at the time. Shortly after arriving at MIT, Summers began working as a research assistant for Martin Feldstein, the star Harvard economist known for his tax policy expertise and his ties to the Republican Party. Summers revered Feldstein. The only activity he prioritized over debate was crunching numbers for the Harvard don. (Classes came in a distant third.) "He was forever running into debate meetings a few minutes late, saying he'd been finishing up something for Marty," recalled one debate teammate.[15]

But Summers's conservative associations weren't limited to his choice of mentor. As a Harvard PhD student, he was always on the lookout for agile-minded undergrads to put to work on his own research projects. He frequently gravitated toward young conservatives and libertarians who, by virtue of their minority status in a sea of dorm-room liberalism, tended to have well-conceived worldviews and were articulate in defending them. In 1978, for example, Summers hired a staunch libertarian named James Buchal. The two would talk late into the night about public policy and academic economics.[16]

By the early 1980s, conservatism was no longer a minority position, at least not outside Cambridge, Massachusetts. Reaganism was ascendant as the public increasingly associated liberalism with government overreach and weakness abroad. For Summers, the most significant consequence of this shift was that Feldstein soon found himself chairing the president's Council of Economic Advisers. Summers followed him to Washington to serve as a senior staff economist.

In itself, a tour in the Reagan CEA revealed little about one's leanings. Staff economists are nonpolitical appointments, typically drawn from the academic ranks. The chairman often doesn't even know the partisan affiliation of the person he's hiring. But Feldstein had taken over from a Reaganite named Murray Weidenbaum, who'd stocked the agency with staunch libertarians and supply-siders—devotees of the "voodoo" creed that tax cuts raise revenue. When Feldstein replaced Weidenbaum, whom Reagan abruptly fired in 1982, he kept most of his predecessor's staff but layered on a cadre of academic stars to manage the workload, including Summers and a young MIT professor named Paul Krugman.

Summers had landed his first academic job in 1979 and had gradually been shedding his youthful conservatism. But living in Washington at the height of the Reagan revolution proved to be a provocative experience.

One day in the summer of 1983, near the end of his term at the Council, Summers attended a lunchtime discussion at the conservative Heritage Foundation on the subject of tax policy. Among the guests were several supply-siders, including Bruce Bartlett, a future Reagan official then working for the Joint Economic Committee in Congress. Bartlett and the others energetically touted a flat tax, which would wring progressivity out of the tax code by charging rich and poor the same income tax rate. Summers sat stone-faced for most of the lunch. Finally, on the ride back to the office with two White House colleagues, he blurted out: "Bartlett's just advocating lower tax rates on rich people because he's trying to protect the class he came from." [17] To Summers, the moment distilled all the defects with Reaganism and sent him searching for like-minded dissenters.

In the mid-1980s, Summers found his way into such a circle. A student of Summers's from Harvard named Jacob Goldfield was working at Goldman Sachs and introduced him to Bob Rubin, then a senior Goldman executive (soon to be the firm's co-CEO). Rubin's first impression of Summers was poor. His curtness during the encounter made Summers worry that he'd blown his chance to win over the older man, already an important figure on Wall Street and in Democratic politics.

But it didn't take long to discern that Summers was brilliant. He and Rubin soon bonded over their aversion to the pompous pronouncements of empty-suit executives, who thought financial success translated one-for-one into knowledge about the world. At times Rubin seemed to luxuriate in Summers's raw brainpower. "Bob used to glow like a proud parent when he'd ask Larry to say something in a meeting . . . knowing it would have show-stopping consequences," recalled one Clinton-era aide.[18] From Summers's perspective, Rubin was a breed of executive he hadn't quite known existed: pro-market but interested in ideas, and unashamedly liberal when it came to social policy.

Ever since his tour at the CEA, Summers had been fascinated by the apparatus of government. He had, in fact, spent much of his year there casing out official Washington. He dropped in on economists at the Treasury Department and got himself appointed to a working group on unemployment benefits with officials from Labor, Treasury, and OMB. "He went off a little bit on his own, making contacts in Washington. He wasn't around much," recalled one colleague.[19]

Now he was increasingly fascinated by politics, too. Through politics, there was a chance to become part of more than just an intellectual elite. There was a chance to be part of an elite with real influence over the country.

In 1987, Summers received a call from an old debating friend named Jack Corrigan, by then a longtime political aide to Massachusetts governor Michael Dukakis. Dukakis was thinking about running for president and Corrigan suggested he retain Summers as an outside economic adviser.

In many ways, the campaign was a transformative experience. For the first time, Summers realized that political communication was a skill that was critical to gaining and exercising power, but that even very smart people could fail to master it. He saw that this failure explained why his fellow academics often had little effect on public policy. His colleagues from the Harvard faculty complained constantly about Dukakis's vagueness regarding the savings and loan crisis: Was Dukakis for deposit insurance? A special resolution mechanism? Why wouldn't he spell it out? It never dawned on them that there were few political advantages, and many disadvantages, to unfurling a position in all its complexity.

At the same time, the campaign brought Summers into close contact with a new species of creature: the policy intellectual who was part operative and part wonk. Young campaign aides like Gene Sperling (a Yale Law graduate) and George Stephanopoulos (a Rhodes scholar) could talk cost-of-living adjustments in one breath and game out how they would play among suburban voters in the next. For Summers, it was another exclusive club to join, one that would put him on a higher plane than the politically naive academics he'd previously known.

Summers reprised his role as economic adviser during the 1992 presidential campaign and landed a senior Clinton administration job for his efforts: Treasury undersecretary for international affairs. As he ascended the Treasury ranks, Summers characteristically sought out people he considered to be of superior insight, knowledge, and experience. In the nineties, that frequently meant the financiers who sent capital gushing into and out of countries like Argentina and Indonesia (and, for that matter, the United States) with a few carefree keystrokes.

Wall Street was hardly alien to Summers before he joined the Clinton administration. In fact, his ties to prominent Wall Street figures extended well beyond Rubin. Jacob Goldfield, his friend and former student, was a rising star at Goldman Sachs (later hired by George Soros to manage his flagship fund). Summers was also close to Nancy Zimmerman, the wife of another former student, who would leave Goldman in the mid-nineties to launch her own hedge fund.

Still, as an academic prior to the 1990s, Summers generally kept an analytic distance from the financial world, as though it were little more than a rich source of data, a laboratory for observing the way markets worked. Wall Street's lingo and norms, its pet practices and conventional wisdom—and certainly its social hierarchy—were of little interest to him.

That was changing by the time Summers arrived at Treasury in 1993, and clearly by the second half of the decade. Once each quarter, the Treasury Department would meet with senior officials from all the leading investment houses, who were key participants in its auctions of government debt. Officially dubbed the Treasury Borrowing Advisory Committee, it was a forum for discussing the technical and legal issues that could arise in such transactions. But the highlight of the meetings was the "courtesy" dinner Treasury hosted the night before. Rubin, who'd spent his whole career among bond traders, would show his face for the obligatory cocktail and disappear after fifteen minutes. Summers, by contrast, tended to stay for the entire meal, eagerly pumping the executives for the latest financial market intelligence. He seemed genuinely curious, but also excited by the chance to mingle with the masters of the universe.

For anyone who saw the top ranks of the financial world as an intellectual elect, Alan Greenspan stood at the very pinnacle. In those days there were few men more revered both in Washington and on

Wall Street than the venerable Fed chairman, and few more convinced of the benefits of free markets and of the financial engineering Wall Street increasingly specialized in.

Summers and Greenspan had a mutual respect that dated back to the earliest days of the Clinton era. Every Wednesday, senior staff members from the Fed and Treasury would have lunch together and exchange views on the economy. As undersecretary, Summers attended frequently. "He went as much as anything to discuss the world with Greenspan," recalled Jeff Shafer, an assistant secretary who was Summers's top deputy at the time. "And Greenspan showed up often, especially when Larry was there."[20] Later, when he was deputy secretary, Summers would accompany Rubin to a weekly meeting with Greenspan, a long-standing Fed-Treasury tradition that had lapsed under the administration of George H. W. Bush.

In Greenspan, Summers saw an intellectual equal, one of the few economists whose musings on policy he instantly took seriously. When the Mexican peso crisis thrust Treasury and the Fed into close consultation in late 1994, Summers and Shafer initially favored allowing the peso to depreciate. They both changed their minds after watching Greenspan lecture the Mexicans on the need to prop up the currency by raising interest rates.[21]

Still, it is Greenspan's influence on the subject of financial regulation that looms large in retrospect. As an academic, Summers had occasionally argued in favor of blunter forms of regulation, like a tax on the buying and selling of stocks. The idea was to rein in speculation by making it costly to transact shares in short, quick bursts.

By contrast, Greenspan's faith in free markets was near theological. It would be tempting to say that Greenspan believed the market was the single greatest technology ever invented for allocating goods and services, labor and capital. But the word "invented" doesn't do justice to his worldview. Greenspan, like any good libertarian, saw the market as the purest expression of human psychology, which impels the pursuit of self-interest. He believed that any attempt at regulation was likely to fail, since it violated not just the laws of economics but the laws of nature. The market had its flaws. But it was as delicate and beautiful an ecosystem as had ever existed.

Rarely was this belief more evident than when it came to derivatives, a market that was growing rapidly throughout the nineties. Derivatives are essentially bets on the future price movements of assets like stocks and bonds: an investor can hedge against a loss by buying a derivative that allows him or her to sell the stock at a reasonable price one year from now, effectively betting that the price will fall. The person who sells the derivative is betting that the price will rise. Elaborating on his views in 2003, Greenspan told Congress that "derivatives have been an extraordinarily useful vehicle to transfer risk from those who shouldn't be taking it to those who are willing and are capable of doing so." [22]

Greenspan's view was less than unanimous even among Wall Street émigrés in Washington. During his Goldman days, Rubin had seen his share of traders blow themselves up using financial instruments they didn't understand, and the experience left him suspicious of financial innovation. He favored tighter regulation of derivatives. But Summers echoed Greenspan. He needled Rubin for being a Luddite and joked that Rubin was like a tennis player who preferred wooden racquets to powerful graphite composites. [23]

Certainly there were ideological differences between Larry Summers and Alan Greenspan. Greenspan was someone who saw regulation as a kind of assault on the natural order; Summers believed regulators were often inept or counterproductive, but occasionally indispensable. Summers was "very much in the world of there's a role for government in laying out the dimensions of the playing field," recalled Ted Truman, a longtime aide to Greenspan at the Fed who became a top Treasury official in the late nineties. [24]

Still, both Shafer and Truman believe Greenspan's optimism

rubbed off on Summers. He already had an innate faith in science and technology. Through his interactions with Greenspan, he began to view financial innovation as a form of technological progress unto itself. "I'm sure [Greenspan] was one of the forces on that side," said Shafer. "I have a number of friends—and Larry is one—where you'd never get him to admit something on the spot. But the next time he comes back, his views are a little different." [25]

For Summers, such high-profile relationships weren't just intellectual; they were also social and political. Summers personally courted Greenspan, playing tennis with him and seeking his support for key initiatives. The connection between the two was such that, when Summers remarried in 2005, Greenspan spoke at a reception for him at the Willard Hotel in Washington.

To be among the top ranks of government insiders, to be a friend and peer of Alan Greenspan's, was to belong to an elite society, and Summers exulted in the status this membership afforded him. The currency crisis that Mexico stumbled into in 1994 required a bailout of tens of billions of dollars. After he took over as secretary, Rubin was intent on sending someone to size up the country's president, Ernesto Zedillo, to whom the U.S. government was about to entrust an enormous sum. He chose Summers for the sensitive assignment—the delegation had to slip into and out of *Los Pinos*, the Mexican White House, unnoticed so as not to arouse local antagonism toward the American intervention. Summers pulled it off without a hitch, reporting back that Zedillo struck him as calm and thoughtful and very much in control.[26] On the eve of the Obama inauguration some fourteen years later, Summers still delighted in telling the story of his secret Mexican mission.

Summers seemed to derive as much satisfaction from the pomp and circumstance of these encounters as the substance. As Treasury secretary, he had enjoyed the copious perks of the job. "He liked having a car, bodyguard, flying on his own plane," said an Obama White House colleague. "He seemed to miss it a little bit when he and I would ride in the back of those Chryslers"—the sedans that ferry around government officials who, unlike high cabinet officers, don't have their own limousines or SUVs. After he returned from another trip to Mexico, this time with Obama himself, Summers told fellow White House aides about how they'd been treated like visiting royalty.[27]

In some ways, Summers had undergone a transformation during the 1990s. When he turned up in the Clinton administration in 1993, he was chronically disheveled. His attire rarely survived a meal intact, as if he'd chosen his brand of personal hygiene to maximize the chances a stranger could discern the menu. He often chewed with his mouth open. By the late nineties, he was far more put together. One night, after he'd finally ascended to the top spot at Treasury, Summers invited his old high school friend Mark Moskowitz to a formal dinner with a variety of senior officials. Summers was dressed in an elegant suit and had impeccable dining etiquette. He seemed practically graceful. Midway through the meal, he turned to his friend and jokingly observed, "I've come a long way, huh?"[28]

But in other respects Summers was very much the same person all along: keen to be a player, to be involved not just in the biggest economic decisions but in the backroom political discussions as well. In 2000, the Clintonites worked feverishly to make permanent the country's trade relations with China. At a key moment in the congressional debate, the West Wing was desperate to find credible surrogates to help make its case. Summers suggested inviting Greenspan, since no one commanded more authority on matters of economic policy. He worked behind the scenes to arrange Greenspan's appearance at a Rose Garden pep rally. "Chairmen don't [usually] get themselves involved in what is a political event," said Ted Truman.[29] But Summers's connections made it happen.

• • •

On December 16, 2008, Obama gathered his economic advisers around a square conference table at his transition headquarters in Chicago to make the first major economic decisions he faced. The president- and vice president–elect sat on one end, the wonks on the other, and senior political aides—Rahm Emanuel, David Axelrod, and Robert Gibbs—filled in the space between them. The memo Summers had prepared with the help of the economic team served as the basis for presentations on housing, the auto industry, the budget, the bank crisis, and the bleak contours of the recession.

In each case, the economists stressed that there was more danger in doing too little than too much. When it came to the stimulus specifically, Romer mentioned her preference for over a trillion dollars. Summers allowed that bigger would be better. But these points were made in passing. "I don't remember that as part of the discussion," conceded one member of the economic team in attendance.[30] The memo had framed the debate around two basic choices—roughly $600 billion and roughly $800 billion—and these were the focus of the conversation. "The option of going well above $800 billion was certainly raised, but it was not discussed extensively," Romer later recalled. "We felt the most important thing was to make sure the president-elect was on board with a plan as large as $800 billion."[31] Obama had little reason to suspect that this amount was perhaps $1 trillion too small.

When the meeting ended, Emanuel joined the economists at their end of the table to finalize the size of the package. Someone suggested asking Congress for a range of $675 billion to $775 billion. Emanuel responded that "we're not doing a range, it'll just go to the top of the range," and decreed that the number would be $775 billion. The whole conversation lasted roughly two minutes.

Summers was not displeased. He believed he'd brought the president's handlers up as high as they would go with their opening bid, given the political constraints. Only later would it become clear that the opening bid was far too small to fill the gaping hole in the economy.

Summers had considered his fluency in both economics and politics to be an advantage amid the competing considerations an NEC director must weigh. But while this might have been true for most NEC directors, for Summers, the logic was flawed. Unlike the typical NEC director, Summers was regarded as the most formidable economic thinker in the administration, if not all of Washington. When he pronounced on a topic, the president and his top aides assumed they were getting the soundest possible economic advice, not economic advice mixed with political handicapping. Even if they solicited the opinions of other economists, including one as respected as Christy Romer, the president and his aides were inclined to discount them, especially if these opinions veered too far from what they wanted to hear. "Larry was telling me what the economy needed," Emanuel later said of their early interactions. "No one had ever heard the number eight hundred. If we came out with it, we had to kind of figure out a strategy. But the president's view, shared by the vice president and myself, was, 'If the economy needs it, do it.'" [32]

In Emanuel's mind, the division of labor was clear: Summers did the economics, and he did the politics. "My job as chief of staff was to give him an assessment of what the political system could absorb," he said. [33] But it turned out Summers had already factored this assessment into his analysis. Summers's recommendation at the December 16 meeting didn't reflect what he deemed the best course of action for the economy—that would have been well over $1 trillion. It reflected what he deemed the best course that was politically feasible. Yet because Emanuel and the president assumed Summers was largely giving them the former, they believed they were closer to the ideal than they actually were.

5

WILDEBEESTS AND CHEETAHS

Understandably, given the source of the crisis, no corner of the U.S. economy consumed the incoming Obama administration more than Wall Street. The economic team spent the presidential transition agonizing over the fate of the banks even as it was deciding on the provisions of the stimulus. But before the new administration could do anything about the banks, it would have to secure more money, and this would not be easy.

When Congress had passed the $700 billion bailout—the Troubled Asset Relief Program (aka TARP)—the previous October, it made the first half available to George W. Bush's Treasury Department, but reserved the right to block the second half if both the House and the Senate saw fit to do so. Since Bush had informally agreed to leave this portion of the money to Obama, the task of lining up votes would also largely be his.

The president-elect and his transition aides had focused on this challenge almost immediately. In the economic team's memo to Obama in December, Geithner wrote, "There is a risk of another acute episode of panic over the course of the next several weeks, particularly if . . . markets come to believe that the political will to make the next $350 billion of TARP funding available is lacking." Geithner also understood the heroic sales job that winning the money would entail. "Unfortunately, the credibility of TARP is so damaged it will be difficult to secure the second $350 billion and achieve our goals. Phil Schiliro"—Obama's chief liaison to Congress—"suggests we consider repealing TARP and replacing it with a new program." [1]

Obama ultimately decided to stick with TARP—the team felt coming to Congress with its own legislation would create an even bigger mess. But in early January 2009, he learned that the window for action was narrower than even his aides had realized. The occasion was an introductory call on House Speaker Nancy Pelosi, and the meeting in her office began with a light, almost jovial tone. Obama opened the proceedings disarmingly, introducing himself to Pelosi and her aides as if he were some anonymous constituent—"I'm Barack Obama," he said. About halfway through, the president-elect complained about Emanuel's incessant knuckle cracking. Emanuel marched over to Obama and, in his inimitable way, cracked his knuckle loudly in Obama's ear. [2]

But before it was over, Pelosi offered the president-elect a sobering piece of advice: He should press to hold the TARP vote even before he was inaugurated. The atmosphere on Capitol Hill was curdling so quickly that it would soon become impossible to extract the additional funds. If nothing else, it would be better politically for Congress to act on Bush's watch. [3]

Thereafter, Emanuel turned the full force of his manic energy to locking down the money. Pelosi and her Senate counterpart, Harry Reid, had asked Obama to write a letter attaching several conditions to its use—such as leaning on the banks to expand small business lending, and limiting executive pay at bailed-out firms.[4] Emanuel drove the economic team to produce this document like a proctor at a British prep school, ceaselessly invoking the dire consequences that would accompany delay. He lived in constant fear of being unprepared for another bank run.

Perhaps more than any other issue, the question of how to help struggling homeowners loomed over the discussion. Politically, it was difficult to justify spending hundreds of billions of dollars to prop up failing banks while millions of homeowners faced foreclosure, and congressional Democrats regarded the Bush administration's neglect of housing as a key reason for TARP's unpopularity. When they spoke of demonstrating that TARP was "under new management," as Democrats like Senate Banking Committee chairman Chris Dodd of Connecticut often did in these days, housing was central to what they had in mind.

But substantively, too, the housing market was of enormous consequence, arguably as central to the fate of the banks as any economic force. It was, after all, losses on *mortgage* securities that had sent the banks staggering into bailout territory. Someone observing from a distance could be forgiven for thinking that even the banks would want the government to spend as much money shoring up homeowners as it was spending on keeping the banks themselves afloat.

For its part, the Obama economic team saw housing as a separate issue, one that was initially a distraction from the more urgent task of financial triage. The team did not consider housing unimportant, to be sure. But if a million homeowners defaulted tomorrow, that wouldn't unleash a small fraction of the economic chaos of a single failed megabank, like Citigroup or Bank of America. In this view, the only reason to grapple with housing so soon was that Congress had made it a condition for releasing the extra bailout money.

An internal Treasury memo prepared for Geithner in late January 2009 about obtaining more money beyond TARP made the point starkly. On the one hand, the memo explained, Treasury would need to show the markets that it understood the source of the financial panic and had the money to fight it. On the other hand, Treasury would need to appease Congress over housing, lending, and executive compensation in order to obtain the funds. If Treasury appeared overly preoccupied with these legitimate but still secondary concerns, then the markets would deem it out of touch, and the panic would intensify. But if it was too focused on impressing the markets, Congress would grumble and deny it additional funds. Perhaps not surprisingly, the memo counseled vagueness.[5]

It was a reasonable posture, but not one that sat well in the House and the Senate. With Geithner not yet confirmed, Summers became the administration's chief emissary to Capitol Hill. He spoke constantly with senators and their staffs, calling them at all hours of the day and night to urge approval of the money. But his efforts did not much endear him to the country's elected representatives, whose poll numbers seemed to sink in tandem with the value of their constituents' homes. "There was a lot of skepticism among Senate Democrats about whether we should do this," said one senior aide to a senator who was influential in the discussion. "I was a little bit surprised by how widespread the cynicism toward Summers was among a diverse group of Democrats."[6] Summers, many senators felt, had pushed some of the Clinton-era regulatory changes that helped cause the crisis.

In the run-up to the TARP vote on January 15, the atmosphere in the Senate was becoming poisonous. At one point before the vote, John Kerry angrily convened a meeting of senior senators—among them, Dick Durbin and Chuck Schumer, the chamber's second- and third-ranking Democrats—in a room off the Senate floor. The Senate aide recalled that Kerry said something like, "Why the hell should I listen to Larry Summers? If he calls me one more time about this, I'm going to blow up."[7] The other senators spoke up in agreement. In the end, they supported the administration only because they believed the consequences of not approving the money could be another market catastrophe. Politically, at least, it was an inauspicious start to the Obama era.

While Congress and the country puzzled over the way the bailout appeared to favor the biggest banks at the expense of ordinary Americans, Wall Street was having its own equally intense debate, although a far narrower one. The question of the moment was whether or not several major banks were on the verge of insolvency, and the answer hinged on the banks' portfolios of mortgage securities, the pieces of mortgages that had been sliced up in order to be sold off as investments (but that banks often gorged on themselves). If the securities were really as worthless as they appeared, then the banks were doomed. But there was also the possibility that the drop in prices had been an overreaction—the work of irrational pessimism. If the securities were only temporarily depressed amid the frenzied sell-off, the banks might recover just by waiting it out.

The debate had excited violent passions on Wall Street since the market first lost altitude in 2007. The big firms like Citigroup and Merrill Lynch and Morgan Stanley refused to believe the securities they'd heaped onto their balance sheets could be worth less than 100 cents on the dollar. Their critics pointed out that the securities were nothing more than claims on the mortgage payments of millions of subprime borrowers, who were defaulting in droves. Yes, the mortgages had been cut up and repackaged in ways that ostensibly eased away the risk—that was the magic of "structured finance." But it was hard to see how much help that would be now that the housing market had self-immolated.

Around this time, the hedge fund manager David Einhorn asked the CEO of a major financial firm why he still valued the company's mortgage securities so richly. The executive told him that it was because the securities were rated triple-A. This was true enough: the ratings agencies *had* blessed them as virtually riskless. The problem, as was becoming increasingly obvious, was that this didn't mean they *were* riskless; it meant just that the ratings agencies hadn't understood the risks. When Einhorn insisted that the securities weren't worth more than 60 or 70 cents on the dollar, the CEO quickly backed down, according to Einhorn's account at a conference in 2008. The CEO conceded that he had to say the securities were worth close to 100 cents because otherwise his accountants would force him to acknowledge the huge loss.[8] It was one of the most surreal conversations of Einhorn's life.

The same bitter divide over mortgage securities that cleaved Wall Street ran straight through Team Obama. The person with the most to say about the fate of the banks early in the administration was a former investment banker named Lee Sachs. The person most determined to prevent him from saying it was Larry Summers. Sachs believed the mortgage securities had significant value, even if he couldn't say with confidence what the value might be. Summers held a similar conviction in the other direction.

The debate may have sounded esoteric, but it had enormous implications. If the securities were close to worthless and the big banks were insolvent, then what lay in store for them was highly unappealing. At best, they'd need a good deal more money from either the government or private investors than anyone was talking about. But there was only so much money either source was going to give them unless they wiped out their current stockholders and fired their executives. At heart, then, the debate between Lee Sachs and Larry Summers was a debate over how much pain the banks might have to endure, with Sachs suggesting less and Summers more.

Though they'd been friends since the late 1990s, Sachs and Summers could hardly have been less similar by disposition. Sachs, whom Geithner had brought in as his top financial consigliere, was as courteous and conciliatory as Summers was gruff and pro-vocative. While working late one night during the darkest days of the crisis, Sachs trooped out of the Treasury building to observe a Secret Service agent confiscating his Chinese food—no after-hours deliveries, apparently. Here was one of the two people most directly responsible for staving off global financial apocalypse, and yet Sachs did not pull rank or risk confrontation. He did not so much as raise his voice. The opportunity cost of the time it took to quietly negoti-ate his dinner's release may have run into the hundreds of millions.

For Sachs, there wasn't an underling too lowly to thank, a battle that wasn't worth avoiding. A Treasury communications official once persuaded him to cooperate in a magazine profile despite his painful aversion to self-promotion. Thirty minutes into the interview, an aide came in and handed him a piece of notebook paper. Sachs quietly glanced at the paper and set it aside. Fifteen minutes later, the aide came in with another paper. Sachs glanced at the paper and set it aside, too. After a few more minutes the journalist was on to such world-historical matters as Sachs's tennis game. Another aide came bursting through the door. "Lee, the secretary needs you right now!" Lee Sachs, for whom few things are less appealing than discussing personal details, had been too nice to stop an interview for the secre-tary of the Treasury.

Sachs had been one of the first economic officials in the Obama headquarters after the election—his old friend Dan Tarullo, the head of economic planning for the transition, asked him to produce a set of options for fixing the banks. A few weeks later Summers showed up, having been named Obama's top economic adviser, and began ordering him around like a deputy or a research assis-tant (Summers often blurred the two positions). The arrangement wasn't unprecedented; Sachs had been an assistant secretary when Summers ran Treasury near the end of the Clinton administration. He choked down the first few assignments with typical Sachsian good cheer.

By day two, even Sachs, he of the inexhaustible patience, could take no more. It was one thing to embark on a Larry Summers treasure hunt when you had all the time in the world, another when you were trying to hold the markets together with the policy equivalent of a glue stick. Sachs had noticed that Summers's old Harvard chief of staff, Marne Levine, was ensconced at Treasury on a worker-bee transition assignment. He called three times in twenty-four hours pleading with her to come step in for him as Summers's gofer. On the final call, he threatened to drive over to Treasury and personally retrieve her. When she finally arrived, he went back to his office and resumed operation glue stick.

Within the financial world, the big banks' chief adversaries were money managers like David Einhorn. The typical hedge fund proprietor was a nimble-minded financier sitting on billions of dollars in capital with few limits on how to deploy it. The hedgies saw the big banks as plodding, herdlike creatures that slavishly followed the latest fads and relied on sheer size and political influence to save them from their own stupidity. It surprised few people in the hedge fund world that several banks had piled into every variety of real estate asset just before the entire market cratered, by which point many hedge funds had positioned themselves in the opposite direction.

When the Citis and Merrills (and Lehmans) fell on hard times in 2007 and 2008, the hedgies were right there to bet on their collapse by short-selling their stock. One got the sense it was only partly in hopes of profiting from the banks' possible demise (you could never be sure that the government wouldn't prop them up, after all). The more visceral reason was to register their disdain toward these thick-skulled behemoths. In the metaphor of the savanna, the banks were the wildebeests and the hedge funds the cheetahs.

It was no accident that Larry Summers identified with the hedge funds. He'd counted some of the industry's leading figures as his closest friends and had joined its rarefied ranks between stints in public service. While still president of Harvard, Summers took on a consulting gig at Taconic Capital Advisors, run by two Goldman Sachs alumni who were prominent Democratic donors. Then, in 2006, he joined DE Shaw. The firm's founder, the computer scientist David Shaw, was a pioneer in using sophisticated mathematical algorithms to profit from patterns in the market. By 2007, many of the so-called quant funds that deployed such strategies were being hammered—few of their gee-whiz models had anticipated the fallout from the credit crisis. Summers, who received a lucrative stake in the fund as compensation, began joking to friends about the novelty of losing half his net worth in a given day.

Summers worked hard to learn his new vocation. When he met with friends and colleagues who knew something about finance, he pumped them for information. One recalled a series of questions about carry trades—a strategy in which investors borrow money cheaply in the short term and lend at a higher interest rate over the longer term. Later on, when Summers joined the administration, co-workers noticed that he'd been influenced by his time among the hedge funds. He once debated a colleague over the social utility of high-frequency trading—a technique, favored by certain "quants" like Shaw, that rely on a computer to buy up stocks a split second faster than humans can, then turn around and sell to them at a profit. The colleague thought this was a high-tech version of "front-running": the computer sees which stocks humans are trying to buy, then buys them a split second faster, before the price goes up. Summers said the practice helped ensure that people would be able to buy and sell the stocks they wanted when they wanted to.[9]

But Summers's views on the merits of banks derived from sociology rather than self-interest. Sooner or later, the most brilliant minds on Wall Street tend to leave the big institutions to start their own hedge funds. They typically find the bureaucracy of the big banks confounding and the conformity oppressive. The culture of this world appealed to Summers. "He, like a lot of people in this business, worships smart," the colleague said.[10] While interviewing for his job at DE Shaw, Summers was asked by one of the firm's partners to take a kind of IQ test that consisted of three logic puzzles.[11] The former Harvard president was not offended by this. He took it as a sign he'd come to the right place.

Before joining the administration Lee Sachs had also worked at a hedge fund: the multibillion-dollar Mariner Investment Group, run by a prominent money manager named Bill Michaelcheck. But Sachs was not a hedge fund *guy*. He wasn't one to dig into a corporate balance sheet and find hidden sources of value or risk. He wasn't known for spotting subtle market inefficiencies—an undervalued currency, an expensive government bond—from which to profit. Sachs chaired the investment committee at Mariner and offered broad-based advice.

Sachs's formative professional experience had been at a Wall Street investment bank: Bear Stearns. Bear lacked the pedigree of Morgan Stanley or the gilded name of Goldman Sachs. The company's longtime chairman and CEO, Alan "Ace" Greenberg, loved to muse that while he would consider job candidates with MBAs, he much preferred recruits with PSD degrees: poor, smart, and with a deep desire for great wealth. The Bear brass could be cartoonishly garish, even by the standards of the nouveaux riches. Greenberg once donated $1 million to provide Viagra for the poor. ("I own stock in Pfizer," he quipped to the *New York Times*.) His successor, Jimmy Cayne, left work every day promptly at five to play competitive bridge and once spent months tracking down the precise variety of cigar smoked by the prime minister of Lebanon. He liked to savor the $150 Cuban contraband in his office even after New York City banned workplace smoking in 2003.[12]

Bear had long cultivated a reputation as one of the more iconoclastic houses on Wall Street—and, in turn, the financial establishment derided it as vulgar and vaguely corrupt. Bankers at other firms complained that there wasn't a deal Bear wouldn't do if it boosted the bottom line, no matter the conflict of interest or cost to its reputation.[13] Nonetheless, Bear was a large bureaucracy with thousands of employees when Sachs worked there in the eighties and nineties. Its antiestablishment sensibility went only so far.

There were two ways to thrive in such an environment: as an adrenaline-addled trader willing to plunk down tens of millions of dollars on a hunch—to be a star, in other words—or as someone willing to labor scrupulously within the organization. Lee Sachs was the latter. At Bear, he was known as tireless, inoffensive, and above all trustworthy. He was smart enough to grasp any deal or line of business, but not so brilliant that he inspired awe or resentment. He had an intellect built for upper management, if not the charisma for the corner suite. "The way in which the firm has been characterized is exaggerated," said one former colleague. "But even if you accept that, he was still among the most soft-spoken people within the firm."[14]

Sach's shot at the fast track had come in the late 1980s. At the time he was a junior banker on the company's capital markets desk, helping to advise companies on their issuance of debt. One day a top Bear executive showed up on the trading floor and asked Sach's boss to point out his best employee. Sachs soon got a tap on the shoulder. The banker was working on one of the company's most lucrative deals: slicing up and selling off pieces of Israeli government debt, which the U.S. government had guaranteed under the 1979 peace accord with Egypt. The banker needed someone to follow him around and "shovel all the shit," as one colleague recalled.[15] Sachs would be the shit-shoveler.

It fell to Sachs to negotiate with the Israelis and with the other U.S. banks underwriting the deal. He had to work with the traders who'd price the debt securities and the salesmen who'd sell them. For Sachs, the deal was about logistics and ego management as much as high finance. He found he had a gift for corralling people who couldn't see how there might be something more important than what they were doing at any given moment. The transaction took months to execute. In the end, Sachs shoveled every last turd.

Not long after, Bear made Sachs head of capital markets, the group where he'd been toiling away before the Israeli deal. A few years later, he came to the attention of the firm's future president, Warren Spector, who added the company's corporate bond-trading business to Sach's management portfolio. To an outsider, this might have seemed an unremarkable promotion. To anyone familiar with the sociology of Wall Street, it was the ultimate test of political skill.

No divide on Wall Street was more brightly drawn in the 1980s and 1990s than the one between bankers and traders. The bankers had traditionally been the in-house aristocracy, practiced in the schmoozing of CEOs whose business they meant to attract. The traders were the upstarts, it having suddenly dawned on Wall Street firms that there was money to be made buying and selling securities themselves rather than simply placing orders for clients. The traders were, as a class, more voluble, more direct, more vulgar. Whole investment banks, like Lehman Brothers prior to its takeover by American Express in the mid-1980s,* fell apart because one group

---

*Lehman Brothers became independent again in 1994, when American Express spun it off. For more on the collapse of Lehman in the 1980s, see Ken Auletta, *Greed and Glory on Wall Street: The Fall of the House of Lehman* (New York: Overlook, 2001).

refused to be led by the other. Suddenly it was Sach's job to manage both. He was barely in his thirties.

In this, Sachs had the great advantage of being liked by all sides. The traders had affection for him from his days on the capital markets desk, when he'd been one of a small handful of investment bankers to sit with them on the trading floor. He'd learned their rites and rituals, their distinctive patois. The bankers liked his thoroughness, the care with which he chose his words. You could send Lee Sachs to meet with any client, and he'd never fail to make a good impression. The clients rather preferred someone who wasn't effortlessly brilliant, who'd really studied their material. It made them feel more valued.

Sachs was a man who could go far in an organization not because he'd figured out who he needed to suck up to and who he needed to kneecap, but precisely because he hadn't. He was, in fact, almost completely lacking in guile, as was obvious the second you met him. This made him unthreatening to those with power, people who were often threatened by one another.

Sach's patrons got all the benefits of a bright, ambitious protégé with none of the costs. If you told him what you needed, you knew he'd kill himself to make it happen, not thinking about where it was getting him and whether there was a faster way to get there. Sachs wasn't mindless; he had opinions. But he didn't waste time asking more questions than it took to do the job.

So there was, at heart, a conservatism about Lee Sachs. He had a respect for the way things were done, for the rules and norms that made bureaucracies function. If you knew the rules, you knew what it took to succeed. Then it was just a matter of executing—of being thorough and exacting, which Sachs had always been. It was this intellectual conservatism that put him on a collision course with Larry Summers.

• • •

If a bank has $100 billion in assets (such as mortgages and mortgage securities, but also safer instruments, like cash and U.S. government bonds) and $80 billion in liabilities (money borrowed from bond-holders, depositors, and other lenders), it has $20 billion in capital (100 minus 80). The capital is like a cushion that exists to absorb losses. Insolvency occurs when the losses drag the value of the assets below $80 billion, wiping out the capital and foisting losses onto the bank's lenders. In the months before the 2008 election, Summers had become convinced that the bursting of the real estate bubble had made the big banks insolvent. He worried they were merely conceal-ing their hobbled state from the public and that they might need to be topped off with heaping sacks of government cash to survive.

The reason this wasn't obvious to outsiders, Summers surmised, was the dubious way the banks valued their assets. Under traditional bank accounting, a bank didn't have to concede it had lost money on, say, a mortgage security as long as it intended to hold that se-curity for years. The going price could plummet to 60 cents on the dollar. So long as the bank had no plans to sell, it could blithely pro-claim the value to be the full dollar it had paid.

That might be fine if the securities were likely to recover. But if, like Summers, you thought the mortgage securities were as doomed as all the homeowners who were skipping their monthly payments, or that they were at least deeply damaged, then bank accounting amounted to an elaborate form of denial. Summers believed there was more information to be gleaned from a practice known as "mark-to-market accounting," wherein the bank would have to ac-knowledge short-term price swings. And if you marked the banks' portfolios to market—that is, valued them using the latest market prices—you got a pretty frightening picture.

This method of accounting was especially popular among hedge fund managers. The hedge fund industry could be maddeningly opaque: prior to 2011, the hedgies didn't have to enlighten regulators about their investors (typically the very wealthy) or their bets (often very risky). But their ethos was fundamentally meritocratic. Those that made money thrived; those that consistently lost money met with a brutal demise.

Central to this ethos was the practice of mark-to-market accounting. Anyone who entrusted a hedge fund manager with money would receive regular updates on how much his or her portfolio was worth *at that particular moment*, not when the assets were purchased, or at some vague future date when they might be sold. No small part of the hedge funds' low regard for big banks were the rules that, in their view, allowed the banks to paper over enormous losses. There was no reason why a hedge fund that had bet mindlessly on real estate should go out of business while a bank that had made the same bet should continue on as though nothing had happened.

To Sachs, such arguments were of mild intellectual interest but useless as a practical matter. The way the banks did their numbers might be vaguely perverse. There might even be an argument for tweaking the accounting rules at some future date to make the system more intuitive. But it was lunacy to insist that the rules be changed *in the middle of the game*. The banks had bought their securities and managed their capital expecting to account for it the way they always did. Now Summers was suggesting they be held to a different standard. If you were the one who had to deliver the news to the banks themselves, as Sachs suspected he would be, how would you propose such a thing with a straight face?

Beyond the obvious unfairness, changing the rules would make the problem look far, far worse than it already was. Sachs believed the banks had indeed suffered losses on their real estate portfolios, but he also believed the market was overreacting. And the difference between losing 10 or 20 cents on the dollar, which struck him as plausible, and losing the 60 or 70 percent the latest market prices implied, was the difference between losses in the hundreds of billions and losses in the trillions when you added them up across banks. Sachs was already killing himself figuring out how to fill the smaller hole. He didn't see the point in making his own job three or four times as challenging. The "hedge fund view," as it became known around Treasury, was fine if you were trying to shock people in an argument. But if you actually had to solve the problem—had to sit around a conference table somewhere in the bowels of the Treasury building and put terms down on paper—it had little use.

Underlying all this was that old question of pain. Summers wasn't averse to seeing the banks suffer in the short term to put them on sounder footing for the long haul. The way that would happen was by "marking down" the value of their assets, which would foist losses onto existing shareholders and force them to raise more capital. Sachs worried that, during a crisis, there was only so much short-term pain the banks could handle. Any more and you might kill them.

And so, within the administration, a great free-for-all broke out a few weeks after the election, and it quickly became epic. The Sunday after the inauguration, Sachs and Summers brought the economic team together to discuss the banks. The group met in the transition headquarters because Geithner wasn't yet confirmed as Treasury secretary. Summers was flanked by two aides who shared his zeal about bank losses: Mary Goodman, a former Clinton Treasury official who'd spent the previous decade at a hedge fund; and a Harvard finance professor named Jeremy Stein.

Sachs, for his part, was joined by Geithner, who echoed the views of his lieutenant. The two men had been close friends since they'd first overlapped at Treasury in the late 1990s, and Geithner often deferred to Sachs on financial market questions, never having worked on Wall Street himself. Later, as president of the New York Fed, Geithner had regulated some of the country's biggest banks. This, too, had given him sympathy for Sach's conservatism. As a regulator, you never wanted to drop too many surprises on the banks, lest you provoke a violent reaction. Geithner had also brought a small contingent of colleagues from the New York Fed who were helping to staff him at Treasury.

For six hours they went back and forth about bank losses with no resolution in sight. At one point Stein argued that if the losses were as large as he and Summers feared, then the banks' shareholders weren't the only ones who might have to endure some pain. The people who had lent the banks money—their bondholders, traditionally a more protected class of investor—would have to lose money as well. Sachs bristled at this, saying that foisting losses onto bondholders had only made the crisis worse when it was tried a few months earlier, in the case of Washington Mutual. The New York Fed officials were uncomfortable with squeezing even the shareholders. In any case, Sachs and his allies didn't think the losses were likely to be as large as Summers and Stein assumed.

The debate was really only beginning. It persisted along roughly the same lines, with the same lack of evident progress, for another six weeks. Every few days, Sachs would take a few hours off from his day job of triaging the financial system and gamely trek over to Summers's office on the second floor of the White House. Summers would have sent an aide to go off and study the minutiae of bank accounting, only to have concluded, when the aide reported back to him, that it was "crazy." He would then proceed to hold Sachs personally accountable for all its sins.

Sachs, for his part, would protest that if you went back and applied Summers's preferred rules over the last fifty, sixty, or seventy years, then the number of times the system was flat broke would be too numerous to count. There was a reason banks didn't do their numbers like hedge funds, he'd insist. Invariably, Summers or an aide would then demand to know what the reason was, particularly since the banks had begun to behave like hedge funds, with all their exotic trades. "People were fond of saying, 'You don't understand. The reason we have banks is because they can't mark to market,'" recalled one aide. "I was never sure what it meant." [16]

The conversation would then devolve. Summers had an annoying habit of narrating the debate even as he participated in it. "Lee, you're losing this argument!" he would announce. "You're getting crushed!" Sachs would sputter that Summers was holding an academic seminar, that Summers had little grasp of how financial institutions actually worked, and what point was there in debating the rules anyway if no one was going to change them.

Here, at least, Sachs did have a point. Even if Summers was onto something, he was maddeningly inept at translating gut feeling into action. There was no one better at finding fault, but when it came to actually generating a workable plan, he was next to hopeless. That meant the practical upshot of all the back-and-forth was mainly to slow the entire process down. Outside the White House, meanwhile, the banks grew sicker and the country grew angrier.

6

THE SUCCESSION FIGHT

The longer the bruising debate over the banks went on, the more administration officials suspected that Lee Sachs was only the proximate target of Summers's verbal pummeling. The actual target was Geithner. "My guess is part of why Larry would take on Lee as forcefully is he didn't want to take Tim on as forcefully," said one witness to several of the exchanges between Summers and Sachs. "It was a way of debating a viewpoint without having to say, 'I think the Treasury secretary is wrong.'" [1]

There was much to commend this theory. The Treasury secretary had long since adopted Sachs's view of the banks, and it formed the basis of the plan he was formulating. If the real estate securities were more valuable than the market was acknowledging, then the banks' losses would be significantly smaller than Summers assumed, and the amount of capital they needed would be a lot less daunting. So much less daunting, in fact, that Geithner believed the banks would be able to raise it without government help, merely by selling more shares to private investors.

The centerpiece of the Geithner plan was the so-called stress test, in which regulators would posit a far bleaker path for the economy than most forecasters predicted, then calculate the effects on the banks' balance sheets and the amount of capital they required. Geithner conceived of the stress tests as a way to show investors that the situation wasn't nearly as dire as they imagined. If the banks looked as though they'd be in decent shape even after two hypothetical years of abysmal economic growth and unemployment, then the typical financier might consider them a sound investment. To put his money where his mouth was, Geithner would offer government cash to any bank that couldn't raise enough capital from investors to fill whatever shortage the stress tests uncovered. The logic of the plan was the logic of the parent who sings the culinary praises of split-pea soup, then pledges to eat it himself should the child—the investors—still refuse.

Summers, for his part, worried that the market would regard the stress tests as every bit the sham most children regard their parents' pea soup salesmanship to be.[2] He was heartened to see Geithner struggle to sell the plan internally, gleefully telling friends that Emanuel had closed one meeting by saying, "Does anyone understand a fucking thing Tim Geithner just said?" But though Summers rarely spoke up for Geithner in these cases, he was loath to challenge the Treasury secretary directly. Hence the appeal of teeing off on Sachs.

Still, the bank debate was woefully insufficient as an explanation of the Geithner-Summers tension. By the time they joined the Obama administration, Tim Geithner and Larry Summers had packed all the intimacy and dysfunction of close family relations into a convoluted fifteen-year history. To chalk up the rift to a disagreement about bank policy would be as misleading as merely calling the Summers-Geithner friendship "textured," as aides and colleagues sometimes did.

When the Clintonites swept into office in 1993, Geithner was working for George H.W. Bush's Treasury assistant secretary as a special assistant—a post for a young man whose elders want to bask in his future. As the incoming undersecretary, Summers had his own candidate for the position, but the Treasury staff raved about Geithner. Finally, the new undersecretary decided he had enough work for two promising young men. It wasn't long before Summers deemed his accidental assistant the indispensable one, at which point he became the elder who reveled in promoting Geithner.

The mistake subordinates often made with Summers was to assume he wouldn't tolerate dissent. In fact, he craved pushback, at least when it came to policy and strategy. Geithner saw that he could deliver this while others instinctively shrank from it. "When you're talking to the Treasury secretary or the under secretary, there's a strong tendency for everybody to leap on what that person is saying and agree," one former co-worker recalled. "Tim's fundamental function was to interrupt that process." Years later, after enough time had passed to make the line funny, but not so much time as to make it painful, Summers would joke that Geithner was the only person who'd walk into his office and say, "Larry, on this one you're full of shit." [3]

Summers could be a good boss. He didn't overrate experience. He trusted his aides with great responsibility long before they'd have trusted themselves with it. The trouble was that he never quite stopped thinking of them as aides. Even after they'd risen through the ranks, their job was to execute his will, even if he didn't put it in those terms and they didn't consciously view it that way. The entire global technocracy wanted to know what Larry thought about this or that; it was no small source of prestige that the former aides could divine the answer. Better still if they could do it without so much as speaking with him.

In 1999, Summers became Treasury secretary and Geithner his undersecretary, the department's highest-ranking international official. Like anyone who'd spent his twenties and thirties winning one promotion after another, Geithner could be forgiven for thinking he was ready to be his own man. But, unofficially, Summers hung on to the international portfolio even after he was ensconced in the top job. "It was like Larry continued to be undersecretary, and David [Lipton, Geithner's predecessor] and Tim were his two assistant secretaries," said one former colleague. "That creates problems."[4]

By the time the two men turned up in Washington in late 2008, Summers understood that his posture would have to change. Geithner hadn't just beaten him out for the job of Treasury secretary. He'd spent the previous eight years leading two major bureaucracies—the New York Fed and, before that, the IMF's influential policy planning department—without a patron peering over his shoulder. Geithner wasn't exactly looking to resurrect the old arrangement. During the transition, when Emanuel suggested he come aboard as Summers's deputy at Treasury, Geithner informed him it wasn't worth moving his family to reprise his role as a sidekick.[5]

There was a part of Summers that really did want to accommodate this new reality. When *Fortune* magazine tried to pull him into a photo shoot in the Treasury secretary's office, Summers protested extravagantly. "I don't want to be photographed in the secretary's office," he said. "That's Tim's office now." And yet there was something about the sheer molecule-displacing bulk of the Summers persona that refused to be budged. "He viewed Tim as junior to him," said one former Obama economic official. "While he respected the office, he thought of Tim at some level as a grad student who needed feedback and critiques."[6]

The White House had circled February 10, 2009, as the date for Geithner to share his bank fix with the world. Given that Geithner was the lone Senate-confirmed Obama official at Treasury, the turn-around would have been tight for a high school commencement address. For a speech supposedly outlining the solution to a once-in-a-century financial crisis, the timetable was positively brutal.

As if this backdrop weren't sufficiently dramatic, the moment seemed to call forth all of Summers's ambivalence. When Geithner forwarded him an early draft of the speech, Summers responded that "it doesn't sound like a Treasury secretary." Geithner and his aides abruptly lost confidence in their speech and frantically reworked it.

More so even than as a struggle to become Obama's alpha adviser, the Geithner-Summers psychodrama may be understood as a competition to succeed Bob Rubin, the paterfamilias, as the paragon of centrist economic thinking in Washington.

That Rubin had shaped the Obama economic team was beyond question. Mike Froman, his former Treasury chief of staff and Citigroup colleague, had, after all, been the person in charge of hiring for the entire Obama administration. And though Rubin had little direct role in selecting Summers, Geithner, and Orszag—he actually urged Summers for Treasury when Obama called to ask—they were all former protégés, as were Sachs, Jason Furman, and Gene Sperling, who also claimed senior economic positions. Rubin remained in contact with many of them. Anyone who spent much time in the White House complex became accustomed to seeing Rubin wander through every few weeks for another consultation. Rubin had even lent his longtime communications aide, David Dreyer, to help prep Geithner for his confirmation hearings.

Still, Rubin was no longer a figure a Democratic president and his inner circle were eager to associate with publicly. Already there had been long-standing animus toward Rubin on the left. Beyond his symbolic importance as the father of Clinton-style neoliberalism—a worldview liberals deemed too centrist, too market-oriented, and altogether corrupt for its association with Wall Street—liberals detested

Rubin for a more specific pair of sins. They believed he'd persuaded Bill Clinton to sign laws deregulating derivatives and burying New Deal–era restrictions on bank consolidation.* And he later accepted a sinecure at Citigroup, the chief beneficiary of the new bank law.

But by November 2008, when Citi earned itself a government bailout made necessary partly by the extra risk taking Rubin had advocated internally, Rubin was no longer anathema only on the left. Rubin-hatred had gone mainstream. The *New York Times* ran an extensive autopsy of Citi's decline expounding on Rubin's role.[7] Across the political spectrum, the idea that such a person would enjoy outsize influence in a Democratic administration—especially the administration of a self-proclaimed outsider—was nothing short of galling.

Even some of Rubin's former protégés had begun to feel differently about their former mentor. It wasn't that they blamed him for Citi, or that they were embarrassed by their association with him. Most still welcomed his calls, still solicited his advice, and still identified themselves as Rubin alumni. It was just that his aura had dimmed.

In their minds, Bob Rubin had always cut a kind of Olympian figure: detached, disinterested, above it all. With Rubin, there had never been an angle other than what was right in the strictest platonic sense. They could all summon the image of Rubin dutifully scribbling down input from colleagues on his trademark yellow legal pad, of him earnestly weighing pros and cons.[8]

In their memories, Rubin was an almost pure distillation of rational ego. He seemed practically immune to grubbier human needs, like physical comfort and affirmation, to say nothing of fame, power, and status. His daily lunch had consisted of an undressed

---

*The truth is somewhat more complicated, as Rubin had already left the administration when Clinton signed both laws. But it's certainly true that Rubin wasn't a voice of internal opposition while Congress was crafting the measures.

salad, which he'd wash down with a bottle of water.[9] When he had nothing of consequence to share with the president, he voluntarily gave up his face time, easily the most precious currency in Washington. He seemed positively scandalized when confronted with evidence of cynicism or political expediency. In 1996, he nearly guffawed when George Stephanopoulos confided that Republican Medicare cuts would be the centerpiece of Clinton's reelection pitch. How "small and insufficient," he complained to Larry Summers.[10] (The pitch would prove wildly successful.) Even his extravagances were almost embarrassingly mundane. On those instances in which Rubin splurged for dessert, he'd treat himself to a few scoops of currant sorbet.[11]

Above all there was *process*: Rubin was fanatical about good process. Clinton had hatched the National Economic Council during the '92 campaign to institutionalize his laserlike focus on the economy. Before Rubin signed on as director, half the wise men in Washington told him it would be a quagmire. The likes of the Treasury secretary and budget director would never abide him standing between them and the Oval Office. So warned, Rubin felt a quasi-historical responsibility to make the NEC work. Every principal would get a seat at the table; everyone's views would be heard and faithfully conveyed to the president. No one's input—including Rubin's—would receive undue weight. It was thanks to Rubin that the term "honest broker" was reintroduced into the political lexicon,[12] where it survived long enough to haunt Larry Summers sixteen years later, when all of official Washington wondered if he would be up to that part of the NEC job.[13]

Even as Treasury secretary, Rubin organized processes as prolifically as Georgetown matrons organize cocktail parties. During the second term, labor began to lobby for steel tariffs, which Rubin strongly opposed. Rather than weigh in with Clinton privately, in that grand tradition of Treasury secretaries and presidents, Rubin ordered up a full-blown process. Meetings were convened, memos written, and the full complement of arguments presented to the president. All so that Rubin could say in good conscience that tariffs were a dumb idea.[14]

In the eyes of some of those who'd long revered him, the problem with Rubin's tour at Citi wasn't that it compromised him morally. It was that it tainted this towering, ecumenical figure with a whiff of parochialism. In your head, you still imagined Bob Rubin scrupulously adding up the pros and cons on his trusted yellow legal pad. But in your gut, you had to wonder if the calculus weren't tilted ever so slightly, if subconsciously, in the direction of his employer. Rubin still sounded and acted like the Rubin of old, still carried himself with that trademark Rubinesque thoughtfulness. It's just that his pronouncements became faintly more self-serving.

It turned out Rubin had always had one genuine human need, which was to influence the course of events, or at least the people who did. When a former Treasury secretary joined Goldman in 1969, the other bankers largely shunned him as a has-been; Rubin befriended the man and relied on his Washington contacts. Rubin wanted to work in the White House so badly that declining his first offer, a poorly conceived job directing the wage and price council, pained him almost as much as the back injury that immobilized him for nearly a year and would have made it impossible to accept.[15] After he left the Clinton administration, Rubin told one friend he joined Citigroup so he could keep having lunch with anyone he wanted. Rubin meant it figuratively: thanks to Citi, he might meet the Korean finance minister on a trip to Seoul. But the idea was the same: he craved being in on the action.

Rubin had taken the job stipulating that he wanted no managerial responsibility. He'd schmooze clients, chat up government officials around the globe, keep his door open to any Citi executive who came looking for advice.[16] But he would not oversee any of the hundreds of thousands of employees, the millions of activities, the hundreds of billions worth of transactions, that made Citi run from day to day. Rubin would be a private sector elder statesman—floating above the factions as he'd done in Washington. Because he had no particular book of business, he'd have no book to talk. He could be, if not as detached and disinterested as he was at the height of his Clinton-era powers, then as close as you get on a corporate payroll.

But by 2007, one could detect the cracks in this plan. Rubin had always been an aphoristic thinker. During his Goldman days, those aphorisms had a way of challenging Wall Street conventional wisdom, at least insofar as people on Wall Street issued such challenges. When colleagues refused to sell a stock because they believed the market had bottomed and would soon rebound, Rubin would instruct them: "Sometimes the bottom isn't the bottom." The market may seem wildly off—stock prices preposterously low—but you couldn't assume you knew better. That was just pride or perhaps self-delusion.

But when it came to the real estate assets Citi owned, the company seemed to be in collective denial, and Rubin was no exception. Citi's numbers guys had assured him the risks were "de minimus." [17] "What we knew was that they were triple-A securities," he later said. "The people doing the [valuing] did do a lot of analysis. Their judgment was that these things were properly rated." [18] To those who warned that the losses could endanger the firm, Rubin insisted that the losses suggested by market prices were wrong. "If there were real markets, it would have been one thing," Rubin said. "But they were small, highly illiquid markets. I thought on those, the market didn't necessarily tell you what they were worth." [19]

Another old Rubin aphorism: "Raise capital when you need it, not when you have to." From his Goldman days, Rubin knew firms had a bias toward believing they could absorb their losses without additional money from investors. That was when they *should have* raised it. By the time they were proved wrong, the terms on which they could raise the money would invariably be worse, if they could raise it at all. But now when outsiders pleaded that Citi should aggressively raise capital, it made little impression on Rubin.

Citi had actually raised more than $20 billion, including some $7 billion from the government of Abu Dhabi, in the fall of 2007, a quarter in which its mortgage securities shed $18 billion in value.[20] But in the year that passed before a new round of losses sent it scurrying for a bailout—$45 billion in taxpayer money, plus another $300 billion worth of government insurance—the company was chronically slow to raise more and undershot when it did.

It was one thing when Lee Sachs opined about the value of mortgage securities. There was at least some distance between him and the banks, even if it wasn't enough for the administration's critics. But with Rubin, you couldn't entirely be sure where the old, detached Olympian left off and the Citi executive picked up. Citi wasn't paying $15 million a year to subsidize Rubin's elder statesmanship—to preserve him as a national treasure after he'd moved on from government service.* Citi was paying Rubin to vouch for it with clients and foreign governments and even, on occasion, the American public; this was partly the idea behind hiring him not long after the controversial merger that created the megabank. Citi was paying for exclusive rights to an icon named Bob Rubin— for the commercial benefits of taking all that legendary detachment and disinterest and wrapping it around the company like patriotic bunting. It was a transaction, in which Rubin transferred something of great value to Citi and was compensated in return. Not for nothing did the Citi board press him into service as chairman in late

---

* Rubin received a base salary of $1 million and a "guaranteed bonus" of roughly $14 to $16 million per year. In 2007 and 2008, he voluntarily gave up his bonus.

2007, after his predecessor's head rolled because of the company's $10 billion loss. Rubin should have known as well as anyone that you can't simultaneously sell an asset and keep it for yourself.

The tragedy was that it had all been so unnecessary. Rubin didn't need the cash. He didn't need the extra stamp on his curriculum vitae or the chance to burnish his legacy. He certainly didn't need anything Citi could offer in terms of status or attention. In the end, about the best that could be said of the Citi experience was that it crimped his lunchtime roster.

Though Rubin was now nearly as toxic as the assets that brought down Citi, the debate that raged within the Obama administration in early 2009 was in many ways a debate between a restorationist Rubin faction, led by Geithner, and a reformist Rubin faction, led by Summers.

Geithner was the fresher face, but had always been the more orthodox Rubinite. This was no surprise, as Geithner had taught himself to be a Treasury honcho through close observation of Rubin at the height of his powers. Geithner sometimes came off as a compelling impersonation of the secretary, down to the physical mannerisms and verbal tics. Like Rubin, he'd shun the head of the table at meetings with subordinates, preferring instead to pace around the room firing questions.[21] Rubin would preface his comments with characteristic self-deprecation: "Well, I don't know much about this, but . . ." Geithner favored an almost identical formulation.[22]

Geithner also had the acolyte's way of elevating everyday wisdom into catechism. Rubin coined the term "optionality" to describe his preference for deferring decisions until the last possible moment. If you had until Tuesday to commit $20 billion to Mexico, "preserving optionality" meant waiting till then, on the off chance some later development would change your calculus. At Geithner's Treasury

Department, there was no matter too small to warrant optionality. Small business lending programs, proposed bank fees; whatever the decision, Geithner was a man determined to optionalize.

Rubin had a fondness for seemingly neutral formulations that often decisively tilted policy debates. He liked to say that a serious country should be willing to do X—whether X was intervene in Korea or shrink its deficit.[23] Geithner deployed the serious-country argument liberally. He invoked it against reneging on bonuses to bailed-out bankers (respecting contracts being a "hallmark of an advanced economy") and against kneecapping uncooperative mortgage lenders ("We don't want to be Bolivia, we want to be the United States").

Summers, with his wider-ranging intellect, had always been more comfortable departing from Rubin's Word. Large deficits might generally be something to be feared, as Rubin warned, but not amid persistently high unemployment. Large government programs might not be efficient, but the health care market was even less so. Expensive government infrastructure projects might seem crude and unsophisticated; but if you couldn't upgrade your crumbling roads and bridges when interest rates were at historical lows, when could you do it? Summers came to disagree with Rubin and, to a lesser extent, Geithner about all these things. At the meeting in Miami on September 19, 2008, the Obama political hands found Summers refreshingly engaged with the reality most voters lived. They were mildly put off by Rubin's economic abstractions.[24]

The split between Geithner and Summers was, suffice it to say, something short of a clash of civilizations. But its resolution was of monumental importance, particularly as it related to the banks, where the economic team divided most cleanly into pro- and anti-Rubin camps.

Whereas Geithner shared Rubin's view on the value of the mortgage securities, Summers had occasionally clashed with Rubin over this question as the crisis evolved through 2008. He'd periodically wondered whether banks like Citi were honestly valuing their portfolios. Rubin was unyielding—soon there was no way to pursue the topic with him without picking a fight. Even after Rubin conceded that the securities were worth less than 100 cents on the dollar, he believed the issue was being trumped up. Rubin felt that the hedge funds wanted to pressure the banks to sell so they could snatch their securities up at fire sale prices. He began to wonder if Summers's views weren't being skewed by *his* ties to DE Shaw.

The internal jockeying became intense on March 15, 2009, when the president gathered his senior aides in the Roosevelt Room to decide the fate of the banks. The meeting started at three on a Sunday afternoon and for several hours the two sides went back and forth.[25] Geithner argued from the premise that the banks' shortage of capital was manageable, and that they could overcome it by raising money from private investors. Summers worried that the shortfall was likely to be hundreds of billions, maybe trillions, of dollars, and that pretending otherwise might only extend the problem indefinitely. Summers derided the Geithner plan as timid. Geithner responded: "You could not want to do something that bold more than I do," before explaining why the boldest course was not, in fact, desirable.[26]

Geithner and Sachs worried that employees and customers would desert banks en masse in the event of a government takeover, which seemed to be the logical endpoint of Summers's criticism, even though he stopped short of recommending it. This would leave the government shouldering the banks' losses, but with no way to generate revenue and no way to sell the banks back into private hands. Fearing nationalization, investors might start to flee healthy institutions, forcing the government to intervene there, too.

When they felt the argument drifting away from them, the Treasury team shrewdly turned the questioning back at Summers. "There are hundreds of billions of dollars of value in these institutions,"

Sachs said. "If you're going to go and destroy that, you'd better know there are WMD there"—you'd better be sure the banks are insolvent.[27] Summers could not be sure. Geithner pointedly asked, "What's your proposal? How would that work?"[28] Before long, the other Obama aides began to feel that, as withering as his criticisms were, Summers had little in the way of a concrete alternative. "There's no doubt that Larry . . . wanted to be associated with doing something that was more transformative and cleansing and big," said one participant. "But he had no options he was prepared to advance in support of that objective."[29] The only certainty was that a bolder approach would require hundreds of billions more taxpayer dollars—the amount of additional capital Summers feared the banks needed.

Between 5 pm and 7 pm, the president stepped out to get his hair cut and eat dinner with his family. "You all don't have this right," he said before excusing himself. "I'm going to leave and come back. When I come back, let's see if we can start putting this together." While he was gone, Emanuel announced that no more government money was likely to be forthcoming for the banks. "The public sector was done propping them up," Emanuel later recalled. "I wanted everyone to know that this ain't going to happen."[30] The conversation would lurch on until ten o'clock in the evening, but the wonks in the room realized the matter was now effectively decided. With no more money available, Geithner's plan to coax cash from private investors was the only viable option on the table.

Geithner had once quipped, "If you don't have a choice, you don't have a problem." The saying summed up the mood in the room. Obama seemed to have no choice but to follow his Treasury secretary's lead. Whether or not there might be a problem remained to be seen.

7

THE FALLACY

For nearly forty-eight hours after the Obama team had settled on a stimulus price tag between $675 billion and $775 billion back in Chicago on December 16, 2008, the figures remained a secret. Then, on December 18, two senior Obama aides had trekked to Capitol Hill to trade ideas with congressional staffers. The price range promptly showed up in the next morning's *Washington Post*.[1] It was a small but telling development—in some sense the de facto end to the campaign. From Chicago, the Obama brass could control information and, on occasion, events. In Washington, the very first step of the very first new initiative had resisted stage management.

Emanuel was furious, having instructed his staff that he did not want the stimulus defined by its size, and the Obamans tried to reimpose order. The transition trotted out Summers to caution, appropriately enough, that the broad outline was still fluid. "I don't think you can regard this simply as a numbers game," the economic adviser subsequently told the *Post*, invoking that ancient refrain of officials confronted with figures they didn't intend for public consumption.[2] But within a week the exercise proved pointless, and the Obama brass dropped the pretense that it had no target in mind. In this battle, at least, Obama would bend to Washington rather than vice versa.

The $775 billion figure had been deemed, in the collective judgment of Team Obama, the biggest opening bid Congress could absorb without an acute case of sticker shock, which could put an end to the whole effort. But the number reflected two additional assumptions. First, that there was a bipartisan resolve to fight the recession—that, in fact, large numbers of Republicans would have no choice but to join in the stimulus making. "We all believed that the vote [in the presidential election] was so strong from the public that we needed change ... that Republicans would have to be bipartisan," recalled one White House aide, echoing several others. "That they would feel tremendous pressure from voters to be viewed as constructive, engaged, collaborative, willing to negotiate."[3] Second, and partly as a result of this bipartisan uptake, that the size of the package would rise once Congress accepted the initial proposal, as opportunistic members from both parties piled on their own pet projects. A $775 billion starting point would be likely to yield $900 billion once the dust settled.

So the Obama figure was in many ways a guess about what would happen in Congress. There is, unfortunately, no such thing as a straightforward guess about Congress. In the best case, a guess about what Congress wants is really a guess about what Congress understands public opinion to be, an inherently unstable proposition. Given that Congress is indispensable to producing legislation, guessing at its mental state is nonetheless a reasonable way to proceed in most cases. In a time of crisis, however, public opinion—and therefore Congress—becomes even less predictable than usual, just as the policy becomes more critical. In those times, there is something to be said for taking a more forceful approach, one that tries to shape more than it tries to anticipate.

It wasn't long before Team Obama had its first whiff of this dilemma, though at first the whiff hardly seemed ominous. For several weeks, the Obama wonks brooded that they were being too optimistic in predicting what the Hill would bear. As of mid-October, Nancy Pelosi, the Democratic Speaker, was musing about a $300 billion stimulus package.[4] Only in mid-December had she pronounced herself open to doubling the amount.[5] Now the Obamans were asking her to raise the price by almost another third. The day in early January that Summers and Emanuel went to ask Pelosi and her Senate counterpart, Harry Reid, for their imprimatur, the economists at the transition office were practically nauseated with angst. For all they knew, Pelosi would have a change of heart, pharaoh-style, and send them back with half of what they were asking for. The transition team steeled itself for disappointment.[6]

Instead, the two Obama emissaries brought back good news: Pelosi and Reid hadn't flinched. In fact, they'd said anything under a trillion dollars would be workable, giving the administration considerable breathing room. "I remember them coming back, saying, 'We got them to a trillion.' I thought it was a miracle," said one Obama economist.[7]

But, as encouraging as it was that the leadership was open to going higher than expected, it did raise a somewhat troubling question: If the Obama transition had been wrong about this assumption, was it also wrong about the other two? Would the bipartisan support pan out? Would the size of the stimulus really rise as it moved through Congress?

• • •

To the Democratic elders watching from the House and Senate, the Obama phenomenon could be mystifying. A black man who'd gotten himself elected president was clearly a force to be reckoned with. The same went for the political team that helped pull it off. "Axelrod was like the guru back then," recalled one Senate leadership aide. "He was the message maven who just steered Obama to this convincing win. So [the senators] were giving him a whole bunch of deference."[8] But all this talk of changing the tone in Washington, the insistence on engaging the other side—it all seemed pie in the sky, even if the Democrats wanted to believe it would work.[9]

For Obama, though, there were few convictions more deeply held than the idea that politics could be civil. Back in 2004, his Republican rival, Jack Ryan, was outspoken about his opposition to the death penalty. Before a sex scandal brought Ryan down, Obama's political aides considered Ryan's views on capital punishment his biggest vulnerability. They urged Obama to seize the issue. But he'd waved them off. A cheap shot, he thought.[10] "That was something about him [Ryan] that I respected," Obama later said in an interview. "Because my own views on the death penalty are very complicated."[11] Whether he'd have held this high ground with the race slipping away is impossible to know, but that was irrelevant now. He'd made it to the Senate without authorizing a genuine hit, and this meant it must be possible to practice a different kind of politics.

Still, for Obama, the new politics weren't just about civility. They were about your entire identity. If you were an unabashed partisan, it meant you cared most about your own tribe. The public interest did not much concern you. In Obama's mind, "partisan" equaled "parochial," even "corrupt."

He'd first come to believe this during his community organizer days in the mid-1980s. Back then, he'd dripped with contempt for the white machine hacks and the black ward heelers—not just the conventional pols but also the pols who masqueraded as civic leaders. There was, for example, a nattily attired pastor named Smalls. Obama wanted the police to clamp down on gang violence after a teenage boy had been shot by a gang member on the South Side. He enlisted the local black ministers to pressure the city. But this was just after Harold Washington had been elected, and the Reverend Mr. Smalls wanted no part of hassling the city's first black mayor. "Things have changed with the new mayor," Smalls told Obama. "I've known the district police commander since he was a beat cop. The aldermen in this area are all committed to black empowerment. Why we need to be protesting and carrying on at our own people?" [12]

When Obama showed up in the Senate, he saw Smallses everywhere—the tribalism was oppressive. To his staff, he'd complain that everyone was dug in, that no politician would take on his own party's interest groups. "You live here," he'd say to his aides. "Why is that?" He resolved to break the pattern: if being partisan meant being parochial, then being bipartisan must mean the opposite.

Of course, as a black man with national aspirations, Obama had his own reasons for shunning tribalism. Any hint of it and whites would assume it wasn't *their* tribe he favored. The only way for a black man to win white votes was to be devoutly ecumenical, and so that's what Obama would be.

And there was a second way bipartisanship served Obama. Lashing yourself to a political party meant waiting your turn, seniority being the party's true currency. Obama was a man in a hurry. Not for him were the decades of dues-paying membership. In the Senate, he preferred to operate as a party of one, joining with Democrats often enough, but warming to Republicans when the cause was right. Of course, Hillary Clinton, that other political celebrity, had courted GOP allies during her own Senate assimilation. But Obama drew conspicuous attention to his post-partisan dalliances. Before long, he'd produced a book—an instant best seller—preaching that each side had much to learn from the other. He launched a national publicity tour to promote it.

Obama was betting that voters regard partisan attachments the way coeds regard the male obsession with sports: quaint at best and often tedious and distracting. A politician who disavowed them would sound as refreshing as an underclassman who professed an interest in poetry.

So Obama ran for president as a transcender of party—"a different kind of politician"—both because he deemed partisanship to be genuinely corrosive, and because rejecting it served his personal ambition. By late 2008, the two motivations were so intermingled it was impossible to sort them out. Obama's bipartisanship wasn't a conscious pose but a deep-seated reflex. "People anticipated that a president elected as a Democrat, who has two houses of Congress under Democratic control, would not spend any time at all trying to work with the other side," said a former Obama White House official. "It was so important to the president that he do that." And the stimulus would be the ideal vehicle. "Rahm's job was to go to Capitol Hill and figure out a way to get Republicans onto the stimulus. To honor the fact that [Obama] wanted to be a bipartisan president," said the official.[13]

On Monday, January 5, the president-elect made his first pilgrimage to the Hill to meet with both parties' leaders in the House and Senate. Obama had come prepared with a symbol of his goodwill: of the $775 billion package he proposed, he would devote roughly $300 billion to tax cuts, the perennial Republican sweetener. True to form, he instructed the leaders that "the monopoly on good ideas does not belong to a single party. If it's a good idea, we will consider it."[14] The gestures appeared to have the desired effect. On their way out, the two GOP leaders, John Boehner and Mitch McConnell, praised Obama's solicitude. "I thought the atmosphere for bipartisan cooperation was sincere on all sides," McConnell said afterward.[15]

It was Pelosi and Reid who were left to stew. Obama was making huge concessions before the negotiation had even started, they thought—before it was even clear what the negotiation would be about. "It did bug her," said a longtime Pelosi aide. "You have to get there"—compromise—"in the end. But just as a tactic, you don't get there right away, you don't show your hand. You want to get something for it: 'We'll go there, give you that, if we get something else.' " [16]

Pelosi was right. The practical effect of Obama's preemptive concession wasn't to defuse the GOP's criticism, but to redirect it elsewhere. Instead of incessantly demanding tax cuts—the Republican solution to virtually any problem that might interest Congress—Boehner, McConnell, and the rest of the Republican critics spent much of the next six weeks criticizing the spending portion of the package and its overall size. Boehner himself telegraphed the attack in his statement after the January 5 meeting. "I remain concerned about wasteful spending that might be attached to the tax relief," he told reporters.[17] Obama's bipartisanship was already looking uncomfortably one-sided.

No stimulus is ever a pure exercise in Keynesian economics, and the Obama version was no different. Even in conception, the Obama stimulus had two not entirely consistent goals. The first was to boost the economy and employment as quickly as possible. The second was to ensure that the Obama presidency left a lasting imprint on the country. Or, as the economic team wrote in its December 16, 2008, memo to the president: "The short-run economic imperative was to identify as many . . . high-priority items that would spend out quickly and be inherently temporary. The long run economic imperative, which coincides with the message imperative, is to identify items that would be transformative, making a lasting contribution to the American economy."[18] The economists mainly preoccupied themselves with the first goal. The politicos, naturally, were preoccupied with the second.

In early December, the economic team dutifully prepared a list of drab but high-bang-for-your-buck outlays and sent it off to Emanuel. The list included such consciousness-raising activities as $20 billion to repair existing roads and bridges, $5 billion to repair public housing units, and another $5 billion to upgrade sewage treatment facilities.[19] All were noble causes that would inject money into the economy immediately. Few were projects whose completion a president could commemorate with a speech before cheering throngs.

Emanuel's brother Ezekiel, a doctor who was joining the administration as a health care adviser, happened to be staying with the future chief of staff when the list arrived via fax. He helped himself to a preview. "There's nothing that really gets my heart racing," the brother later complained. "What would get your heart racing?" Rahm Emanuel asked glumly. "I don't know. How about high-speed rail—getting from New York to DC in ninety minutes?" Within days, some $20 billion in high-speed rail investments had immaculately materialized on the internal list. When Orszag saw it, he did some quick arithmetic and realized the government would be spending roughly $100 million per mile. The veins practically lurched out of his forehead. (Congress eventually scaled back the amount to $8 billion.)

More often, the legacy items advanced some policy goal Obama had touted on the campaign trail. There was $20 billion to help doctors and hospitals digitize their medical records, slicing a source of inefficiency out of the health system (ultimately approved by Congress); $2 billion to seed the production of batteries that could power electric cars (also approved); $7.7 billion to "green" federal buildings (later cut to $4.5 billion). From the perspective of the economists, the problem was that years could pass before these projects were completed and the money was fully spent, whereas the need was most acute in the here and now.[20]

Energy was a particular obsession of the president-elect's, and therefore a particular source of frustration. Week after week, Romer would march in with an estimate of the jobs all the investments in clean energy would produce; week after week, Obama would send her back to check the numbers. "I don't get it," he'd say. "We make these large-scale investments in infrastructure. What do you mean, there are no jobs?"[21] But the numbers rarely budged. The U.S. clean energy industry was so microscopically small that even doubling or tripling the size of it, a major accomplishment that could take years, would produce an insignificant number of jobs relative to the size of the country's workforce.

Still, all things considered, the Obamans were relatively restrained in their desire to build monuments to their time in office. By one internal estimate, about 90 percent of the cost of the stimulus paid out within three years. Predictably, the lard tended to accumulate in Congress. A mid-December e-mail from Reid's chief of staff cautioned colleagues, "Only those items that spend out quickly, create jobs, and constitute sound national policy should be considered for inclusion in the package."[22] But, of course, there isn't a successful politician alive who can't rationalize his pet cause as job-creating and sound. As for the rate of spend-out, well, you could always tell yourself that this was just a matter of will.

Congressmen and senators who regularly described themselves as fiscal hawks happily piled on with all manner of questionable requests. Nebraska Democrat Ben Nelson, whose complaints about the overall size of the package later grew progressively shrill, insisted on the traditional assortment of roads and bridges for his home state, few of them long enough in gestation to make them an imminent source of jobs. Georgia Republican Johnny Isakson insisted on a $15,000 tax credit for homebuyers at a cost of some $20 billion that would mainly benefit people who were already planning to buy homes, many of them people with high incomes, and some who'd already bought a home. (It was later scaled back to $6.6 billion.)

New York's Democratic senator Chuck Schumer was an especially dogged advocate of his personal policy obsession, college tax credits. To a man, the Obama economists scoffed at the idea. The credit was a highly inefficient way to make college more affordable for children of low-income families, who have to pay tuition in September but don't receive their tax refund until the following spring. The best way to increase college enrollment among the neediest students was to beef up Pell Grants, the workhorse of a program that dated back to the 1970s, which makes the money available immediately. But topping off a seventies-era aid program didn't exactly sound visionary.

One night during the stimulus negotiations three administration economic aides—Jason Furman, Brian Deese, and Jeff Liebman—began conspiring to eliminate the credits. They buttonholed Summers when he returned from Capitol Hill around midnight and prosecuted their case. "You don't understand," he told them. "We need Schumer on this." The insurrection fizzled.

Even so, these were run-of-the-mill congressional boondoggles—really the cost of business for such a large spending package. There was, however, one uniquely corrosive congressional add-on: a $70 billion reprieve from the Alternative Minimum Tax (AMT). The AMT is the floor below which the taxes of high-income earners are forbidden to fall. Congress first enacted a version of the measure in 1969, to prevent the wealthiest Americans from shedding their tax burden by taking advantage of various loopholes and shelters.[23] But thanks to inflation and changes to the law over the years, it had increasingly hurt unsuspecting middle-class families that hadn't been trying to game the system. Washington's way of dealing with this was to exempt millions of families from the higher AMT burden. But because no one wanted to go out and replace the trillions of dollars that would be lost to the U.S. Treasury by fixing the problem for good, Congress was in the habit of approving one-year reprieves, albeit year in and year out.

As early as January 5, Iowa Republican Chuck Grassley had proposed replacing some of Obama's preferred tax breaks with the AMT exemption.[24] A collection of House Democrats initially embraced the idea, too, before Obama informed them his own tax proposals were nonnegotiable. This shut down the conversation in the House, which wasn't keen to cobble together $70 billion in savings to make room for the AMT reprieve. But in the Senate, Grassley's friend Max Baucus, the powerful Democratic Finance Committee chairman, simply tacked the AMT measure onto the rest of the package, no offsets necessary.

Including the one-year AMT fix in the bill had zero stimulative value because Congress was certain to attend to it in 2009 whether or not the stimulus passed, just as it had done annually since 2001.[25] But senators like Baucus felt there was at least no harm in addressing the AMT issue a bit earlier in the year than usual. They couldn't have been more wrong.

By the week after the inauguration on January 20, the administration had largely given up on winning over Republicans in the House, where the rank and file tend to fall in line behind the party leadership. The particular moment that the White House abandoned this hope came on Tuesday, January 27, when the president ventured to Capitol Hill for a discussion with Republicans. Just before Obama arrived, Boehner told his caucus that he planned to vote against the stimulus and urged them to follow suit—a curious warm-up for an ostensibly bipartisan occasion. "Boehner said, 'No one's going to vote for it,' as we're walking into the room," recalled an incredulous White House aide.[26]

To some in the White House, the Senate seemed equally hopeless. The week before Boehner's stunt, the West Wing had dispatched Jason Furman, one of Summers's two deputies, to meet with Republican chiefs of staff in the office of Mitch McConnell. Rather than even pretend to carry on a high-minded discussion, the Republican aides simply recited their party's talking points and took shots at the whole concept of a stimulus. It was clear they had zero interest in engaging.

Still, when the final negotiations commenced in the first week of February 2009, the White House believed it could pick up 8 to 10, perhaps as many as 15, Republican votes in the upper chamber.[27] That wouldn't quite net the 80-plus votes the administration had hoped for at the outset (that is, including Democrats), but it would be an impressive achievement nonetheless. "We thought we were going to have the moderate Republicans till the very, very end," said a second White House aide. "We knew we were not going to get 80 [overall]. But I think we were aiming for 70."[28]

By midweek, however, this too had become inconceivable. As of Wednesday, February 4, the Senate version of the stimulus had swelled to $920 billion, appearing to vindicate the Obama expectation of upward drift. But the vindication was achingly brief. By now, all but three Senate Republicans had announced their opposition, while the three still in play—Arlen Specter of Pennsylvania and Olympia Snowe and Susan Collins of Maine—were demanding massive cuts.

Emanuel was furious. He cursed the Republican special pleaders whose demands he'd met—Johnny Isakson on the homebuyer tax credit, Chuck Grassley on the AMT patch—but who were now intransigent. "I don't understand the Senate," he fumed. "How could you get a major amendment associated with [the stimulus] and not vote for it? In the House, you'd have to vote for it." For his part, Reid conceded that he didn't have the votes to pass the stimulus without the three Republican defectors. With the backing of the White House, he quietly blessed a negotiation between Collins and Ben Nelson, a conservative Democrat, as a way to attract them.

By the end of the week, Collins and Nelson had banded together with Specter to present their formal demands: $100 billion off the final price tag. (The third Republican, Olympia Snowe, piggybacked on the effort without getting directly involved.) Shrewdly, they didn't insist on specific cuts, but simply presented the Senate leadership with a list of items they favored and left it to them to find savings elsewhere. Emanuel and Orszag, under instructions from the president to reach a deal, rushed to Harry Reid's office to do the requisite nipping and tucking. When they finished, they'd cut tens of billions of dollars in aid to states, and billions more in health care subsidies to the jobless and tax cuts for low- and middle-income workers—all potent sources of stimulus.

The AMT fix, which appeared prominently on the Nelson-Collins protection list, stood intact. That meant the final, trimmed-down bill didn't pack the $820 billion of stimulus it appeared to; it had no more than $750 billion. The senators would eventually lop off another $30 billion when merging the package together with the House version (mostly by scaling back Isakson's home-buying credit). Instead of rising from $775 billion to $900 billion or more, as Team Obama had expected, the stimulus was now effectively $50 billion *below* where they'd started. The original proposal had "set the ceiling," in the words of one White House aide.[29]

Nancy Pelosi learned what the White House and the senators had agreed to only when Reid announced the deal from the Senate floor, and she promptly lost her mind. Before long, Reid and a contingent of White House aides were scurrying across the Capitol to contain the fallout. When they arrived at her office, Pelosi singled out the White House congressional lobbyist, Phil Schiliro, for special abuse. "Phil," she bellowed. "You can't let the Republicans dictate the terms!" Pelosi pleaded for a vote in the Senate on the full $920 billion package, on the theory that the three Republican deal makers clearly believed a major stimulus was critical and wouldn't vote against it. Reid apologetically explained that he couldn't consider the idea because he couldn't guarantee that the stimulus would pass.[30]

The White House had assumed that it could start with a modest figure, which would rise as the legislation moved through Congress. It had assumed that the GOP, instead of obstructing the process, would be a willing and constructive participant. But this was at best half-right. Legislators from both parties had larded on proposals, driving up the cost of the legislation by $150 billion. Then, when it became clear Republicans would largely oppose the bill, a tiny handful of moderates were empowered to scale back the price by roughly the same amount. In the process, they left many of the most dubious additions intact and pared back some of the bill's key features.

"In hindsight, it looks naive," said one White House aide in 2011, looking back on the quest for bipartisanship. "The reality is, the state of normal now is completely new. . . . Only in the last two and a half years has voting with a Democratic president become a mortal sin in the Republican Party."[31] But this was not entirely true. Republican obstructionism dates back at least to the early Clinton era, when Republicans unanimously opposed his deficit-cutting package and derailed his health care reform bill. The oversight was a tragic mistake.

Harry Reid and the White House were right to move ahead with the vote on the $820 billion compromise. Though it's possible that Collins, Snowe, and Specter were bluffing, this wasn't a chance Democrats could take. "If the stimulus failed, it would have had huge consequences. Remember what happened when TARP failed," said the same White House aide, referring to Congress's initial, market-murdering rejection of the bank bailout.[32] Worse, the failure would have been Reid's and Obama's—for refusing to make concessions to close the deal. The only thing the gambit would have accomplished would be to send Reid and Obama crawling back to the Republican swing senators, by which point the price of their votes would surely have risen.

But the fact that there was no path to a larger stimulus in February 2009 doesn't mean that there was no path to a larger stimulus. It means that the time to have forged the path was earlier. To sell a bigger package, the White House might have exploited Obama's popularity in Maine and Pennsylvania, the states from which the GOP swing senators hailed, and which Obama had carried by double-digit margins the previous November. Ads might have been cut, phone messages recorded, a president dispatched for town hall meetings—whatever it took to raise the cost of opposing him on the stimulus. Had the three Republican swing senators found themselves plainly on the wrong side of public opinion in their home states, their incentives would have changed.

But, of course, this wasn't a strategy that could be conjured into existence during the final day or two of a negotiation. It would have required at least a few weeks to execute. The White House may have even wanted to open with a strategically high offer—$1.2 trillion, say, rather than $775 billion—with the hope of eventually compromising in the $850 billion to $900 billion range.

As it happens, there was precedent for this approach. In 2001, George W. Bush came into office proposing an eye-popping $1.6 trillion tax cut. Between his inauguration and early April, Bush headlined campaign-style events in twenty-two states. The GOP ran ads on local radio stations and badgered voters with robo-calls. The *New York Times* accused Bush of "tactics reminiscent of President

Bill Clinton's 'permanent campaign.'"[33] But far from hurting his chances for bipartisan success, it clearly helped them. Bush won 85 percent of what he wanted—$1.35 trillion—*and* 12 Democratic votes in the Senate. He demonstrated that the opposition responds to raw calculations of self-interest, which he was able to alter, rather than to goodwill or constructive give-and-take, of which he offered little.[34]

There's a reason to believe a similar strategy would have worked for Obama. Bush had been able to exploit "reconciliation"—the Senate rule which allows budget-related measures to pass with a simple majority (and which was unavailable to Obama because the Senate hadn't yet passed a budget). But Obama also held key advantages over Bush. His election victory had been more convincing, his popularity was higher,[35] and he started with a caucus of fifty-eight senators, versus fifty for Bush. Although both presidents needed to win over moderates in their own parties, the number of votes Obama needed from the other side was much smaller.

Even if the hard-line strategy hadn't produced an additional cent of stimulus, it would have yielded real benefits. Above all, it would have stamped each side's position into the country's consciousness, making clear that the stimulus ended up smaller than Obama preferred, and that the reason for this was his Republican opposition. If the economy subsequently underperformed or unemployment stayed high, Obama would have positioned himself to blame Republicans for holding down the size of his stimulus package, and to argue for more.[36]

But because the Obama strategy was to pick up votes by appealing directly to Republican senators rather than ginning up outside pressure, he was committed to embracing the stimulus even as it became significantly weaker. "This thing was very, very close to not passing," said a White House aide. "If we were going to gainsay the thing even as we tried to pass it, the reluctant folks on board were likely not to stay on board." [37] The upshot was that when the economy later underperformed, Republicans could blame Obama's stimulus. He'd gotten what he'd wanted, after all, and yet it hadn't done the job.

White House aides say there simply wasn't time to deploy a Bush-style strategy: Congress didn't pass Bush's tax cut until late May 2008; Obama was aiming to pass the stimulus within weeks, if not days, of the inauguration. For good measure, he also had to deal with a faltering financial system and comatose automakers. "You sit here [saying], 'You ever think of going campaigning up in Maine?' Great idea," Emanuel quipped in an interview. "Where were you on my credit crisis when I needed you? How were you on the auto review?" [38]

And yet the reason the White House didn't play hardball had little to do with logistics. The reason was that playing hardball simply wasn't who Obama was. "There were definitely people at the White House who would play ball like that—the Rahm contingent," said a second White House aide. "But that's not the president's style. It's never how he would do it." [39] It was no more useful to bemoan this fact than it would be to blame a bike for not being a car, however much you might need one when you have only the other.

There was something truly noble about Obama's quest for bipartisanship—a real hunger for a more redemptive form of politics. But it was also deeply confused. Contrary to what Obama assumed, "partisan" is not, in fact, synonymous with "parochial"; being partisan doesn't necessarily mean putting party ahead of country. In fact, when the other side has adopted a strategy of reflexive opposition, as the GOP had by early 2009, then partisan muscle-flexing may very well serve the public interest, since there's no other way to pass legislation. The stimulus was a disturbing early example of this confusion. It wouldn't be the last.

8

BAIT AND SWITCH

By the time he joined the Obama administration, Tim Geithner had settled on a narrative of the financial crisis that had the virtue of being nearly correct. As Geithner saw it, the government had faced two imperatives during that tumultuous time. The first was to stop the panic and save the banks. The second was to satisfy the country's bloodlust toward Wall Street. Geithner believed—and this was his real insight—that you could do only one or the other. Anything truly vengeful, such as cleaning out whole floors of executives or other forms of what Geithner called "Old Testament justice," could destroy the institutions you were trying to save. But anything merely symbolic—a firing here, and a perp walk there—the public would dismiss as a stunt.

The trouble with politicians was that they instinctively shrank from this choice. They clung to the delusion that they could fix the banks while keeping the people behind them. Almost invariably, they succeeded at neither. Geithner prided himself on his maturity, on his ability to look soberly at such trade-offs. It was no doubt repugnant to protect the bankers, "repugnant" being another favorite word of the Treasury secretary's. But just as there was no military victory without collateral damage, there was no financial peace without bailed-out financiers. It was petulant to pretend otherwise. The country would accept this in the end, although, one had to concede, the end could be a very long time coming.

And yet, when Geithner traveled a few hundred yards from his office to the White House for the daily senior staff meeting—the Treasury secretary was the only department head with a standing invitation, a tradition that began under Rubin—he was surrounded, as it were, by petulance. The president's top aides were desperate to solve the crisis. They were just as desperate to position the administration as resolutely anti–fat cat. They pleaded with Geithner to fire a bailed-out CEO. They begged him to hack away at executive pay.

The case of Bank of America's Ken Lewis was instructive. Along with Citigroup and AIG, BofA was the most notorious of the financial problem children, having sucked up $45 billion of government cash and a $118 billion government insurance policy (the latter was never officially finalized even though it benefited the bank). Lewis, moreover, was an even fatter target than his peers at these other companies. By early 2009, AIG was on its third CEO since the start of the crisis. Citigroup's CEO, Vikram Pandit, had taken over well after his predecessor, Chuck Prince, set the bank's near demise in motion. Only Lewis had presided over the decisions that wrecked his company: the acquisitions of Countrywide Financial, a major source of BofA's vast portfolio of battered subprime mortgages, and, under pressure from the Fed, Merrill Lynch.

Lewis seemed destined to become the scalp the West Wing politicos—"Tammany Hall," Larry Summers called them—craved. He'd grown isolated from his own board of directors and was unlikely to survive as it was. The substantive cost of firing him a few months prematurely appeared to be next to nil. Yes, it would be tawdry, akin to taking credit for the tidal movements. But the political logic was unassailable, almost elegant. The idea filled David Axelrod and Robert Gibbs, the president's two powerful aides, with Machiavellian glee. Some of Geithner's own aides endorsed it. Even Larry Summers spoke up for its merits. But Geithner dug in and prevailed.

In these internal debates, Geithner often invoked practical reasons for his resistance. Always there was the concern that it would be next to impossible to find a qualified replacement: who would give up a successful career to run one of America's most reviled companies? In the particular case of Lewis, Geithner invoked the stress tests. The premise of the tests was that each bank would have a chance to correct the deficiencies that the regulators uncovered. Firing Lewis before the results were in would send the wrong signal to the other banks.[1]

But lurking just beneath the pragmatic arguments was a closely held Geithnerian principle: that the governments of First World countries ceded a patch of high ground any time they behaved capriciously; that there were steps it was simply beneath the United States of America to take, even if the fallout were minimal. One sometimes had to strain to find consistency in the principle's application. (Geithner hadn't opposed the firing of General Motors CEO Rick Wagoner on March 27, 2007.) And it was hardly the only principle relevant to the discussion. (Rewarding catastrophic misjudgment offended Axelrod's own principles.) But there is little doubt that Geithner believed himself to be acting on it. After administration lawyers could find no legal reason to stop the $165 million in bonuses AIG owed employees of its failed financial products unit, an aide suggested that Geithner put a stop to them anyway. The secretary shot him a look befitting the teller of a racist joke: pure, affronted disbelief.

The AIG bonus episode epitomized the difference between Geithner's instincts and those of the administration's operatives. When the bonus news broke in March 2009, an aide responded the way political aides respond to such things: by leaking exculpatory information. In this case, the aide told *The Washington Post* that the Federal Reserve had known about the bonuses for months but alerted the administration only days before the payments came due.[2] The implication was that the administration might have stopped the bonuses had it had more time to deal with them.

In retrospect, the leak was tactically suspect: Hadn't Geithner been president of the New York Fed when it first learned about the bonuses? (He had.) Wouldn't the Fed now claim it had informed Treasury of the bonuses well in advance? (It would.) More important, the question of timing missed the point: Geithner's decision to pay the bonuses would have been the same whether he'd had five days or five months to consider it. "If I would have tried to intervene to stop those payments . . . it would have been terrible policy," Geithner later said in an interview. "I don't think I would have made that judgment differently if I had more time."[3]

Geithner believed a political uproar during a financial crisis wasn't just inevitable but a validating sign. A year into his job as Treasury secretary, Geithner would tell *Newsweek* that he'd been shaped by the experience of helping to bail out Mexico and Asia in the 1990s. He regarded the political turmoil from these earlier episodes as a badge of honor. "The surveys were 9-to-1 against almost everything that helped contain the damage. And I watched exceptionally capable people just get killed in the court of public opinion as they defended those policies on the Hill," he said. "The test is whether you have people willing to do the things that are deeply unpopular, deeply hard to understand, knowing that they're necessary to do and better than the alternatives."[4]

It was here where Geithner's logic could swerve uncomfortably close to fallacy. On one level he was right: doing what was necessary *did* mean courting public outrage. You simply couldn't fix the system while meting out justice to every greedy banker, every grubby mortgage broker, every blinkered credit analyst. But the converse wasn't true: the fact that your actions provoked public outrage didn't necessarily make them right. Sometimes the popular thing was also necessary. Sometimes the people had a point.

It was a great irony of Tim Geithner's career that he became reviled as a creature of Wall Street. Television anchors, newspaper columnists, congressional inquisitors—all assumed he'd come to Treasury by way of a white-shoe investment bank. The mayor of New York publicly alluded to him as an alumnus of Goldman Sachs. At a dinner party, the wife of Rahm Emanuel once remarked that he must be eager to return to Goldman's gilded boardrooms.[5]

In fact, Geithner had never worked a day in the financial markets, something he took pains to point out. At a weekend retreat for House Democrats in early 2009, Geithner, already dogged by his apocryphal past, stood before the caucus and announced, "I never worked for Goldman. . . . I don't come from money." One senior House aide recalled that "people were taken aback that he'd be so direct about it."[6] The truth was that Geithner's mistakes were not those of a Wall Street insider, but those of an official distinctly not from Wall Street who nonetheless found himself having to save it.

A few days after Lehman Brothers declared bankruptcy in 2008, Steve Shafran, an adviser to Treasury Secretary Hank Paulson, began a series of phone conversations with Geithner and his top aides at the New York Fed. The fallout from Lehman had begun to resemble an enormous bank run. Not quite a traditional run, where frantic depositors lined city blocks to demand their savings from banks, which couldn't pay because they'd lent the money out. But close. The day Shafran called, the stampede had reached all the way to a group of money market mutual funds, which had been considered a risk-free place to park cash but were suddenly staggering around. Investors frantically withdrew their money; the funds couldn't make them whole because they'd lent the money elsewhere. In some cases they'd lent it to Lehman, so they were hard-pressed to get it back.[7]

In principle, stopping a run was easy: someone with deep pockets could simply proclaim himself good for all the cash. The clamorers would relax, realizing their money was guaranteed. Fortunately for them, the government had begun to prepare just such an assurance for the money market funds in those early post-Lehman days. The question wasn't whether to bail the funds out, but *how*. Geithner believed the government should directly guarantee every last dollar residing in the money market accounts, nearly $4 trillion in all. Shafran, a former Goldman Sachs executive, wasn't so sure. He knew that money market funds were usually attached to large corporations. He knew that these corporate parents had traditionally bailed out their money market subsidiaries rather than watch them go broke. If the bailout was designed the right way, the corporate parents could be made to share the burden with the government.[8]

For a few days, the two sides went back and forth, with Geithner and the New York Fed arguing that the bailout must be firm and unambiguous and Shafran arguing for his more subtle approach. Finally, because Treasury, and not the Fed, was putting up the money, Shafran got his way. The corporate parents would do their part if necessary. The world did not end. Account holders didn't lose a single dollar. The run on the money markets ceased.[9]

It was, in the end, a debate about the old doctrine of "overwhelming force." More to the point, it was a debate about precisely how overwhelming was overwhelming enough. Since the 1990s,

Geithner had placed himself on the more forceful end of the spectrum; since Lehman, his appetite for megatonnage had reached
nuclear proportions. If the point was to save the financial system,
you shouldn't just err on the side of doing more rather than less. You
should do everything you could possibly do, then go back and think
about what else might be done and do that, too. Lehman had been a
profound experience in that way. Geithner spoke of having "stared
into the abyss" that the government created when it let the firm collapse. As Treasury secretary, he vowed that he would never again
tolerate such a mistake. Bailout critics who hadn't lived through the
crisis he derided as "chickenhawks."

Even within Geithner's own Treasury Department, there were
dissenters. Gene Sperling, Geithner's all-purpose kibitzer and deputy
on matters of fiscal policy, would mordantly observe that you could
fire the CEOs of car companies, threaten them with bankruptcy,
even saddle their creditors with losses. No one would bat an eye.
But the second you looked crosswise at a major bank, people would
scream about "systemic risk" in the financial markets. "Anytime
someone says the words 'systemic risk,' everybody's IQ drops fifty
points," Sperling joked in meetings.

But administration liberals like Sperling were hardly the only
ones worried that Geithner was too quick to bolster the banks, that
he was too resistant to anything that might cause them a twinge of
pain. There were, for one thing, academics like Jeremy Stein, the
Harvard finance professor Summers brought with him to the NEC.
Stein believed that banks and their investors could do more to shoulder the cost of their own bailout.

Perhaps more curiously, so did some of the Treasury hands most
skilled in the art of financial engineering. One of the undisputed
stars of the Geithner Treasury was a young Wall Street alumnus
named Matthew Kabaker, who'd arrived by way of Blackstone, the
massive money management firm. Kabaker was a Blackstone manag-

ing director, Wall Street-ese for "made man," by his early thirties and hadn't turned thirty-five when he left to become Lee Sachs's top lieutenant at Treasury. At Blackstone, the CEO was given to rhapsodizing about his supple intellect as a "four standard-deviation event," [10] which, taken literally, would mean that a Matthew Kabaker showed up at the firm about once every hundred and fifty years. (Even adjusting for Wall Street's flawed understanding of statistical probability, that would be very high praise.)

Around Treasury, Kabaker was known by those with market experience as a "banker's banker," the finance equivalent of an haute couture designer, and by the rest as the man "with the pen." Officially, Lee Sachs was the Geithner aide tasked with orchestrating the financial rescue. But while Sachs was out being lacerated by Larry Summers, or listening to the sob stories of Wall Street eminences, it was Kabaker who often sketched financial plans in longhand. In February 2009, Citigroup's stock was in free fall and the company pleaded with Treasury to take an ownership stake of roughly one third. The government would do this by converting the roughly $25 billion that it already held in preferred shares (which pay a dividend and don't imply ownership) into shares of common stock (which confer ownership), rather than giving the company more money. Sachs figured he should hire an outside adviser to vet the transaction, but the bureaucratic red tape proved insurmountable. Instead, Treasury tapped the financial advisory firm named Matt Kabaker.

All of which is to say that Kabaker was no radical. He was, in some respects, a highly evolved form of market wisdom. And yet when he thought through exactly how generous the government would need to be to the banks in order to solve the crisis—how much force the bailouts should bring to bear—his conclusions sometimes looked more like Gene Sperling's than Tim Geithner's.

When it came to Citigroup, for example, Kabaker had mapped

out a crude version of what's known as a good bank/bad bank plan.[11] This was a way of salvaging what you could of a company rather than letting its toxic assets drag the whole enterprise down. The government would take all of Citi's valuable assets and house them in one institution (the "good" bank) and all the toxic assets and wall them off in another (the "bad" bank). The good bank could then resume lending and investing as though nothing had happened. The bad bank would eventually be shut down, but might need a few tens of billions, if not hundreds of billions, of dollars to cover its losses in the meantime.

Kabaker believed there was a way to set this up without a huge infusion of government cash: foisting the losses onto the owners of certain types of Citigroup debt. The debt holders would be given "haircuts," in the Wall Street vernacular, meaning they'd receive less than 100 cents back for every dollar they'd lent Citigroup, and maybe a lot less. Kabaker had a similar idea for AIG.

Kabaker wasn't exactly enthusiastic about such measures. He knew there was a chance they could unsettle the market. If, for example, investors in the other banks' debt began to fear haircuts, that could trigger a sell-off. But he also considered this approach to be doable. If Citi or AIG deteriorated further, that was certainly preferable to some of the other options available—not least, hundreds of billions more dollars from the government. In any case, the point was academic. When Kabaker broached the subject of haircuts with Geithner, the secretary was immovable. "I may be scarred by the experience of the fall of '08," he said, referring to the fallout from Lehman's failure, "but we're not going to do it. It would hurt our credibility deeply."

Of course, if Kabaker were in Geithner's position, with all the responsibility the secretary carried, he might have felt the same way. It was arguably Geithner's staunchness in these matters that had saved the financial system the previous fall.

Geithner's problem wasn't so much any one decision as his absolutism, his conviction that anything that might cause the banks discomfort could tip the whole financial system back into chaos. This was defensible, perhaps even necessary, immediately after Lehman. But over time it became a kind of crutch, more a matter of emotion than case-by-case judgment. And it was the Wall Street alumni who often saw this most clearly. Precisely because they had the financial market experience Geithner lacked, they were confident the banks could recover while enduring a modicum of pain.

In February 2009, Treasury approached a prominent hedge fund manager named Frank Brosens about joining the department to oversee TARP, the $700 billion bailout program Congress had approved the previous October. Brosens was well known to Team Obama, having donated tens of thousands of dollars to the party during the presidential campaign and traveled to a dozen states to knock on voters' doors. He'd also forged a relationship with Larry Summers, who had worked as a consultant to his firm, Taconic Capital Advisors, between 2004 and 2006.[12] It was Summers who had recommended him for the Treasury post.

At first glance, Brosens looked like exactly the wrong person to manage Treasury's dealings with Wall Street special pleaders, having spent fifteen years at Goldman Sachs. But Brosens had less obvious credentials that made him an intriguing choice, not least a reputation for genuine foresight. Brosens had, for example, spotted the rot in the Japanese economic system as early as the late 1980s, well before the country's stock and real estate bubbles burst (and nearly a decade before the Japanese would acknowledge it themselves). It was thanks to him that Goldman made hundreds of millions of dollars betting against the Japanese market once it began to falter in 1990.

To the surprise of no one who knew him, Brosens had been

worked up about the U.S. financial crisis. But, unlike his would-be colleagues in Washington, Brosens wasn't worried about deploying too *little* force in defense of the banks and their hobbled assets. He was worried about deploying too much. Since the start of the crisis, he'd been groaning that the government had been too generous in handing over money and guarantees to Citigroup and its ilk. He believed it would create a political backlash against the entire banking system. Soon Geithner was giving him additional reasons for heartburn.

When Geithner had addressed the country on February 10, he had laid out two proposals for shoring up the banks. One was the stress tests, in which the government would assume that the economy would underperform even its meager postcrisis trajectory, then calculate the effect this would have on the country's nineteen largest banks. Any bank that looked shaky under the "stress scenario" would have to scrounge up more capital as a cushion against the losses it would suffer if that ugly hypothetical situation came to pass. The second idea was to have the government partner with private financiers to buy up the banks' lousy loans and mortgage securities. This was the so-called Public-Private Investor Program, or PPIP.[13]

For several weeks in the winter and spring, the world assumed that the banks and, by extension, the Obama administration would rise or fall on the success of the second idea, since the toxic assets were presumed to be the nub of the problem. Tellingly, the markets wilted when Geithner's vague speech in February left investors wondering if the government partnership would be worth their while. They bounced back six weeks later, on March 23, when Geithner finally bared the details. Not only would the government put up cash alongside the buyers; it would lend the buyers money they wouldn't have to repay if the investments soured. It was a head-turning deal for anyone coveting the banks' sludgy inventory. Between the government loans and the money Treasury and its partners would pool together, the Geithner plan imagined up to a trillion dollars in purchasing power. Lee Sachs often spoke about the need for enormous "firepower" when he described the plan.

Though Brosens would ultimately decline the Treasury job, he went deep into the hiring process before bowing out, and this made him someone the administration consulted more often than other financiers about PPIP. The idea of massive firepower left him cold. As a believer in free markets, he thought it could be construed as market manipulation. He felt Treasury would be signaling that investors should snatch up the securities because Treasury would soon be buying them in such epic quantities that the price would shoot up and investors could sell to the government at a profit.

Worse, since there was no way Treasury could ramp up the program so quickly, Brosens believed the end result would be a *failed* attempt at market manipulation, which would badly damage its credibility. Indeed, the Paulson Treasury Department had junked plans to buy assets from banks the previous fall when it realized it wouldn't be able to spend money quickly enough to matter—that is, to get the assets out of the banks before the losses crippled them. Paulson's team figured it would be able to buy only $5 billion to $10 billion worth each month, even once the program was fully up and running.[14]

For his part, Brosens favored a comparatively humble approach, what amounted to a $50 billion government-owned fund that would buy up the banks' battered holdings. By itself, the fund wouldn't be big enough to drive up prices very much. There were just too many subprime mortgage securities to make that plausible. (Well over a trillion dollars worth, depending on how you valued them.) But it just might restore a little confidence to the market. If other hedge funds saw the government buying, even on a smallish scale, they might worry less about the price collapsing further and start to open their own wallets. And if not, well, $50 billion wasn't *so* much to spend on a worthy experiment in the grand scheme of things. In any case, the government would be able to hang on to the assets as long as it took to get its money back.

By mid-March, Brosens had taken himself out of the running for the TARP job, reckoning that Geithner didn't need a hedge fund manager to run the partnership program, since Treasury would be piggybacking on the decisions of private investors, not actively buying and selling securities. That would make the head of TARP into more of an administrator, and Brosens figured it wasn't worth missing his youngest son's high school years for a job that didn't suit his skills. He decided to stay put in New York.

Geithner's grand ambitions were fizzling, too: investors started to worry that the political mob would turn on them if they made out too well under Geithner's deal. Meanwhile, the banks were loath to sell at a loss at the bottom of the market. Most decided they were better off taking their chances that the assets would recover. Treasury finally launched a scaled-down version of the program in September 2009,[15] which had deployed only $20 billion by the end of 2010,[16] a far cry from the trillion Geithner once envisioned.

The entire debate now seemed academic. Except that Brosens had raised a troubling question, and it lingered long after the TARP job was filled: was there a danger in trying to revive the banks *too well*?

The stress tests had barely provoked a reaction when Geithner first proposed them. But with the quiet downsizing of PPIP, they became the main channel for stabilizing the banks. In Treasury's telling, the tests would be a kind of platonic exercise, shielded at all costs from the grubby calculus of politics. The financial wizards at the Fed and FDIC, independent agencies whose leaders can't be fired by the president, would first determine how much another rough economic patch would hurt the value of commercial mortgages, credit card loans, auto loans, and every other asset down to the dodgiest sub-prime mortgage security. Then the Fed's corps of grim-faced supervisors would politely ask, in the way that mob enforcers politely ask, the banks to spell out how much of each asset they had.

By matching up the hypothetical losses to the banks' actual portfolios, the Fed and other regulators could figure out how much each bank might lose overall if the economy stalled during the next two years, and, therefore, how big a cash cushion each would need to ensure its survival. So, for example, if the regulators believed residential mortgages would be worth 80 cents on the dollar by the end of 2010, and a bank had $100 billion worth of such mortgages that it valued at 100 cents, the bank would be looking at a $20 billion loss in that category alone. Once all the potential losses were tallied up, the government would then "ask" each bank to raise the money to cover them. Any bank that couldn't raise enough money by selling shares to private investors, who might worry that the bank was just too big a risk, would be advised to take government money instead, with various strings attached.

The key feature of the exercise would be the integrity of the numbers: the data would go in, the predicted losses would pop out, and anyone who cared to know could see how much a given bank was short of cash. There wasn't a thing any banker or government official could do to alter the result.

The upshot would be credibility. If the regulators certified a bank to be hale and hearty—which is to say, in need of little or no capital—then the financial world would embrace it as such. And if the regulators identified a shortage of tens of billions in capital, then God help the bank that failed to come up with it. The ensuing run could make Lehman look like calisthenics.

That was the preferred narrative, in any case. In practice, while the tests were reasonably pure by the standards of the banking industry, there were several ways for the government to skew the results in one direction or another.

The most important was the question of how thick a capital cushion the banks actually needed. Capital is measured as a ratio. For example, if a bank has $1 trillion in assets, and the regulators require a capital cushion of 6 percent, then the bank must keep at least $60 billion in capital on hand. If the bank has the minimum amount of capital and suffers a $10 billion loss, it must replenish this by raising $10 billion.

Under the stress tests, however, the regulators had to decide how much capital the banks needed in order to cover *expected* losses, not actual ones, which was a slightly different question. The regulators might expect the bank to suffer a loss of $10 billion over the next two years, but that didn't necessarily mean they should ask the bank to raise $10 billion. They could press for $20 billion instead, effectively raising the capital requirement to 7 percent in our example, on the theory that predictions are uncertain and it never hurts to err on the side of caution.

Largely unappreciated at the time was that the rule for how much capital a bank needed wouldn't be set in advance. Instead, it would be debated right up until the end of the stress tests, by which point the regulators and the Obama administration could see how it would affect the results. Or, put differently, the government could first pick the amount of money it wanted the banks to raise, then set the rule that would elicit that amount. It would be a bit like the IRS announcing income tax rates only after all the taxpayers had filed their returns, at which point the government could set the rates so as to raise whatever amount it wanted.

But, of course, this meant that the administration first had to decide what the right amount was. In the run-up to May 7, when the

Fed planned to announce the results, Geithner convened three grueling meetings to consider possible outcomes. Summers, with his conviction that the banks' real estate misadventures had saddled them with crippling losses, believed the stress tests would be credible only if the regulators prescribed heaping doses of capital to cover them. If the numbers were too upbeat, Summers brooded, the markets would dismiss the tests as a thinly concealed cover-up. "Larry and the NEC always thought stress tests are a bit of a symbolic exercise designed to say all the banks are strong," recalled one Summers aide. "Larry thought of them as a big charade." [17]

Lee Sachs's concerns ran in the opposite direction. Believing the banks' mortgage securities to be more valuable than was commonly assumed, he worried that prescribing eye-popping amounts of capital would only depress investors, not reassure them. The angst-ridden investors would shun the banks' stock, leaving the banks no choice but to tap the government for the money. If, on the other hand, investors were told that the banks' losses were manageable with a moderate amount of capital, they'd happily buy shares in the banks on their own.

Less than a week before the final results were to be released, Treasury finally had a chance to look them over. The regulators had prepared four separate scenarios based on the size of the capital cushion they could ask the nineteen banks to hold. The mildest scenario would have required the banks to collectively raise about $35 billion, the next mildest $75 billion, then about $125 billion. The toughest option would be about $125 billion. It now fell to Geithner and the regulators to decide which figure to endorse.[18]

Hours of conference calls ensued at various levels of government. Many of the regulators, like Fed chairman Ben Bernanke and vice chairman Don Kohn, worried about asking the banks to raise more than private investors were likely to give them. They favored the lowest number. Characteristically, Lee Sachs agonized over changing the rules on the banks in midstream and also argued for the lowest number. But Geithner, perhaps reflecting Summers's influence, argued for the second lowest number: $75 billion. "If the other guys . . . were in one place, he'd want to be incrementally a little tougher," said one Obama economic official.[19] A handful of bank examiners within the Fed did recommend $125 billion. But no one at the decision-making level broached this figure, much less $175 billion. "It was like, 'Woah,'" said one participant of the largest number.[20] With fewer than forty-eight hours before the May 7 announcement,[21] Geithner's position carried the day.

From the perspective of the markets and the banks, the $75 billion figure hit a sweet spot. Many pundits and investors pronounced the amount tough and credible. But it was not so tough that the banks had trouble raising the money. Within a week, they'd already raised $20 billion. They would go on to raise over $100 billion more before the end of the year, during which time one popular index of bank stock prices would climb more than 20 percent. For the first time, the bank recovery seemed reasonably secure.

In retrospect, the stress tests were a brilliantly executed bait-and-switch. The portions of the exercise that were visible to the public—namely, the estimates of losses on mortgages and other loans—looked like the work of a cool, impartial hand, which they largely were. Meanwhile, the portions of the tests that hinged on gut feelings and armchair analysis were mostly hidden from view. "In a way it was a hell of a trick," said the Obama economic official. "The part of the process that was not corrupted were the loss estimates. . . . They drew people's eyes to that stuff, were realistic about this thing. Then, here's where rabbit goes into hat"—the debate over $35 billion versus $75 billion or $125 billion.[22]

The stress tests worked because a combination of these two elements—a credible, objective process masking a final number that the powers-that-be could control—created confidence in the banking system at a time when confidence was lacking. And that confidence, in turn, propped up the banks.

In the fall of 2009, Rahm Emanuel summoned the administration's top operatives and policy makers to his office for a meeting on communications strategy. Emanuel's management style had a frenetic quality. He would lunge at causes he deemed essential in their importance, then abruptly drop them, only to reconsider a few weeks later when the urgency returned. The public's anger toward the banks was a leading candidate for this treatment, and Emanuel wanted to know what could be done to defuse it. It was a question he'd been asking in recent months with rising desperation.

The conversation soon settled into thinly veiled recriminations. Axelrod and Gibbs bleated that the president's options were limited. The country's rage was legitimate given that the administration had awarded the banks hundreds of billions of dollars. This moved the normally placid Geithner to protest: "We didn't give the banks any money. We forced them to go raise it." It was one thing for the man on the street to labor under such misimpressions, Geithner thought. For the president's top aides to suffer from the same false consciousness was altogether alarming.[23]

Geithner was referring to the stress tests, of course. And, in a narrow sense, he was right. The Fed had asked the nineteen banks to raise $75 billion by selling new shares of stock. This watered down the value of their existing shares, as each share now represented a smaller fraction of the company, and left the existing stockholders (many of them top executives) poorer. The so-called dilution had been most severe for the banks with the most money to raise: Citi, Bank of America, Wells Fargo, and GMAC, which collectively needed $65 billion.[24] This had the felicitous effect of singling out shareholders in two of the most notorious banks, Citi and BofA, for the harshest treatment.

Better yet, singling out shareholders was eminently fair. Unlike a bank's bondholders, who have lent the bank money and expect to be repaid in full, the shareholders generally understand that their investment is riskier. As partial owners of the corporation, they know going in that they will benefit (that is, the stock price will increase) if the company becomes more profitable and suffer (the stock price will decrease) if the company becomes less profitable. This is the reason that, when a company goes bankrupt, the bondholders and other creditors get the first claim on its assets. Whatever is left over after they're made whole, which is often nothing, goes to the shareholders.

Geithner could also point to the fact that TARP, the $700 billion taxpayer-funded bailout, was no gift. The banks were on the hook to repay with interest any money they received from TARP. If they didn't repay, it said right there in the law's fine print that the government would hit the banking industry with a fee to recover the difference. In any case, most of the nineteen largest banks would settle up by the end of 2009; all but one would by 2011.

But Geithner was wrong in a broader sense. Since the beginning of the crisis, the U.S. government had showered banks and other financial institutions with trillions of dollars in benefits, only a small fraction of which the firms would ever pay for. Many of these benefits came in the form of guarantees and subsidies that average pitchfork-wielding Americans only dimly understood, if they were aware of them at all, but whose cumulative effect was to trigger a collective gag reflex.

Most head-turning were the largely below-market-rate loans the Fed had made to financial firms through a variety of programs beginning on Bush's watch in late 2007.[25] The balance of the loans peaked at $1.2 trillion in December 2008. According to documents obtained by Bloomberg News, the country's ten biggest banks and investment houses alone collectively borrowed $669 billion from the Fed around the same time.* Two large European banks, the Royal Bank of Scotland and UBS, of Zurich, borrowed over $160 billion between them.[26]

In the white-knuckle aftermath of the Lehman bankruptcy, the Bush administration had layered on additional freebies, like the government guarantee of money market mutual funds. But some of the subsidies traced their origins to the Obama administration. In late February 2009, Treasury and the Fed, along with three smaller agencies, released a statement pledging to "preserve the viability of systemically important financial institutions."[27] Many private investors read this to mean that the government would prevent another major bank from failing, the equivalent of an enormous insurance policy for which the recipients never paid a cent. The banks benefited from this in the form of lower borrowing costs, since bondholders assured of repayment will accept a lower interest rate.

Even the stress tests featured their own version of this insurance arrangement. Under the terms of the test, the banks would first try to raise money from private investors. If investors balked, the bank could turn to the government, which would buy stock in the bank at 90 percent of its average price from late January and early February. That could turn out to be a bargain for a bank whose stock had subsequently tumbled—a bit like someone offering to buy your house for 90 percent of what you'd paid for it anytime you wanted to sell. Having the option to sell at that price would be valuable even if you never actually used it. It would guarantee that you didn't lose more than 10 percent on your investment, a form of insurance any private insurer would charge for. This was in essence what Treasury did for the country's biggest banks, except without the charge.

So it turned out that Axelrod and Gibbs were onto something.

---

* All the figures reflect the largest amount that a bank borrowed from the Fed in a given day.

The administration may not have given the banks any money, strictly speaking. But what it had given them would have cost plenty had the banks been asked to pay for it, far more than they could collectively afford. That was the whole point of the exercise. As Geithner never tired of explaining, it was far cheaper for the country to save the banks than to let them topple over and smother the economy.

But that was a different question from how much of the burden the banks should have to shoulder themselves, even if they couldn't have come close to paying back the government entirely. It was this figure that Treasury and the Fed consistently lowballed. There was, for example, a way to charge the banks for the insurance policy they received under the stress tests. This would have involved issuing the banks a type of preferred stock prior to the tests: stock on which they would have had to pay the government a dividend, and which could convert to common stock for those banks that later needed it. After some initial enthusiasm, Geithner sided with his counterparts at the Fed in rejecting the idea, according to a former Fed official.[28]

There was also the matter of whether the banks, having been saved, should enjoy such a rapid return to health. And whether their owners, the shareholders, should make out so well in the bargain. It was one thing to save the banks from collapse; another to restore the edenic days of yore. The former was never going to be popular, but voters might grudgingly accept it. The latter flaunted the banks' special treatment while the rest of the economy wheezed.

Again, the stress tests provided a telling example. To Axelrod and Gibbs, Geithner had cited the tests as evidence of Treasury's toughness toward the banks. But that wasn't entirely correct. The point of the stress tests hadn't been to inflict pain on shareholders, though that was a welcome by-product. The point had been to restore confidence in the banking system. Geithner favored asking the banks to raise $75 billion because he believed it was the lowest amount the markets would find believable, not because he deemed it the most cosmically just. It was a bit like responding to a job interviewer who inquires about your greatest weakness: you want a flaw that's credible, but not so big that you inspire second thoughts.

Had Treasury and the Fed wanted the shareholders to suffer more, they could have asked them to raise as much as $175 billion. It's hard to believe the larger amount would have shattered market confidence, given the ease with which they subsequently raised money. And any bank that couldn't raise the money from private investors would have been able to raise it from the government.

The biggest concern under this scenario would have been Bank of America, which already had to raise $33 billion, almost half the $75 billion amount for all nineteen of the stress-tested banks. BofA had managed this relatively easily, but asking it to raise another $20 billion or $30 billion might have made it look so weak that few investors would have wanted to touch it. Still, as a practical matter, Treasury had the money available to step in, though it could have ended up owning a sizable chunk of the company if the shortfall was large.

On the other hand, the beauty of forcing BofA and the other stress-tested banks to raise more money is that it would have diluted their shareholders even more, eliciting howls of protest which would have only been good for the bailout's legitimacy. In the end, the stress tests were a missed opportunity to correct the public's sense of injustice while putting the banks on a firmer footing.

9

THE BIG DIVERSION

By the spring of 2009, a group of administration Cassandras had begun to worry that the economy's problems were overwhelming the therapeutic powers of the stimulus. Christy Romer was the first to confess these anxieties, at least in the company of the president. In briefings as early as April, she harped on the staggering job loss since the fall—over 700,000 per month in the first quarter of 2009,[1] far worse than the economic team had predicted—and warned that it would take another big dose of medicine to ensure a strong recovery.

A few months later, Axelrod was preparing Romer for a Sunday talk show appearance by peppering her with sample questions. By this point in the administration, many outside economists were voicing doubts about the size of the original package, and so Axelrod asked: "Was the stimulus big enough?" Without hesitating, Romer responded: "Abso-fucking-lutely not." She said it half-jokingly, but the joke was that she would use the line on television, not the underlying sentiment. Axelrod did not seem amused.

Inside the Obama economic team, Romer wasn't alone in that view. Her fellow worriers included Jared Bernstein, the vice president's chief economic adviser, who'd long echoed Romer's calls for a larger stimulus and was dismayed by the trajectory of the economy since it passed. Alan Krueger, a widely respected Princeton professor then serving as Treasury's top economist, was also shocked by the bodies piling up on the unemployment rolls. In May, Krueger quietly began sketching ideas for boosting job growth.

The following month, Bernstein and Krueger found themselves briefing the president on the chances that the recovery would be of the jobless variety. Krueger dwelled on a slide with two columns. The first listed reasons that the joblessness could linger for years, and it ran on at some length: the layoffs had mostly hit permanent employees rather than temps, and the former are rehired more slowly; the housing crisis was making it difficult for workers to move in search of new jobs; the length of people's unemployment spells was at record highs. The second column listed the factors that could make jobs unexpectedly plentiful, and included precisely one argument: companies were now so lean they would have to hire in order to produce more.

When Summers argued that the lone upbeat indicator could overwhelm the other factors, the president was not reassured. "Larry, if you're right, you get a ten-dollar bonus," he said. "But we shouldn't count on it."

Obama worried that the jobless recovery could define his second year in office and wanted to address it proactively. The problem was that the chances of passing another several hundred billion dollars of stimulus were looking increasingly remote. When Romer dwelled on the idea later in the year, the frustrated president came close to losing his temper. "Well, the American people don't think it worked, so I can't do it," he groused. At best, the president felt, Congress might be able to pass some scaled-down measures, such as giving companies targeted incentives to hire, maybe some additional infrastructure investments and money for "greening" old buildings. But given the direction of public opinion, even this would soon look ambitious.

Politically, there were three giant cinder blocks weighing down the stimulus. The first had been obvious to the Obama brass from the get-go: Franklin Roosevelt had become president at the bottom of a four-year-old recession. By the time he ushered in the New Deal, the situation could only really improve. By contrast, Obama had slipped into the presidency with the economy spiraling downward, but well before the average voter grasped the steepness of the drop. The ordering of events most people observed in 2009—first Congress passed the stimulus, *then* unemployment hit twenty-six-year highs—made it look as if Obama had worsened the problem, when the truth was the opposite.[2]

The two other problems were self-inflicted. The stimulus Congress passed in February was $150 billion to $200 billion below what the administration had hoped for, which was itself far less than the $1.8 trillion Romer believed it would take to solve the problem. But the administration had shied away from making this case as Congress finalized the legislation. And it remained silent as the months went by. "We were never allowed to say the stimulus wasn't big enough," said one economic official of the spring and summer of 2009.[3]

The Obamans had calculated that to concede the inadequacy of the stimulus would be a provocative show of weakness, or at least a confusing message. "The notion that we were going to pass this, the largest economic recovery act in history, and upon signing it say, 'This isn't adequate, we need to do more,' doesn't comport with reality," said one White House aide.[4] The White House also believed that, if it needed to come back for more stimulus, the way to boost its chances was to argue that the first one had been a smashing success.[5] In fact, the reverse was true: it was not conceding the flaws in the stimulus that proved debilitating. If the stimulus was the best of all possible worlds, Americans could ask themselves, then why was the economic pain still so acute? The administration was in no position to explain.

Finally, there was the endlessly frustrating matter of "Romer-Bernstein," as it became known, a January 2009 report by the two White House economists touting the recession-fighting capability of the stimulus.[6] The document's centerpiece was a table showing that $800 billion of stimulus would hold unemployment to 8 percent or lower, versus 9 percent without such a package. The actual unemployment rate surged after the president signed the bill into law, reaching 9.4 percent within three months and a high of 10.1 percent in October.[7] Suddenly "Romer-Bernstein" loomed as a monument to administration incompetence.

The Romer-Bernstein forecast had been a source of some dissension within Team Obama. Romer had been intent on producing it and Emanuel thought it would help sell the bill on Capitol Hill. But Summers believed it was political malpractice to release a specific prediction that could be thrown back in the administration's face, something that was highly likely, given the uncertainty involved.

Still, the attack for which Romer-Bernstein provided the fodder was highly dubious. To anyone vaguely acquainted with the logic of an economic forecast, the numbers didn't mean Romer and Bernstein had overhyped the stimulus. It was equally plausible that the economy had been in much grimmer shape than they'd realized when they'd made their prediction. If a world without stimulus would have suffered 11 percent unemployment rather than 9 percent, then holding unemployment to 10 percent would have been a bona fide achievement. The only error would have been the starting point for the analysis—the so-called baseline. The effect on unemployment would have been more or less as predicted.

This is, in fact, precisely what had happened. The government's initial report on the final three months of 2008, published a few weeks after the Romer-Bernstein projection came out in January 2009, found that the economy had shrunk by roughly 4 percent. When the same data were revised for the last time more than two years later, they showed that the economy had actually shrunk by nearly 9 percent.[8]

Even as early as February 2009, though, it was clear that the recession was much deeper than anyone had realized only a month or two earlier,[9] and most economists adjusted their forecasts accordingly. But by that point the administration was stuck. The original 14-page Romer-Bernstein document attracted political opponents like chum attracting sharks in the ocean; no amount of updating could fend them off. By early July, when the previous month's unemployment rate clocked in at 9.5 percent, House Republican elders like John Boehner and Eric Cantor mirthfully recalled how the administration had "promised" to keep the figure a point and a half lower.[10]

The irony is that the stimulus really was working. The economy started growing again sometime in the summer after almost two years of shrinkage. And although unemployment kept ticking upward, the job losses that had gushed forth in January and February had nearly stopped by the end of the year. All of the nay-saying notwithstanding, a sustained but honest campaign by the White House might have laid the groundwork for another substantial round of jobs-related spending. But that proved impossible. The administration by then had its hands full with something else—something that would rival even the dreaded stimulus for the scorn it inspired in voters.

• • •

No administration official, not least the president, ever decided that health care reform would take precedence over the economy. Team Obama simply never imagined itself to be facing such a trade-off. In the master plan Rahm Emanuel had drawn up, the administration would notch its health care victory before Congress adjourned in August, then "pivot" to employment. "We were going to be done, under the plan, by the summer doing health care and energy," said a White House aide. "Then we'd return to the economy in the fall. That would be highlighting parts of the Recovery Act [aka stimulus] that worked, and it would be discrete proposals . . . to help the economy and jobs."

Better yet, since most of the health care action would unfold in the House and Senate, the president could spend June and July ramping up for the fall push. "In an ideal world in the summer, he is going out in the country once or twice a week, like he does, to do economic events," said the same aide. "We wouldn't have to do health care events, because health care would be happening on the Hill." [11]

Even so, there was always something too pat about this timeline, as though it grew less out of an assessment of what was possible than a desire to prove that health care was compatible with minding the recovery. In more candid moments, top Obama advisers conceded that the two goals might be at odds, and that, at the very least, health care would be a diversion from voters' more immediate concerns. They questioned the wisdom of embarking on it.

The nervousness had first set in after Obama formally clinched the Democratic nomination in 2008. Up until this point, the Obama high command had regarded the candidate's preoccupation with health care as a plus, given the hunger within the party's base for universal coverage. But with the general election under way, the political gurus began to view health care as a costly indulgence. In September 2008, the campaign's chief pollster, Joel Benenson, briefed his colleagues on all the ways the issue left Obama vulnerable, most of them having to do with the ease of labeling him a big government liberal. "So why are we doing health care?" many of his fellow consultants wondered. "Because the candidate wants to do health care," Benenson reminded them.

The politicos had begun to panic—the entire health care crusade was frankly getting a bit nutty. Axelrod had begged Obama to dial down his rhetoric for the sake of his election prospects. The senator responded that he wouldn't have a mandate to pass health care if he didn't champion it as a candidate.[12] A compromise was eventually struck. If Obama was determined to talk health care, the campaign would give him cover, but of a slightly unorthodox variety. Instead of making the case for Obama's plan, the campaign would attack John McCain for his health care heresies—from the right. McCain had proposed nudging workers onto the open market by taxing employer plans. Obama would therefore spend tens of millions of dollars branding him a health care tax raiser. "We managed to position ourselves in the middle of the spectrum on the health care debate," recalled a senior aide. "That was the right place to be."[13]

Of course, this didn't resolve the internal conflict; it only deferred it. Axelrod believed Obama owed his victory to the financial crisis and to a desire for cleaning up Washington. "He didn't think people voted on health care," said one of his colleagues.[14] As a pure political proposition, Axelrod advised Obama to dedicate himself to the economy and maybe education, that perennial political winner. Now Axelrod suddenly had reinforcements elsewhere in the new administration. At a meeting in January 2009, the vice president begged Obama to make his early presidency about jobs. The people who'd given him his mandate would understand that times had changed, Joe Biden said. "They'll give you a pass on this one."[15]

The economic team also radiated skepticism. The economists

moped through meetings on health care like children forced to sit through a performance of avant-garde ballet. Like Biden, Romer worried that the issue would distract from the economy. Others, like Geithner, brooded that expanding coverage to the uninsured would balloon the deficit at a time when the recession was already plumping it up. "He kept narrowing the playground," said an administration wonk. "You couldn't deficit-spend; the whole thing had to be paid for. Then you had to bring down the [overall spending] number." [16] Only Orszag was enthusiastic, believing that health care reform would save money over time.[17]

Still, the man with the most important vote was unmoved. Obama told his aides that if he couldn't reform health care, another generation would pass before a president tried again. Even waiting a year or two was out of the question. "The president's view was, yes, we had to deal with the economic emergency at hand," said a White House aide. "But if we didn't move on health care in the first few years, we'd probably never be able to get it done." [18]

Not long before the administration jumped full force into health care, Romer issued one of the blunter appeals for postponing the undertaking. "I know this isn't what you wanted to do when you came into office," she told the president, "but this is the hand you were dealt. Saving the economy is enough of an accomplishment." Before the president could say anything, Emanuel interjected: "If you look at what people accomplish in their first year, it's most of what they accomplish. If you want to do this, now is the time," he said.

The great strength of Rahm Emanuel was his pragmatism. The great weakness of Rahm Emanuel was his pragmatism. Emanuel was a pragmatist with every ounce of his being, at every level of cognition: micro and macro, strategically and tactically, on matters weighty and picayune, G-rated and X-rated. When Emanuel ran the Democrats'

House campaign committee in 2006, a candidate asked him to clear the field of primary challengers as a condition for running. "Well, I guess if I can take care of Bill Clinton's blow jobs, I can take care of that," Emanuel responded.[19] Once, during a White House meeting with business executives to plot strategy on climate change legislation, Emanuel stopped by to lay out his principles for the bill. There was, in fact, just one, he said: "Success." He did not mean whether or not the bill stopped global warming.

The problem was that all these different pragmatisms had a tendency to collide with one another. Emanuel was pragmatic enough to see that health care was a loser in a time of rising job loss. He was also pragmatic enough to recognize that he had a president who wouldn't be separated from his top priority. Not being able to resolve this tension, he resolved to fix both problems at once.

Emanuel's relationship with Obama had always been based more on perceived obligation than magnetic attraction. He was not exactly *of* Team Obama, like Axelrod and Robert Gibbs, but a man enlisted by Team Obama to get things done. When Obama won his Senate primary back in 2004, Emanuel, already an Illinois powerbroker as a freshman congressman, was dispatched to give his campaign manager, Jim Cauley, a two-hour grilling about the general election: how would he raise money, hire employees, scale up the turnout operation? The message was clear: Cauley could keep his job, but the leash would be short. "Everyone understood where we were," Cauley said.[20]

The thanklessness of this arrangement wasn't lost on Emanuel. In 2006, members of the Illinois establishment backed a wounded Iraq War veteran named Tammy Duckworth in a suburban House race because they assumed she stood the best chance of winning the traditionally Republican seat. When Duckworth narrowly defeated a liberal activist in the Democratic primary, the left singled out Emanuel as the culprit, even though Obama had also endorsed

Duckworth and helped throw her a fund-raiser.[21] Emanuel did not accept the abuse gracefully. "You think Obama wasn't involved?" he complained to a reporter. "But who gets blamed? Me. Tough guy Rahm. No one wants to blame Barack, because he is who he is. So fuck you."[22]

The Emanuels were a profane and volatile brood, but with a near-pathological sense of duty. It was the legacy of their immigrant-doctor father, their civil rights activist mother, and heaping piles of Jewish guilt. Emanuel was the fourth-ranking member of the House when Obama and Axelrod petitioned him to be chief of staff. Being two decades younger than each of his senior House colleagues, he could practically taste the speakership. For a full week after Obama and Axelrod approached him, Emanuel ranted implacably about the sacrifice they were asking. "I have a great life. I'm going to rise up in the House leadership, be the first Jewish speaker," he moaned. But they knew they had him. You could make Emanuel feel obliged just by looking solicitously in his direction.[23]

That was the beauty of Rahm: always feeling that it was his lot to organize and supervise, as if it would all go to pot if he weren't nagging and cajoling. Emanuel was the Jewish mother of American politics, a man crushed by burdens often self-imposed. After getting demoted from the position of White House political director in the mid-1990s, Emanuel took it upon himself to solve the party's perception problem. Middle America thought Clinton was soft. And so Emanuel, from his perch as second-string White House counselor without portfolio, excluded from the action on health care, concocted an anticrime campaign almost out of thin air.[24] Suddenly cops and mayors from across the country were descending on the White House. Relatives of assault weapons victims were being honored at Rose Garden ceremonies.[25] Before long, the president began asking his aides, "Why am I not doing more of Rahm's events?"[26] A crime bill passed Congress in August 1994.

Emanuel had a manic need to save the Democratic Party from itself, or at least to feel as though he were doing so. The centerpiece of his 2006 strategy for retaking the House was "the Fighting Dems," a VFW hall full of ex-military and law enforcement types who could withstand the charge of French-sympathizing defeatism that had done in John Kerry. (Never mind that Kerry himself was a Vietnam veteran.) Emanuel recruited them to run in swing districts across the country, several dozen in all. There were Patrick Murphy of Pennsylvania, who'd been decorated in Iraq; Andrew Horne of Kentucky, a Marine for three decades; and Jeff Latas, a Gulf War veteran from Arizona. In Emanuel's mind, they were the answer to a situation the polls had homed in on: voters were souring on Iraq, but they didn't entirely trust the Democrats' opposition to it.[27]

When the party retook the House, Emanuel dashed off a volume of memos—really more of a distillation of Rahmian anxieties into prose—begging the leadership not to misinterpret its mandate. Democrats believed they'd won by flaying the Bush administration over Iraq, with some help from the stench of Republican corruption that culminated with the indictment of House majority leader Tom DeLay. Emanuel concluded that it had mostly been about voters' bank accounts. He thought voters had sensed the economy stalling out as early as 2006, and that they would stick with Democrats only as long as the party addressed these economic concerns. "He talked about the degree to which we were renting the majority," recalled one aide. "In all these districts where all we had done was rent independents, it didn't represent some kind of new world order."

Two years later, during the Obama transition, Emanuel was quick to unearth this epistolary record. "He already had that on his brain, harkening back to what we put in the early memos to the Speaker," said the aide. At a retreat Emanuel organized for incoming White House staffers in early December 2008, he was as preoccupied as ever with the economic concerns of fickle independents. He warned that the administration would have to speak to them even as it teed up legislation on health care and climate change.[28]

When the spring came and went with no end in sight on health care, Emanuel's agita was becoming palpable. By the end of June 2009, not a single one of the five congressional committees with jurisdiction had so much as voted on a bill. Worse, to the surprise of many in the West Wing,[29] the House had taken up climate change legislation first, deferring health care in the one chamber where it might have moved quickly. As the Emanuel aide recalled: "I would say he was good and concerned by the time the energy bill passed"—in the House in late June—"that we were steering too far away from pounding jobs day in and day out."[30]

Finally, in mid-July, Emanuel began to see signs of the momentum he craved in Congress. Three committees approved health care bills in rapid succession; approval from a fourth was imminent. Still, the holdout, Senate Finance, was easily the most important. It was Finance that had effectively killed Clinton's health care hopes back in 1994. This time around, the committee's Democratic chairman, Max Baucus of Montana, had spent months negotiating with his Republican counterpart, Chuck Grassley of Iowa, with exceedingly little to show for it.

Emanuel was beside himself. The plan all along had been to strike quickly in Congress so as to avoid a protracted public brawl. Not only would a months-long stalemate divert the administration even further from the economy, it would crimp the chances of passing health care itself. There were just too many smelly details tucked away in such a complex piece of legislation. Public opinion was sure to collapse as opponents unearthed them. For that matter, it already was collapsing.[31]

Emanuel gathered his top aides and searched for a way to hurry the process along. The Senate Labor Committee had produced its own health care bill. Perhaps, he wondered, majority leader Harry Reid could bypass Baucus and bring it to the floor? Or maybe Baucus could just stop bargaining with Grassley and move a more partisan version of his bill?[32]

But the president brushed the idea aside, decreeing that Baucus should press ahead in search of Republican partners.[33] Whether or not Emanuel's plan could have worked, rejecting it ensured that the administration would miss its August deadline and cede the initiative to the right. "Basically we went for the quick kill on health care and missed," said a senior White House aide. "The danger of going for the quick kill is that we didn't prepare the country for [a long debate]."[34]

In August, conservative activists flocked to town hall meetings to hector Democratic congressmen and bully supporters of reform. You almost had to admire the nihilistic genius at work, at least if you weren't counting on universal health coverage. Opponents seized on two relatively unconnected provisions—one that subsidized optional end-of-life counseling, another that created a new agency to study the effectiveness of medical treatments—and fused them into "death panels." Though the "death panel" was no less mythical a mash-up than the centaur or the mermaid, suddenly all the right-wing baby boomers in America expected to be hauled before a council of technocrats on their sixty-fifth birthday and told whether they would live or die. As smelly details go, the odor was damn near asphyxiating.

By late summer, Emanuel and other White House officials were sufficiently alarmed that they considered abandoning health care altogether. When Obama returned from vacation on Martha's Vineyard on August 30, he convened two meetings to gauge the odds of success. Among his top aides, the consensus was that passage was still possible—Democrats had 60 votes in the Senate, after all—even if they couldn't see the precise legislative path.[35] This was all Obama needed to hear. Around the White House, he was fond of recalling that he'd traveled to all fifty states during the campaign and personally spoken to over 2 million people. Overwhelmingly, he said, they'd wanted health care, and he'd made a promise to give it to them. "This is my priority, what I want to do," he told his aides. "If there was a chance to do this that was not foolhardy, he wanted to go," recalled one person who attended both meetings.[36] Emanuel dutifully fell in line.

Beginning the week of Labor Day, the White House embarked on the counteroffensive it had always intended to avoid, beginning with a presidential speech before a joint session of Congress. The new push clearly saved reform, which would finally pass the following March. But having bumped the economy off the agenda for the summer, health care would now repeat the feat for the fall. "No one thought we would have to take every element of the administration and dedicate it to health care both publicly and privately," said the White House aide. "Which is what we ended up having to do [starting in] September."[37]

Outside the White House, however, there were many who'd harbored this concern all along. Before the fateful meetings in August, one frantic senator went to see Obama in the Oval Office to make a final plea for setting aside health care, a move he'd urged since the transition. For forty-five minutes the two men debated with rising emotion on both sides. "Had I been elected president last fall, at the end of my first year in office I would have wanted people to know one thing about me: that I spent the entire year working to find a way to put people back on payrolls," the senator said. "What they're going to know about you is that health care is the most important issue." The president responded that he had a once-in-a-lifetime

10

THE PURIST

To anyone outside the Obama economic team, the biggest obstacles to putting another round of cash in the pockets of workers and businesses were the unpopularity of the original stimulus and the stumbles over health care. Within the economic team, however, the biggest holdup in the spring and summer of 2009 was a rising anxiety about the deficit that would linger once the recovery took hold.

Perhaps not surprisingly, given Treasury's institutional bias toward budget hawkishness, Tim Geithner was an early advocate of tamping down the budget deficit. Since the transition, he'd favored a plan that would reduce it to 3 percent of GDP, the level most economists considered "stable," during the president's first term. With the worst of the recession and the financial crisis now over, Geithner began to argue that it was time to take deficit reduction seriously.

But even the Treasury secretary wasn't the most outspoken exponent of the traditional Treasury view. That honor fell to Peter Orszag, the director of the White House Office of Management and Budget (OMB). Orszag had been head of the Congressional Budget Office (CBO), the government's official arbiter of the cost of legislation, prior to joining the administration and was an avowed deficit-scold. During the transition, he'd worried that the sheer size of the stimulus could undermine the confidence of businessmen and money managers, who would fear an endless expansion of government spending and would delay private investments as a result. Unless the administration quickly announced a plan for taming the ten-year deficit, this would weigh on the economy and could make the stimulus self-defeating.

The preoccupation with "confidence" was pure Rubinism. Orszag had been a young White House aide when Rubin was Treasury secretary and had cultivated Rubin as a mentor upon leaving the Clinton administration. He'd internalized the wise man's near-physical discomfort with deficits, but the concern wasn't universally shared among Rubin's disciples. Back in the fall of 2008, Orszag and Summers had spent thirty minutes heatedly debating the importance of "confidence" to the economy while several of their new colleagues looked on. Orszag insisted that confidence mattered independently of basic economic fundamentals: it could hurt growth even when wealth and income were high, or boost it when they were in short supply. Summers thought this was mostly nonsense.

Even before you actually reined in the deficit, Orszag believed, it was important to show that you intended to rein it in. He was fond of symbolic gestures that would bolster the administration's deficit-cutting credibility. Early in the administration, he suggested that Obama ask his cabinet to cut $100 million from their collective budgets, a rounding error in accounting terms. The president made the pitch during his first formal cabinet meeting. Orszag later sold Obama on holding a contest among federal employees to generate the most innovative penny-pinching ideas.[1] (The eventual winner—flown to Washington, Super Bowl–champ style, for a presidential handshake—was a V.A. hospital worker who wanted to send patients home with their medicine rather than throw it away. Total savings: $20 million.) He also urged the president to freeze domestic discretionary spending in his next budget. Orszag reckoned the economic impact would be modest (he put the short-term hit at a mere $10 billion, in a $14 trillion economy), but that it would send an important signal to businessmen and investors.

Whether or not these measures actually established the administration's budget-pruning bona fides is difficult to say. But within the White House, they certainly established Orszag's. In May 2009, the president asked him to draft a secret memo laying out the government's options in the event of a fiscal crisis, in which a runaway deficit sent interest rates spiraling ever upward. No other member of the Obama economic team was even aware of the assignment.

By the summer of 2009, Orszag had become so alarmed by the amount of red ink the government was tallying that he lobbied to put out a new long-term budget with a tough plan for shrinking the deficit. The occasion for releasing it would have been the "mid-session review" in August, normally a pro forma affair in which the administration simply updates its annual deficit numbers. At Orszag's request, the economic team held weeks of meetings on the subject before other senior White House officials decided that August was a lousy time to unveil a new budget plan, especially with the health care debate raging. If anything, an unemployment rate nearing 10 percent strengthened the case for spending on jobs, not ratcheting down spending.

Orszag wasn't opposed to additional stimulus in principle, so long as it was paired with long-term savings. But the practical effect of his deficit preoccupation, and his success at transmitting it to the president, was to narrow the range for action. At worst, Orszag contributed to an internal stalemate that rendered the president a bystander as the economy stalled out months later.

There was no bigger star in the first six months of the Obama administration than Peter Orszag. The media often portrayed him as the kind of nerd Washington periodically invests with power, with his slightly-too-high voice and the mini–office supply store pouring forth from his shirt pocket. He carried two BlackBerries, which he kept holstered on his belt, and his glasses looked both expensive and peculiarly out of fashion. All together, he would not have been out of place on the set of *Apollo 13*.

Within the West Wing, though, Orszag instantly showed himself to be formidable. From his days as CBO director, he carried enormous credibility with Senate moderates like Democrat Kent Conrad of North Dakota, the powerful Budget Committee chairman. The White House traded on this epically. It was Orszag whom Emanuel deployed to Capitol Hill to broker the final stimulus deal in early February 2009. It was Orszag who nimbly guided a budget resolution through Congress with the seeds of a trillion-dollar health care plan.[2] Whenever there was talk of defections by Blue Dogs, the conservative House Democrats, or rebellions over health care financing, Orszag somehow quelled them. Before long, many in the White House felt he could succeed Emanuel as chief of staff.

Reporters and the policy mandarins they quoted were just as reverential. During the summer of 2009, all of Washington took notice when Orszag's successor at the CBO, Doug Elmendorf, began to assail the administration's health care numbers. Elmendorf and his analysts doubted the savings the administration hung on its "game-changers," the tweaks and tinkerings intended to make the system more efficient. In response, Orszag ginned up a minor backlash against the CBO, whose cost projections, he said, undervalued such efficiencies. He even took the campaign against his former agency to his White House blog.[3] None of it mattered a lick to the riled-up seniors whose support the administration was hemorrhaging. But the pundits were by and large persuaded. Thanks to Orszag, the hemorrhaging within the Washington establishment more or less subsided.

Perhaps even more than it came from his savvy and competence, Orszag's power came from the harmony between his worldview and the president's. Both men were fierce anti-partisans; both shunned ideology. The two shared a conviction that technology and ingenuity and old-fashioned common sense could resolve most public policy problems.

During the presidential campaign, for example, Obama touted the computerization of health care records as a way to cut administrative costs and avoid medical errors. Orszag, too, was evangelical about such reforms, which he believed would generate efficiencies by showing doctors how best to spend health care dollars. As a candidate, Obama had leaned heavily on the Harvard economist David Cutler, who'd made his name demonstrating that the quality of health care often has little to do with what we pay for it.[4] Orszag had devoted much of his CBO tenure to corroborating this proposition.[5] Obama was taken with the finding that workers rarely enroll in even generous 401(k) plans, but don't opt out if their employers enroll them.[6] He proposed a savings plan that exploited this so-called status quo bias. Orszag had talked up the idea for years.

Above all was their deficit hawkishness. It was no accident that Obama had ordered up the fiscal crisis memo in May 2009. Nor was it an accident that he tapped Orszag for the job. The two men had a shared distaste for deficits that long preceded the administration. "The president really hates the deficit and wants to deal with the long-run problem," Romer later said.[7] Back in 2006, exactly one senator was invited to speak at the launch of the Hamilton Project, the centrist policy shop that Orszag ran and Rubin helped bankroll: Barack Obama. In his remarks commemorating the occasion, Obama declared, "When you keep the deficit low and our debt out of the hands of foreign nations, then we can all win."[8] At the time, Orszag had recently written a scholarly 55-page study demonstrating how deficits raise interest rates and hurt the economy.

Once the Obama administration was under way, White House aides realized that these affinities explained how Orszag consistently carried the day in discussions with the president, especially with his ideas for deficit reduction. "There were not infrequent times when we'd go into a meeting and basically everyone would be against OMB," said one OMB official. "We'd walked out and the president would decide to go with [our position]."[9]

One of Orszag's health care "game-changers" was an agency that would propose cuts in the cost of treatments, such as MRIs and prosthetic joints, for which Medicare reimbursed doctors and hospitals. Members of Congress often inflated these payments at the urging of smooth-talking lobbyists, even when the White House had hoped to scale them back. Under Orszag's plan, the cuts would take effect automatically unless Congress voted down the entire menu, limiting the opportunities for special pleading. Many a congressional baron was furious at the loss of his price-setting prerogative. Obama's own Health and Human Services department bemoaned the threat to its authority.[10] But the president held firm. "The guy [Obama] was really tough on the payment advisory board," said the OMB official.[11] "It wouldn't have happened without him."

In November 2009, Orszag would tout an idea that divided the economic team and inspired contempt in the political shop: extending for one or two years George W. Bush's middle class tax cuts, which were scheduled to expire in 2011, then letting them lapse unless Congress found a way to offset their costs. During a meeting with Obama in the Oval Office, he casually outlined the proposal. The obvious defect was that it would be likely to break the president's campaign pledge to oppose tax increases on the middle class. Nevertheless, Obama was intrigued by its elegance as a deficit-cutting maneuver, according to two people in the room. He also liked the idea of forcing the Republicans to grapple with the costs of Bush's policies. Only later did the politicos revolt—the vice president, for one, was apoplectic—and the president lost interest.

Orszag could be a stickler: for rules, for numbers, for technocratically sound policy. This helped bolster his reputation and explained his influence in public debates. But, over time, the starchiness of his collar became a source of friction in the White House.

Orszag's most persistent antagonist was Larry Summers, with whom he'd clashed from the get-go. Several weeks after the December 16, 2008, meeting that set the administration's economic agenda, Orszag complained to Romer that Summers had manipulated her to drive up the stimulus price tag to $800 billion: "I know why Larry gave you so much time [at the meeting] in Chicago," he said. "He wanted a big stimulus, too."

Orszag was convinced that Summers's ambitions extended far beyond the NEC's traditional "honest broker" function—that, in particular, he wanted a central role in crafting the administration's budget. He was loath to give in to this territorial expansionism. The two men squabbled over such trivialities as who would send out invitations to meetings and which agency would host them.[12] After a series of fact-finding inquiries from Summers's staff, Orszag prohibited his charges from speaking to officials outside OMB without prior authorization. He enacted a special rule for Summers's deputy, Jason Furman: anyone receiving an unsolicited inquiry from Furman was to alert Orszag's chief of staff, Jill Blickstein. "There was an institutional turf kind of game going on between NEC and OMB," said one former aide to Summers. "I think we liked declaring victory over Peter. I'm sure he did the same."[13]

Within a few months, each man had appealed to Emanuel, who in turn blamed both sides for the stand-off, accusing Summers of being "petty" and Orszag of acting "pretty small." Emanuel told Orszag he could limit Summers's influence over the budget process if the OMB director was truly adamant. But if that happened, Orszag shouldn't expect much input on a variety of other issues, or much of a presence at the daily economic briefing with the president. Orszag said he could live with the trade-off.

Mostly, Emanuel hoped the two former friends, both of whom were Rubin protégés who had collaborated at the Hamilton Project, could solve the problem on their own. Not long after, Summers and Orszag agreed to meet periodically for dinner to ease the tension between them. Yet the dinners tended to produce only a temporary thaw that the next bureaucratic run-in inevitably undid. Sometimes they did not produce even that. During one meal, Summers told Orszag, "You don't want to be the budget director who oversaw the biggest increase in the budget deficit ever, do you?" Summers was being empathetic—assuring Orszag that he understood his predicament. But Orszag interpreted the question as a taunt. He found it odd that Summers would assign him responsibility for a development that was largely beyond his control and that he was actively combating.

By the second half of 2009, the politicos had started in on Orszag, too. Axelrod became convinced that he was leaking to reporters to buff his image as a deficit purist and advance his agenda on the issue. Orszag counted Jackie Calmes of the *New York Times* as a personal friend—they'd gotten acquainted when her daughter babysat for his kids—and Calmes seemed to land one damaging scoop after another. Orszag insisted that he gave Calmes nothing remotely juicy, that he only talked her through budget arcana.

Before long, the signs of tension were everywhere. Axelrod would ask Orszag for cover during a public skirmish on the deficit. Orszag would say he preferred to sit it out, worried about damaging his credibility with dubious talking points. The West Wing would ask Orszag to defend the health care bill on his blog. Orszag would beg off if he felt the argument was misleading. During the summer of 2009, Phil Schiliro, the White House congressional point man, urged him to post a blog item celebrating the fact that, of the administration's expansive list of "game-changers," the House bill included all but a handful. Orszag was unimpressed: the handful the House had omitted were among the most important. He refused to lend his good name to the effort.

For their part, the West Wing politicos chafed at Orszag's indifference to the president's campaign promises. Orszag was one of the administration's leading proponents of taxing employee insurance plans to limit health care spending, the same idea for which Obama had pounded McCain. Axelrod violently resisted reversing course on this question. To illustrate the perils involved, he sat the health care team down and screened a ten-minute montage of every ad Obama had run blasting McCain as a tax raiser. Still, the Orszag view prevailed internally.[14] Axelrod was also dead set against repealing the Bush tax cuts for families making under $250,000, which Obama had pledged to protect. But Orszag didn't see how he could defend the administration's deficit-cutting plans with the tax cuts off-limits.

Increasingly, Orszag's only source of leverage was his uncanny mind-meld with the president. But that gave him more than enough influence to shape the agenda.

Orszag was never going to fit easily into a political operation. It just wasn't in him to smile beatifically while others spouted nonsense, to bow before the authority of blowhards and political hacks. "I get very uncomfortable when I have to pitch lines that are demonstrably not true," he said.[15]

Authority was, in fact, something Orszag had been bucking for as long as he could remember. He wore it as a badge of honor. In the early 1990s, he'd decided to take a break from his dissertation at the London School of Economics to work for Clinton's Council of Economic Advisers. But he nearly flubbed the FBI security check before he ever got in the door. The agent had noticed a tiny gap in his employment history—an unaccounted-for week during his undergrad days at Princeton. "Were you unemployed?" the G-man asked. "No," Orszag told him, before delivering a brief tutorial on economics: "To be unemployed you have to be actively seeking a job. I was out of the labor force." The rest of the interview did not go smoothly.

Upon leaving the Clinton administration in the mid-nineties, Orszag thought he needed private sector experience to round out his résumé. He weighed several opportunities before settling on McKinsey, the prestigious management consulting firm. Within a month he realized he'd made a huge mistake. He bristled at the corporate-speak, struggled through the endless PowerPoint presentations. It was bad enough to be an organization man in your own organization. It was still another thing to toil away in a company that catered to other companies.

But one doesn't just quit McKinsey a few weeks into the job like some clerk in a convenience store. The harder Orszag tried to leave, the more McKinsey tried to keep him. Before long, he found himself in the office of the senior west coast partner, looking out over the bay in San Francisco. The partner told Orszag he was committing career suicide, then finally saw it was getting him nowhere. "We can't make you stay," the partner sighed. "I know," Orszag shot back. "Indentured servitude's illegal."

Even the way he met Bob Rubin bespoke a certain irreverent swagger. He was in his mid-twenties, a junior economist in the Clinton White House, when he was invited to observe a high-level meeting. At one point, Rubin made a small computational error. Orszag scribbled a quick note explaining the mistake and passed it to the Treasury secretary. Two weeks later, Rubin called out of the blue. The great man wanted to acknowledge that Orszag had been right.[16] "We had a democracy of thought, and Peter was a very well-regarded young staff person," Rubin later recalled.[17]

In 2003, at thirty-four, Orszag was ensconced at the Brookings Institution when Senator Conrad put forth his name as the Democrats' candidate to run the Congressional Budget Office. At the time Republicans controlled the House and Senate, so his practical chances were nil. But it was a sign his stock was soaring. He'd cultivated a reputation as a budget savant and his congressional testimony was much in demand. When the Democrats took back the Senate in 2006, it suddenly dawned on Orszag that the job would be his. Sure enough, a Conrad aide called a few days later to make the offer.

CBO director was the best job Orszag ever had, an arrangement that fit him like a Superhero outfit. There were no operatives to fend off, no competing bureaucracies to contend with. Only Orszag and his elite corps of number-crunchers, who could kill legislation just by feeding it through their spreadsheets. God help the senators whose tax credit the CBO deemed more expensive than they'd claimed, or whose budget proposal the CBO said cut half as much as advertised. It was like being a professional oracle: the most powerful politicians in the world cowered before his pronouncements.

And Orszag was good at it—great, even. Previous directors had kept a studied distance from the authors of the legislation they priced. The presidents and senators and representatives never knew why their proposals didn't "score" they knew only that the proposals had come in over budget. Orszag set out to demystify the process. If you were trying to keep a program under a billion dollars, Orszag would walk you through the ways the math could add up: keep this feature in, take this one out. But the analysis never changed. There were no deals to cut; no horses to trade. Orszag did transparency, but he didn't do politics. He had no ideology other than the truth.

There was, indeed, almost a contempt for politics. Just as it was a politician's job to overpromise, to gloss over hard choices with vague prescriptions, it was the CBO director's job to tilt against this with practiced sobriety. Orszag took special pleasure in undermining the politicians' most inflated claims. When congressman after congressman proclaimed that infrastructure spending would boost the economy quickly, CBO showed that very few projects actually had rapid "spend-out rates." Political celebrities like Bill Clinton and Al Gore (and Barack Obama) were fond of talking up the job-creating potential of green technology. CBO discerned that the impact on jobs would be modest, at least in the short term.

There was a part of Orszag that had always thought of politics as grubby and corrupting. His undergraduate thesis was about the subtle ways Congress skewed interest rate setting by the Federal Reserve. He tallied up the number of times the Fed chairman had been hauled before a congressional committee. Then he noticed that it happened most frequently when interest rates were high, presumably so that the congressional overlords could rant at the chairman over his tightwad stance. There was political pressure to keep rates low, in other words. Orszag concluded that less democratic accountability would mean better monetary policy.

Even after Orszag joined the Obama administration, he was fond of saying he didn't have a "license to practice politics."[18] This was of course absurd, as politics had become a central feature of his job. But in a cosmic sense Orszag was being honest. It still gnawed at him the way politicians were always mucking up policy. If you had to summarize his plan for controlling health care costs, you could do a lot worse than "rescuing the system from politics."

In early 2009, the administration proposed cutting tens of billions in overpayments to insurance companies under Medicare. When Iowa senator Chuck Grassley protested the cuts at a hearing, Orszag responded, "I very firmly believe that capitalism is not founded on excessively high subsidies to private firms. That is what this system delivers right now." Grassley reacted no better to Orszag's brief lesson in economics than the FBI agent had two decades earlier, huffing that Orszag had chewed up "half of my time lecturing me on capitalism." [19]

Orszag's views on the deficit came from the same emotional zip code. The budget deficit would inevitably rise from time to time in response to a recession or national emergency—this was as it should be. But over several years, a government should hold its deficit steady as a fraction of the economy, and preferably a small one, so as not to alarm the people who lent it money. Any economist would tell you as much. For that matter, most Americans intuitively grasped this logic. It was only the politicians, with their penchant for overspending and undertaxing, who seemed immune to such basic math.

For most of 2009, Christy Romer had stood alone among Obama's top economic officials in resisting the preoccupation with deficits. She believed that the first halting steps of a weak recovery were precisely the wrong time to talk deficit reduction. In any case, bond markets were relatively sophisticated creatures, she reasoned. They understood that the deficit naturally rose in response to an emergency. In the same way that they'd mostly sat tight when the government piled up debt to fund World War II, they would cut the government some slack while it tried to prop up a crisis-stricken economy. As for the risk of shifting to deficit reduction prematurely, Romer also harked back to the Roosevelt era. She warned that the country could suffer a repeat of 1937, when FDR's deficit winnowing doomed a solid recovery and extended the Depression by several more years. Far from wielding the budget ax, Romer argued, the president should make the case for another round of government spending.

Summers did not disagree with this logic. But he was reluctant to throw himself into Romer's cause. Only a few months after the enormous exertion of passing the first stimulus, Romer's table-pounding was already earning her eye-rolls in the White House. Summers could see that the president's political aides had little appetite for contemplating another go at it when he would privately float the topic. On top of this, Summers believed that conservative Senate Democrats, like Kent Conrad and Evan Bayh, might become more amenable to another short-term economic boost if the administration evinced some interest in tackling the deficit. It might be preferable to lead with that effort.

By the fall, though, Summers had begun to evolve on these tactical questions. One reason he'd been comfortable recommending less than the $1.2 trillion Romer had sought was that, unlike Romer, he subscribed to a concept known as "escape velocity." The idea was that at some point, people would become sufficiently confident in the recovery that they would spend an increasing fraction of their incomes. If they'd spent 60 percent of their salary before, they might suddenly start spending two thirds, and this would lead to more purchases, more output, more hiring. But now it looked as if the economy might not achieve the escape velocity he'd been hoping for.

The fall of 2009 also marked the beginning of a new budget season, making it a natural time to consider new proposals. To aides and colleagues, Summers began to muse about the win-win logic of a big investment in infrastructure. Most impartial experts believed the country's roads, bridges, and ports needed $1 trillion to $2 trillion in upgrades and repairs.[20] Meanwhile, unemployment among construction workers was at an all-time high after the bursting of the housing bubble. Not only did the government have a chance to create jobs in a sector where they were badly needed; it would get its roads and bridges at a bargain, since it wouldn't have to outbid the private sector for the services of these contractors.[21]

Still, in meetings with the president, Summers played his cards close. One of Orszag's pet arguments was that the government couldn't possibly pass enough stimulus to drag the unemployment rate back to the sunnier side of 7 percent, the sort of progress that might turn heads in Middle America. At most, it would slice off a few tenths of a percentage point, in which case why bother? Romer found this mental exercise utterly infuriating. As a rough rule of thumb, she calculated that every $100 billion of spending would produce a million jobs for one year. Taking a million people off the unemployment rolls would be a real achievement even if it didn't solve the entire problem.

When the president repeated Orszag's point during a meeting about additional stimulus, she quickly interjected: "That is oh so wrong." Obama betrayed a flash of annoyance. "It's not only wrong it's 'oh so wrong'?" he wondered. For his part, Summers privately agreed but looked on and said nothing.

As time went by, though, Summers was becoming a bit less tactical, a bit more . . . shrill. Some co-workers dated the beginning of the change to the moment, in August 2009, when it became apparent that Ben Bernanke would stay on as Fed chairman, a post Summers had coveted. "Clearly with Larry, once the whole Fed thing goes down, he starts becoming disheveled again, like the whole charm school wore off," said one White House colleague.[22] Others believed it had more to do with his gradual eclipse by Geithner, who was beginning to consolidate his position within the administration. "If Tim decided to be popular, which he did a fair amount, Larry was always going to lose [when they disagreed]," said a White House economic aide. "It made the job less fun for him."[23]

In truth, Summers had plenty of reasons to feel frustrated. His understanding with Emanuel had been that the National Economic Council would enjoy the same primacy in the economic sphere that the National Security Council enjoyed in foreign affairs. Mostly, this meant Summers's agency would be the key intermediary between the president and all the economic advice percolating through his administration. But in May, Summers learned of the fiscal crisis memo the president had privately asked Orszag to draft. Summers was apoplectic. He marched into Emanuel's office and announced he would leave if the chief of staff didn't put a stop to such advice giving by stealth.

Summers also seethed about Emanuel's retreat from several more specific commitments. Upon taking the job, Summers asked that the NEC's jurisdiction extend to health care and climate change. Emanuel assented, then realized he couldn't deliver. The president had opted for independent health and energy "czars" who would report to him directly.

"Life sucks around here," Summers bleated to Emanuel on one especially draining day in the fall of 2009. "I waited thirty minutes outside the Capitol because you fuckers can't get your motor pool to work right." When Emanuel responded that he would procure a chauffered car for Summers, the economic adviser was instantly suspicious. "Rahm, I would like to have a car," he said. "But don't tell me you can get me a car if you can't." Emanuel insisted that he could arrange the car, only to later discover it was statutorily impossible. (The executive office of the president is only allotted a handful of cars, all of which were spoken for.)[24]

Whatever the cause, something had changed with Summers by the fall of 2009. For several months, he had seemed intent on being the economic adviser whose tactical judgment the president's handlers respected. Now he seemed less concerned about internal politics, more willing to speak his mind regardless of how it reflected on him. Larry Summers the operator had given way to Larry Summers the policy nag.

By late November, there was a second key meeting on the subject of further stimulus. When Orszag offered his familiar refrain about the futility of these efforts, it was Summers and not Romer who objected. "You know, we actually do need more [stimulus]," Summers said. "Every little bit helps." Obama had long revered Summers's economic aptitude. "The president would just show up in Larry's office . . . multiple times a week," said one of Summers's aides.[25] Now that Summers had made the point, the president seemed open to considering it.

In principle, there should have been a way to satisfy both sides. The president and Congress could devise a plan to shrink the deficit over a decade while boosting spending in the first few years, when the economy was still fragile. In fact, it was an idea pretty much every economist inside and outside the administration endorsed. Unfortunately, this was complex to execute in practice. Among other things, Republicans were likely to object that any deficit deal should cut the deficit, period, not raise it for a few years as a prelude to the cutting. There was no way to rebut the argument in a ten-second sound-bite.

Perhaps an immaculately functioning economic team might have succeeded nonetheless. The president, alas, did not have such a team. Summers's talent was for influencing a particular decision at a particular moment. He was not someone with a flair for the long game—for the week-in, week-out slog of bringing colleagues around to his views. His NEC meetings had a persistent aimless quality. The academic-style discourse would drag on for hours without producing a single concrete conclusion; it would yield only increasingly esoteric questions. (Emanuel often complained about how it had taken the better part of a year to generate a modest small business initiative.) For months, Summers and Romer couldn't even agree between themselves on how to give the economy an additional boost. Whereas Summers favored an investment in infrastructure, Romer proposed giving employers a $5,000 tax credit for each new worker they hired. Suffice it to say, there would be no grand bargain emerging from this mire.

Orszag found this dysfunction exasperating and began ducking NEC meetings whenever possible. But the great deficit-versus-
stimulus debate of 2009 had a way of sucking people in each time
they tried to escape. Every few weeks, the economic team would
convene before the president to reenact the same minor melodrama.
Orszag would observe that the administration was publicly saying
the economy was on the mend, and that it was obliged to follow
through on the implications of this position. He pressed for action
on the deficit, often with Geithner's backing, and favored setting up
a commission of Washington elders to recommend trillions in savings over a decade. In response, Romer and eventually Summers argued that the economy was still very far from healthy. They pleaded
for more money for the economy and job creation.

Finally, the economic team arrived at a tentative truce: the administration would publicly embrace another $100 to $200 billion
of stimulus in the short term, then propose to cut the deficit by at
least as much over ten years.

Predictably, the truce quickly unraveled. Seated in the Roosevelt
Room in early December, the president wondered why both sets of
ideas were so timid. Orszag grumbled that it *was*, in fact, disappoint-
ing to offer so little on the deficit front. Summers was just as quick
to seize on the president's dissatisfaction: the economy *was* in dire
need of more stimulus, he said. Each side then labeled the other's pet
proposals political nonstarters, and the conversation descended into
the familiar back-and-forth. Orszag argued that the bond markets
needed a sign the administration was serious about responsible budgeting. Summers and Romer brooded about adopting the rhetoric of
austerity while the economy was still fragile.

The president quickly lost his patience. "You know what, this
is the same meeting we've been having," he said, excusing himself.
"Talk to me when you've thought this through." At which point
Romer and Orszag began yelling at each other. Summers accused

Geithner's Treasury Department of leaking deficit-cutting promises to make them difficult to back away from. After Orszag left in a huff, Romer turned to Geithner and berated him as "feckless" for his tepid stance on more stimulus. The exchange got so voluble that Orszag's deputy, Rob Nabors, lunged to shut the door to prevent the brawl from echoing throughout the West Wing.

Still, with no agreement forthcoming, it was Orszag who had filled the vacuum throughout the fall. The domestic spending freeze, he could argue, at least created the appearance of progress on the deficit. The deficit commission would be the first step of a longer-term plan. These ideas irritated Summers to no end. He worried that the fiscal commission would box the president into ill-conceived cuts. "McChrystal risk," Summers dubbed it, after Stanley McChrystal, the general whose report urging more troops for Afghanistan the president couldn't easily reject.[26] Meanwhile, the spending freeze could affect programs that served the most vulnerable. "We're Democrats," Summers harrumphed. "We believe in these things." Besides, both ideas struck him as gimmicks unworthy of a president. To colleagues he complained that "what's really important in life is not to believe your own bullshit."

In both cases, however, the president sided with Orszag. The ideas might be gimmicky, but at least they were crisp and actionable. That was more than could be said for Summers's hazy infrastructure plans.

Like the president, Orszag was right to be exasperated by a White House that constantly deadlocked over how to carry out the first-best solution. But that didn't get either man off the hook for the most gruesome labor market in a generation, a tragedy Orszag too often minimized. Whatever risk the deficit posed—a sudden panic among bondholders and a corresponding surge in interest rates—it was a hypothetical risk, whereas 10 percent unemployment was an unremitting reality.

Politically, too, making the case for additional stimulus was far more urgent than making the case for deficit reduction. Republicans would always be around to sell the public on spending cuts. It was stimulus that needed presidential cover given the GOP's determination to discredit it. Instead, the president's embrace of belt-tightening, however symbolic at this point, shifted the conversation several ticks rightward and launched a budget-cut bidding war that would escalate over the next two years.

It turned out that, in the aftermath of a deep recession, being a deficit hawk wasn't ideologically neutral, as Orszag liked to think. It was itself an ideology. It meant prioritizing budget balance over economic growth and employment. One could argue that the deficit hawk view was preferable. But it wasn't *correct* in some objective sense. It was a question of values, a judgment call.

In fact, the more you poked and prodded on the deficit, the more Orszag's worldview began to reveal its seams. On an issue like health care, where politics really did corrupt public policy, the budget director's intuitions were impeccable. The better you could insulate medical decisions from the health care industrial complex—the insurers, the pharmaceutical companies, the device makers—the better your chances of delivering solid care at lower cost.

But the broader deficit picture was different. Outside health care, there weren't trillions of dollars of irrationality lurking in the government leviathan, just waiting to be hacked away by right-thinking wonks. Maybe there were a few billion dollars here or there in wasteful subsidies and boondoggles; perhaps there were even tens of billions. But that was chump change alongside the long-term deficit. The real problem was that there were trillions of dollars tied up in programs that people relied on daily (Social Security, education, highways) or that they deemed essential to the country (the military, basic research), and not enough money to pay for it all.

There was, in other words, no way to be a budget balancer

who hovered above politics. Really it was more like the opposite: being a deficit hawk *required* politics. Almost every program that cost real money came with a sympathetic constituency, and almost every constituency could lay a legitimate claim to its funds. If not for politics—which, in its own imperfect way, at least adjudicated between competing interests—how would you decide which ones to cut?

Peter Orszag and Barack Obama had gotten along so well because Orszag was the administration's purest distillation of Obamaism, of Obama's technocratic, anti-partisan sensibility. It was what had been lost in the distillation process that could be problematic. Orszag was who Obama might have been had the president never hustled for votes in Galesburg, Illinois, had he lacked the writerly empathy that made his memoir so achingly sensitive.

Like Orszag, Obama believed politics could be maddening and perverse. But he could also see how there might be something redeeming about it: that it could change lives, especially for people who would be hard-pressed to change on their own. Obama told a reporter in 2007 that "there were times when patronage politics worked pretty well for the down and out, and the immigrant end of America. And, you know, maybe the lace curtain crowd didn't like it, but it really helped in terms of upward mobility." [27] It was not a sentiment Peter Orszag would have rushed to embrace. But when Obama strayed too far away from it himself, he put his presidency in the gravest sort of peril.

11

THE ROGUE

The first few months of the Obama administration featured a running debate between Rahm Emanuel and Tim Geithner over one of the chief of staff's pet obsessions: Wall Street reform. Being a fundamentally political creature, Emanuel saw that the public wouldn't stand for spending hundreds of billions on banks without assurances that it would be a onetime event. So, in his characteristically frantic way, Emanuel leaned on his colleagues to hurry up and rewrite seventy-five years' worth of financial regulations. He hoped Treasury would have a bill ready to send to Congress within a few weeks of the inauguration.

Not surprisingly, the financial wonks chafed against this lunatic timetable. In early February 2009, Emanuel dispatched Diana Farrell, the Summers deputy who served as the official White House overseer of reform, to tell half a dozen Treasury aides that the president expected a bill on his desk by April 2, when leaders of the world's largest economies would gather in London. "That's not going to happen," a Treasury official told Farrell. As if the breathtaking complexity of the task weren't enough, Treasury was laboring under a dire manpower shortage, with several top appointees awaiting confirmation in the Senate and a historic financial crisis to stop. "We won't be in one [congressional] committee," the Treasury man said, alluding to the slim chance that the administration would have a draft ready for even the most preliminary step in Congress.[1]

These concerns were shared by Geithner, who added one more worry: that moving too quickly on reform would strain the fragile banks, perhaps beyond their breaking point. "He also had an active point of view that you don't do [financial] reform in a crisis," recalled a colleague from the transition.[2] But as much as anything else, Geithner didn't want to rush because, unlike Emanuel, he didn't want a plan whose only virtue was that Congress was likely to pass it. Having toiled in the plumbing of the financial system during the darkest days of the crisis, Geithner had a particular vision for financial reform. He did not consider it to be the kind of project that could be completed on the fly, much less while his department scrambled to ensure there would even be a financial sector when all was said and done.

Fortunately for Geithner, the dirty little secret of life under Emanuel was that if you could just wait him out, his attention would soon drift to the next major obsession, or the one after that, and you could buy yourself a few months to maneuver. By the time Emanuel and the White House tuned in again, it was spring, and Treasury was ready to engage.

In early May, Geithner attended a meeting with a dozen Wall Street lobbyists in the Roosevelt Room of the White House to sketch out his views on reform. Among his top priorities were new powers for the Federal Reserve to monitor "systemic risk," essentially the risk posed by firms whose failure could shatter the financial system. This was a response to the way that companies like AIG, which weren't traditional banks, had largely escaped oversight prior to the crisis. Geithner also believed the government should have the power, known as "resolution authority," to take over and dismantle financial behemoths like AIG and Citigroup. Not having this power, which the FDIC enjoys over smaller banks, had made massive bailouts the only alternative to a messy, Lehman-style collapse.

Finally, there was the question of derivatives, essentially bets on the movements of other assets like bonds and commodities. AIG had lost tens of billions of dollars betting on subprime mortgage securities through a type of derivative called a credit default swap (CDS), which had forced the government to bail it out. This made derivatives a top priority, too.

But although resolution authority and the monitoring of systemic risk commanded broad support on Wall Street, the big banks were deeply resistant to major derivatives reforms. The sums of money at stake were just too vast. In 2009, the five banks with the biggest derivatives business were on track to hoover up over $30 billion in revenue from unregulated derivatives, according to one estimate.[3] Total revenue for these banks that year was roughly $300 billion.

Geithner was also loath to move too aggressively on derivatives, and this came through at the early spring meeting. When an industry lobbyist raised the subject, Geithner extended his hand to cut him off. "Don't worry about derivatives," the secretary said, according to the lobbyist. "I think you'll like what you see on derivatives."

Derivatives were originally conceived as a form of insurance: a pipe manufacturer worried about what copper would cost him next year could use a derivative contract to lock in the price today. But derivatives had a speculative feature, too. A hedge fund could take the other side of the copper contract, agreeing to sell copper one year from now at this year's price. If the price subsequently fell, the hedge fund would pocket the difference as profit. If it rose, the hedge fund would eat the loss.

AIG's derivatives bets had been more like the latter, speculative variety. Had the real estate market kept rising, AIG would have kept pocketing money from the banks whose mortgage securities it insured. But once the real estate market stalled, the mortgage securities plummeted in value and AIG had to hand over massive amounts of money—collateral—to cover the losses. In principle, AIG might have recovered the money had the securities regained their value. In reality, the company would have gone belly up long before it had the chance.[4]

Of course, if AIG were a threat only to itself, few people would have lost much sleep over it. The problem was that AIG's failure would have affected the banks on the other side of its real estate bets. If AIG were unable to honor its payments, many of them could have toppled over, too. This, in turn, would have rippled out to dozens if not hundreds more companies, all of which were linked by additional derivatives bets. On and on it might have spread, sowing a Shermanesque path of destruction through the financial system. Hence the necessity of bailing out AIG.[5]

This is why, as early as the fall of 2008, the banks realized that derivatives would soon be an inviting target for politicians, and the prospect deeply concerned them. In addition to placing big bets themselves, the big banks served as derivatives middlemen or "dealers," charging hefty fees for connecting people on either side of a bet. (Hereafter, "dealers" and "banks" are cited interchangeably.) As much as anything else, the dealers worried that Washington would come after this cash cow. Before long, executives at these companies—

JP Morgan, Goldman Sachs, Morgan Stanley, Citigroup, and Bank of America—began holding weekly conference calls with their Washington front men to prepare for the inevitable backlash.[6]

The solution they arrived at was to trick Congress with a kind of bait-and-switch. First, the banks would embrace a practice known as "clearing"—that is, requiring each side of a derivative contract to set aside cash (with an institution called a "clearinghouse") in case a bet went bad. In principle, this was an important reform. In the run-up to the crisis, companies like AIG didn't have to set aside a single cent to cover potential losses: this was a bit like letting a car insurer operate as though it would never face a single claim.[7] The beauty of clearing is that it would have stopped the trouble at AIG from spreading across the financial system. The clearinghouse would have used the cash AIG set aside to pay off its betting partners in full.

Done correctly, clearing would inflict real pain on the banks: research by the IMF suggested it would have forced them to raise $200 billion to cover their existing bets,[8] all of which would be tied up in clearinghouses and not available for profitable activities like lending or speculation.[9] By making transactions more transparent, clearing would also have made it harder for the banks to impose hidden costs on their customers. The banks often charged clients extra fees to cover the client's side of the bet, typically a much higher fee than was necessary for this purpose.

From the dealers' perspective, clearing was preferable to an even more radical measure: forcing them to transact most derivatives on exchanges, the way investors buy and sell stocks (and only a small fraction of derivatives at that point). Under the status quo, a dealer could charge the buyer of a derivative contract far more than the price at which it was willing to sell. For example, AIG might be willing to sell insurance on mortgage securities—the credit default swap or CDS—for $150,000 per year per $10 million of insurance. A buyer might be willing to pay $200,000 for this coverage. Without exchanges, the dealer could charge $200,000 and simply pocket the difference. An exchange would put these portly "spreads" on display for the world to see and, presumably, erode them, as buyers scoped out the best deal.

So, clearing was the bait the banks offered up to convince Washington they were serious about reform and to stop the backlash from going any further. The switch would come when, having embraced clearing, the banks turned around and made those rules as weak as possible. To this end, according to one top industry lobbyist involved, the JP Morgans and Goldman Sachses devised a plan they hoped would lighten pressure emanating from Congress. Several years earlier, these dealers had struck an arrangement with the New York Fed to voluntarily clear some of their most standard, least profitable derivatives while leaving the rest untouched. As a public policy matter, it was an improvement over the status quo, but a marginal one. Now, according to the lobbyist, the dealers drafted legislation that simply formalized the arrangement and sent it to the administration.[10] The plan was about "ratifying what they'd already done," said the lobbyist.[11]

For his part, Geithner was acquainted with where the banks stood on derivatives. As president of the New York Fed, he'd led the years-long collaboration with the banks to make the derivatives market more orderly, with clearing as its centerpiece. Like the proposal the banks were shopping in late 2008, his initial plan as Treasury secretary envisioned the Fed regulating the biggest derivatives players and did not require the use of exchanges. The similarities were not lost on the industry. "That was the plan dealers had come forward with," the lobbyist said.[12]

There were others who would have a say in the outcome of financial reform—the U.S. Congress for one. Still, if the House and Senate were the only obstacles standing between Geithner and his ideal vision, then the process might have unfolded relatively smoothly, all things considered. In fact, there was an entirely separate cast of characters poised to influence the direction of reform: the regulators at independent agencies like the Securities and Exchange Commission (SEC) and the Office of the Comptroller of the Currency (OCC). Their independence insulated them from administration browbeating and made them more formidable than even the crustiest congressional don.

The highest-profile challenge came from Sheila Bair, a moderate Republican and former aide to Senate majority leader Bob Dole, who frequently clashed with Geithner from her perch atop the FDIC. The antagonism between the two dated back to the fall of 2008, when Geithner, then New York Fed president, concluded that Bair was more concerned with protecting her agency than pitching in to solve the financial crisis.

Time and again during that fall, Geithner would suggest tapping the FDIC's insurance fund, which exists to make depositors whole when the agency seizes a smaller bank, to bail out the teetering megabanks.[13] Time and again, Bair would resist, requiring the collective arm-twisting of Bush Treasury secretary Hank Paulson, Fed chairman Ben Bernanke, and Geithner to bring her around. Bair hated giving the megabanks a pass on the harsh treatment the government applied to other banks, which the FDIC dismantled under similar circumstances. Often her opposition would kill an idea altogether. For her part, Bair had the distinct impression that the three bailout impresarios consulted her only at the last possible moment, by which point they'd hashed out their proposals and were missing only the money to fund them. They had a way of making Bair feel like little more than a $45 billion piggy bank.[14]

Geithner and Bair continued to clash throughout the first year of the Obama administration, especially when the subject was Citigroup. In February, when Citi approached the government about converting its preferred shares (which don't imply ownership) to common stock—a move that would shore up its rickety balance sheet—Treasury needed a private sector financial adviser to help evaluate the deal. But the FDIC had already retained the most qualified firm and Bair refused to grant a waiver allowing it to perform double duty. Later, Bair made several runs at ousting Citi's top executives, including CEO Vikram Pandit, on the theory that they didn't have sufficient commercial banking experience to manage the company because they hailed from the investment banking world. Geithner defended the Citi executives, who, he argued, had taken over only after Citi had made its most disastrous decisions.[15]

By the time the discussion turned to financial reform, a Bair-Geithner collision was more or less inevitable. One key flash point was "resolution authority," which would empower the government to liquidate failing megabanks like Citigroup in an orderly way, rather than consign them to a panic-inducing collapse. The FDIC already performed this function for all but the biggest banks, and Bair argued, not unreasonably, that her agency should be entrusted with the new powers, too. Treasury believed that it and the Fed should have an ample say over the process and worried that, left to her own devices, Bair would be too punitive in her approach.[16]

At first glance, the conflict between these two bureaucrats should have been no contest at all. Treasury was, after all, writing the legislation. But Bair was a crafty operator with impeccable back-channel credentials. Both Chris Dodd, the Senate Banking Committee chairman, and Barney Frank, his counterpart in the House, counted themselves as admirers.

Throughout the spring, Geithner had recommended giving the Fed new powers to monitor the riskiest financial firms, some of which, like AIG, had escaped attention because they weren't officially banks. On May 6, 2009, Bair proposed giving these new powers to a council of regulators that would include the FDIC, rather than to the Fed alone, as Geithner preferred. When Geithner showed up two days later at the White House meeting with industry lobbyists, the room was abuzz over Bair's proposal. The secretary was quick to pour water on it. "There isn't going to be any fucking council," Geithner grumbled. Five weeks hence, the administration released its outline for financial reform. The council was item I.A. in its "Summary of Recommendations." [17] To this day, Fed officials still refer to it as the "FC," for "fucking council."

Before long, it wasn't just Bair but several other regulators who were campaigning to defend their cherished turf, straining the patience of Geithner and the White House. Many of the regulators feared losing out to the Federal Reserve, which stood to gain new powers. In August, Geithner summoned the whole group to Treasury—Bair, Bernanke, SEC chairman Mary Schapiro, Commodity Futures Trading Commission (CFTC) chairman Gary Gensler (who regulated derivatives), and a few others—for a stern talking-to about team play.

Some of the invitees sensed a setup from the get-go. Normally such meetings were scheduled well in advance, but this one materialized only a few days ahead of time. Each official typically toted along a small retinue of aides, but Treasury held attendance at this meeting to "principals plus one." Sure enough, when they arrived, Geithner unloaded a profanity-laced monologue. He accused them of being "off the reservation" and implored them to air their opinions privately before tattling to Congress. "This is fucking ridiculous," he said. If the hope was to restore order, it wasn't immediately successful. News of the secretary's screed was promptly leaked to the *Wall Street Journal*.[18]

For all of Geithner's searing dislike of Sheila Bair, there was a predictability to her, a perverse kind of transparency. Bair didn't hide her impatience with the megabanks, which she felt finagled goodies unheard of for their smaller competitors.[19] She didn't soft-pedal her desire to see them answer for their catastrophic mismanagement. She was unfailingly blunt about her priorities, the highest of which was preserving the FDIC insurance kitty. You could respect adversaries like that, even if they drove you to distraction.

Someone like Gary Gensler, on the other hand, was more of an enigma, and in a way more frustrating. Gensler was a longtime Goldman Sachs executive who'd first met the future secretary in the mid-nineties, when they were colleagues in the Clinton Treasury Department. Both were later confirmed to the position of under-secretary on the same day in 1999: Geithner for international affairs, Gensler for domestic finance. Even then there had been a whiff of rivalry, as though they understood they might someday be competitors for a bigger job. During the height of the Asian financial crisis, Gensler was dispatched to Greenwich, Connecticut, to tend to Long-Term Capital Management, a massive hedge fund then burning itself to the ground. "So you had to do a bailout, too?" Geithner needled him. "Well, you guys were getting too much attention," Gensler shot back.[20]

When they were reunited almost a decade later, Geithner had risen to the highest altitude of government and Gensler was groping for a place in the bureaucracy. The offer he finally got from Obama was perhaps less than he might have expected a few years earlier—the Commodoties Futures Trading Commission (CFTC) was obscure under the best of circumstances, and had been left to languish under George W. Bush. But it was not without possibility. Geithner himself pointed this out. "You have a chance to lead and shape what's in your lane," the incoming Treasury secretary told Gensler. At the time Geithner had no idea how right he would prove to be.

In the meantime, it wasn't even clear whether Gensler would be claiming the humble office he'd been tapped for. Maria Cantwell, the liberal Washington senator who'd made derivatives her cause, doubted Gensler's fortitude as a reformer. She dwelled on his role shielding derivatives from regulation during his Treasury days in the late nineties and blocked his nomination for months.[21]

The protest was broader than Gensler: Cantwell wanted to register her distaste for the entire Obama economic team. But you couldn't very well sandbag your own party's nominee for Treasury secretary during a financial crisis. Instead, she made a proximate target of Gensler, as fitting a symbol of the president's taste in personnel as anyone else.[22]

Gensler, for his part, wasn't about to be mistaken for a Wall Street lackey, whatever one might say about his colleagues. He embraced the Senate hazing ritual as an opportunity to remake himself into a derivatives tough guy. Gensler argued that all but the most obscure derivatives—say, a yacht manufacturer trying to hedge the price of an exotic species of wood—should be cleared and traded on exchanges. For the small sliver of derivatives this omitted, the dealers would have to hold extra cash in case the bets went sour. If anything, this agenda was even stricter than the dealers' worst fears.

By the time Geithner tuned in that spring, he noticed the gap that had opened up between him and his old colleague. In their conversations, Geithner was decidedly cool to Gensler's thinking, especially on exchanges. But Cantwell was now threatening to expand her insurgency if the administration didn't adopt Gensler's hard-line position. There was talk of placing a hold on Neal Wolin, the nominee for deputy secretary. To defuse the situation, Geithner would have to deal.

What followed was weeks of shuttle diplomacy. Inside Treasury there was grumbling about the way Gensler had suddenly styled himself the Che Guevara of Wall Street. But when a compromise was finally struck, Treasury had come much of the way toward Gensler, agreeing that standard derivatives would have to be traded on either exchanges or similar facilities. The industry was momentarily stunned. "The banks got an exchange-trading requirement they didn't want," said one industry lobbyist. "Gensler was more of a rogue than they thought." [23]

Gary Gensler wasn't an outsider so much as an insider turned inside-out. Gensler had landed at Goldman in 1979, having picked up an MBA at Wharton a mere four years out of high school. He quickly made partner and gave every indication of being groomed for bigger things. In 1991, two top Goldman executives, Bob Rubin and Jon Corzine, assembled an elite group of young partners to rotate through key parts of the firm. Gensler was one of the half-dozen executives they selected for this rite.

Gensler had come up through the investment banking side of the business, where he'd made a name for himself as the company's chief media industry deal maker. He'd brokered acquisitions in Rupert Murdoch's apartment and advised the NFL on the sale of its television rights. Suddenly, Rubin and Corzine were sending him to the company's trading operation, to dwell among the adrenaline junkies who bought and sold securities for Goldman's bottom line. After that, it was off to Japan to run the company's bond- and currency-trading operation. The last stop on this rotation was the finance department back in New York, which Gensler coheaded. In addition to keeping the company's books, Gensler had the final say on the $250 billion balance sheet Goldman's traders risked with every bet.

Gensler had thrown himself into each new vocation with the discipline of a marathoner—which, as it happened, he also applied to marathons. But there was something about him that didn't quite fit the Goldman mold. Not every Goldman partner had to be a gentleman of Wall Street, à la Rubin. Lloyd Blankfein, for one (who'd made partner with Gensler in 1988 and became CEO in 2006), would never have been accused of excessive refinement. He was 50 pounds overweight, smoked heavily, and sported a scraggly beard until the early 2000s. But there were certain faux pas that were tolerated—slovenliness or bravado—and certain faux pas that grated, and Gensler's were of the latter variety.

Gensler struggled with the unconscious rituals of daily interaction. He worked too hard to make a good impression. He was slow to pick up on emotional cues and unwritten rules. He said out loud what was best left unsaid. By the mid-nineties, the Goldman brass became worried enough that they hired a consultant to educate him on such matters. "You have a habit of asking a lot of questions," the consultant said. "About the second-to-third question you ask somebody, think of it as taking them to a cliff and making them look over the edge. . . . You're making them feel uncomfortable." Gensler stopped asking the third question.

Gensler's ambitions were large, but not so much larger than anyone else's. What he really lacked was the basic tool kit for concealing them. He was prone to offhandedly suggesting he should be singled out for praise or a promotion, but in a way that seemed anything but offhand. One Goldman colleague would later remark that had Gensler been half as pleasing to be around as Bob Rubin, he and not Geithner might have been Treasury secretary.

Still, no one could doubt Gensler's intelligence and thoroughness, to say nothing of his sheer force of will. Before Rubin had left for the Clinton White House, he and Gensler had breakfast in Rubin's apartment and took a walk through Central Park. Gensler said he might be interested in joining Rubin in Washington if the right job came along. Four years later, in December 1996, a White House aide called asking if Gensler would consider an administration job. Rubin, now at Treasury, was looking for a financial markets expert. Gensler was the first person he thought of.

Gensler's four years at Treasury—two as an assistant secretary, two as undersecretary—put him at the center of the major economic dramas of the 1990s. But his first tour in Washington would later be defined by precisely one shameful episode: the Commodity Futures Modernization Act (CFMA).

In 1998, the market for so-called over-the-counter derivatives—that is, derivatives that don't trade on exchanges—had grown to some $70 trillion. Brooksley Born, a Washington lawyer who was then head of the CFTC, began to worry that the market had become too risky to leave to its own devices. Her CFTC produced a document raising dozens of questions about the potential dangers, most of which hinted at the need for new regulations.

The tob brass at the Fed, the Treasury, and the SEC flew into a rage when they caught wind of the document. Officially, these agencies worried that the CFTC's questions would raise doubts about whether over-the-counter derivatives were even legal, which could eviscerate the market. Larry Summers reportedly called Born and warned that merely releasing her document publicly could "cause the worst financial crisis since World War II." [24] Unofficially, the other agencies took a dim view of Born's regulatory designs. This was especially true at the Fed, where financial regulation clashed with Chairman Greenspan's pro-market fanaticism. Greenspan was such a revered figure in those days that his mutterings carried considerable weight at Treasury.

Soon the Republican majority in Congress proposed legislation that would once and for all shield over-the-counter derivatives from the prying eyes of regulators. Gensler was sidelined for the early portion of the debate because of his time at Goldman, which had a stake in the outcome. But, beginning in 1999, he contributed to two administration reports on financial markets that endorsed watered-down regulations for derivatives. Then, in 2000, he helped negotiate the final bill, the CFMA, which enshrined the exemption in federal law while also making some practices, like clearing, optional. Congress approved the bill that fall with majorities more befitting the election of an African strongman than two democratic chambers grappling with a complex issue. The measure first passed by a 377–4 margin in the House. It was later tucked into a budget bill that Congress approved in December 2000, the final version of which won "unanimous consent" in the Senate.

In fairness, Treasury didn't deserve all the blame. Rubin expressed reservations to colleagues about leaving derivatives unregulated. Both he and Gensler believed derivatives dealers should be forced to maintain enough capital to cover losses from bets gone bad. Such ideas died silent deaths, however, either from quiet opposition at the Fed, or from the poison darts hurled at them in Congress, where Republican senator Phil Gramm ruled the debate as chairman of the Banking Committee.

Still, the Clinton Treasury was far from innocent. There was nothing forcing Rubin and Summers to defer to Greenspan. Certainly there was no need to accord such reverence to Gramm, who would later leave Congress for a sinecure at UBS, a major derivatives dealer. And yet Rubin persuaded himself that Gramm's opposition to tougher rules made them a nonstarter. After Summers took over as secretary in mid-1999, he was solicitous of the numerous objections Gramm raised, asking Gensler to review each one exhaustively. In the end, the Clintonites accepted the retreat on derivatives either because they didn't feel strongly enough to try to stop it, or because they were skeptical of the regulations themselves.

Years after the fact, even after Lehman and AIG demonstrated the folly of this neglect, Rubin and Summers would resist admitting their mistake in public. The silence from the rest of the Clinton Treasury was nearly as conspicuous. Other than Bill Clinton himself, who later identified the CFMA as one of his real regrets,[25] Gensler was the lone exception.

When Gensler looked back over his career, he had to concede he should have known better. Two years before the CFMA passed, after all, he'd inspected the books at Long-Term Capital Management, the mortally wounded hedge fund. He'd seen how its derivatives bets had linked it to so many other firms that its failure could shake the financial system, the same risk AIG posed a decade later. He'd understood the need for regulation, in other words, but he and his colleagues had allowed Congress to move in the opposite direction.

On paper, Gensler looked to have been a Rubinite in good standing: Goldman partner by his early thirties, Clinton Treasury undersecretary. But he was never entirely part of the club. When Geithner and Summers and Lee Sachs attended tennis camp in Florida, Gensler did not get an invitation. Gensler was one of the few senior Rubin Treasury officials the former secretary didn't either summon to reminisce with him in 2002, in advance of writing his memoirs, or subsequently thank in the book's acknowledgments.[26]

Gensler was never belligerent or antagonistic. He simply wasn't the type who assimilated easily into a group. As one former Treasury colleague recalled, he gave the distinct impression of keeping his options open, of constantly reevaluating whether tribal loyalty served his purposes. In 2002, he wrote a book bemoaning the ways money managers fleece small investors, which was notable for more than the author's Wall Street pedigree: Gensler's identical twin brother managed money for T. Rowe Price, the large family of funds.[27]

But the same qualities that made Gensler an unreliable ally made him immune to the most corrosive group dynamics. When it became clear to just about everyone outside the old Treasury network that the CFMA had been a mistake, Gensler didn't feel bound to keep quiet in solidarity with his old colleagues. In fact, he was eager to put himself on the right side of history. He began his confirmation hearings in February 2009 by proclaiming, "All of us that were involved at the time, and certainly myself, should have done more to protect the American public through aggressive regulation, comprehensive regulation."[28] He would tell reporters that "there's not a day that goes by that I don't think what we might have done differently."[29]

Gensler's great strength was that he was capable of looking at himself through the eyes of an ordinary voter. And when he saw that there was no excuse for his passivity, he didn't get shifty or defensive. He simply admitted it. Gensler may have been lousy at internal politics. But he turned out to be a strikingly good politician.

The big banks spent the spring and summer of 2009 in full diplomatic mode, portraying themselves as pillars of an honest, responsible industry distinctly not in need of more regulation. Derivatives, the banks were at pains to explain, were hardly financial weapons of mass destruction, as Warren Buffett had famously labeled them. They were a vital, mainstream product designed to *alleviate* risk.

From the industry's perspective, the lessons of the financial crisis could be absorbed with only a few minor tweaks, and the dealers were at pains to show that they were making them. Every few weeks, one dealer or another would update Congress on all the ways derivatives were becoming safer. "The banks came to us lobbying many times. 'We're already doing our homework, getting up to speed. Don't worry, we're clearing the stuff that should be cleared,'" recalled one congressional staffer involved in writing the new rules.[30] The message was clear: There was no need for Congress to impose its own ideas.

But behind all the dutiful rhetoric was a more manipulative strategy. Its origins also dated back to the previous fall, when the dealers had first commiserated about the looming regulatory threat. At the time, the banks were already reviled for their role in the crisis. But the so-called end users—customers like the pipe manufacturer who used derivatives to control the price of its raw materials rather than speculate—were sympathetic, and they hailed from every congressional district in the country.[31]

This gave a JP Morgan lobbyist named Kate Childress an idea: Why not build a strategy around the end users? Before long, Childress and her colleagues at JP Morgan were urging fellow dealers to contact their corporate customers and warn them that Congress intended to make their derivatives prohibitively expensive. The anxious end users would be told to register dismay over this potential outrage with their congressmen and senators. The hope, according to a source privy to the calls and to internal planning documents, was that pressure from end users would persuade Congress to craft a bill so weak it would leave huge swaths of the market untouched. "What they wanted was, 'Hey, let's get the dopey end users to go out and be the face of reform,' " recalled another person who participated in the strategizing. " 'We don't have the credibility.' " [32]

Congressional aides with years of experience making policy on derivatives had never heard the term "end user" before. Suddenly they were surrounded by this supposedly benign species.[33] It wasn't until one congressional staffer encountered several JP Morgan bankers at a conference that it became clear what was going on. "They said, 'Oh, you're working on derivatives? ... That's so interesting, because I just did a client meeting with Jamie [Dimon, the CEO of JP Morgan] pitching for an M&A [mergers and acquisitions] deal. He was imploring all of our clients to start calling Congress, get their lobbyists involved.' " [34]

By the summer of 2009, the JP Morgan–led counteroffensive was having an effect. Several House Democrats with pro-business leanings, the so-called New Democrats, seized on the end user complaints to press for a weaker measure. They began to clamor for a bill that preserved the status quo not just for the derivatives the end users depended on, but also for the ones the dealers procured for financial firms like hedge funds.[35]

Geithner and his aides soon aligned themselves with this zeitgeist, submitting a weaker than expected bill to the House Financial

Services Committee in early August because they assumed it was the only bill the committee would pass. "The House committee was where it was," said a senior Treasury official. "We were not keen to draft something up that wouldn't have worked." Gensler, for his part, was unmoved by this logic. A few days beforehand, when the secretary solicited his input, he pronounced the Treasury approach inadequate.[36]

In the normal order of the bureaucratic universe, this would have been the end of the discussion. The obscure regulator, having noted his objections, would have fallen in line behind the Treasury secretary. He would have been grateful simply to have been consulted. He would have considered himself blessed to have prevailed on a number of related turf issues, as Gensler had when the secretary repeatedly favored his agency over the SEC, which also claimed jurisdiction.

But Gensler had little interest in the normal order of things. Six days after Treasury submitted its legislation to the House, Gensler cataloged his reservations in a public letter to Congress,[37] stirring up a scandal in the small world that runs from K Street to Capitol Hill. The problem, he complained, was that the administration's bill included a "major exception [that] may undermine the policy objective of lowering risk."[38] Treasury officials reacted as if he'd curbed his dog on their beloved statue of Alexander Hamilton. "We were definitely surprised when we read it, that I can say for sure," recalled the Treasury official.[39] Or, as one industry lobbyist sputtered, "It's just not done. . . . People don't do that."[40]

Gensler wasn't the only one unsatisfied with the administration proposal. The dealers were, too, except that they considered it too tough rather than too lax and soon upped their demands. The goal was to riddle an already weak bill with loopholes and exemptions. It was a bit like convincing your boss to approve a three-day workweek, then turning around and demanding three months' paid vacation.

By early October, all the additional lobbying had paid off. Barney Frank, the chairman of the House Financial Services Committee, released a draft of legislation that was even weaker than the administration's version. It didn't require any derivatives to trade on exchanges, the step Gensler had fought for back in the spring. And it included the yawning "end user exemption" the lobbyists had been agitating for.

Like the administration, Frank said that he'd had to compromise to clinch the necessary votes on his committee—and that, in any case, his bill would exempt only 15 percent of the derivatives Gensler hoped to capture. In fact, Gensler believed it would leave out closer to half the market. A few days later, he turned up in Frank's committee room testifying that the chairman's compromise "could have the unintended consequence of exempting a broad range of entities," even large Wall Street firms.[41]

It was now clear that Gensler was playing a different game: not a backroom negotiating game, but an outside political game. He was appealing over the heads of bureaucrats and congressmen and making a run at public opinion. Given how esoteric the subject matter was, this would have been an audacious assignment for a president. There are limits even to his megaphone, after all. It was an utterly preposterous undertaking for a second-tier regulator. And yet Gensler approached it with the same relentlessness that had annoyed well-heeled colleagues since his days at Goldman Sachs.

Gensler began giving more than a speech a week to evangelize about his preferred derivatives clampdown.[42] He was as inclined to appear before reform groups like the Consumer Federation of America[43] as to address gatherings of financial executives and insiders. And when he addressed the latter, he often calibrated his message for maximum discomfort, which invariably made headlines. Asked to name the biggest obstacle to reform at one banker confab, Gensler curtly responded: "You." [44]

Everywhere he went, Gensler handed out a photocopied pie chart. It was the regulator's answer to the Book of Mormon, and Gensler was determined to spread the good word. The smallest sliver of pie was green and represented bona fide end users, Gensler explained, like airlines and car manufacturers. He estimated that they made up 9 percent of the market. Alongside that was a hulking red slab of pie—some 57 percent of the market, which included the derivatives used by banks, insurance companies, and hedge funds. Gensler said Congress would be crazy to exempt the red slice, as the industry was urging, when it claimed to want to exempt only the green one.

The upshot of these efforts was to make Gensler uniquely effective at shaming public officials. All the more so when he locked arms with a coalition of reform groups, like the labor-backed Americans for Financial Reform, to which he lent the credibility of an insider. Barney Frank, for one, had always fancied himself a reformer and was stung by the criticism of his bill. Of particular annoyance was a tough *Boston Globe* piece in late October reporting that his measure had come "under blistering assault from consumer groups as well as key Democrats." [45] The piece featured a Gensler quote advising Frank to go back to the drafting table.

In December, the full House passed a bill that was marginally stricter than the version Frank had proposed. But the real signs of progress were the trend lines. After the dustup over his legislation, Frank had proclaimed himself a convert to the cause of derivatives hawkishness. His Senate counterpart, Chris Dodd, had recently unveiled legislation of his own, which took a Gensler-esque hard line. Most important of all, Tim Geithner had finally come around. Testifying in the Senate at about the same time, Geithner retrospectively washed away all the differences between him and the CFTC. He said that while he supported a "carefully crafted limited exception for non-financial end users," he wanted to ensure that such exceptions "don't end up gutting the rest of the framework."[46] As improbable as it would have seemed a few months earlier, Treasury now felt the need to declare that it stood shoulder to shoulder with Gary Gensler.

12

A CASE OF CLIENTITIS

Within the small universe of Obama appointees, there were few personalities more at odds than Tim Geithner and Gary Gensler. Whereas Gensler had turned himself outward, attuned to public opinion, Geithner was a man of the inner corridors, preoccupied with the opinions of technocrats and elites. Gensler could be off-key in intimate settings but was surprisingly deft before a crowd. Geithner could carry any conference table you sat him around but was a leaden public speaker.

Though both men courted the press, they did so in opposite ways. The CFTC chairman was often a presence in media coverage of financial reform. Both in print and on television, he cultivated the image of a former Wall Streeter turned no-nonsense regulator. Even as Treasury secretary, Geithner preferred to shape stories without surfacing in them himself, through private conversations with reporters.

Perhaps most telling was their posture toward colleagues and peers. Gensler thought consensus was overrated; he craved the freedom to position himself in the public eye. Geithner valued loyalty and cohesion above all else. As the Treasury secretary prepared his response to the bank crisis in early 2009, he told his staff he wanted different agencies "to sign [on to the plan] in blood, with no tribal conflict."[1] Gensler preferred to sign in pencil.

From the perspective of the White House, Geithner was the consummate cabinet officer—always embracing the official West Wing line, happy to open himself to abuse when it would protect the president. In the spring of 2010, the administration began prodding the Europeans, or at least the countries that could afford it, to spend more to prop up their economies. Geithner was not a staunch Keynesian. He'd supported the original stimulus as a temporary fail-safe measure, but was skeptical that government largesse could heal a crisis-ravaged economy. He feared large deficits more than he feared slow economic growth.

Even so, he was unwavering in carrying the Keynesian message to Europe, particularly to the masochistic Germans. At the time, an additional round of German spending could have offset the cuts forced on the debt-laden Greeks, Portuguese, and Spanish. Instead, the Germans announced they would join in the austerity. When a German official touted the move as an exercise in pan-European solidarity, Geithner scoffed that it sounded like something Herbert Hoover would do.[2]

Geithner's genius as a bureaucratic operator was that he could sublimate his ego to the broader task at hand. After his universally panned February 10, 2009, speech on the financial crisis, Emanuel began to treat the Treasury secretary like a half-witted student in need of remediation. Often he would summon Geithner to the White House twice a day and check in by phone between visits. The day before the secretary released details of his toxic-asset purchase plan in March, Emanuel spoke with him five times.[3] If Geithner was miffed by this treatment, he did not betray it. His posture, recalled one Treasury colleague, was, "If Rahm wants to think he's in charge, that's fine."[4]

Such low-maintenance behavior was the reason that, despite being a newcomer to Obamaland, Geithner remained one of the most popular members of the administration internally even when his public standing was at its shakiest. In January 2010, news leaked that Geithner had neglected to pay payroll taxes on income from the two-plus years he worked at the IMF, a frequent oversight for Americans employed by international organizations. The revelation sent cable commentators and senators into fits of righteous outrage but, said a senior transition staffer, "From the inside, it didn't feel like he ever lost his footing."[5] Daily White House staff meetings featured Axelrod joking affectionately about Geithner's apocryphal past at Goldman Sachs, and the approximate date of his future firing from Treasury. "I hope they do it soon," the Treasury secretary would quip, ever the dutiful straight man.[6]

Geithner was just as skilled at managing down as up. He played basketball—the reigning sport of Team Obama—with Dan Pfeiffer, a young strategist then being groomed for the role of White House communications director. He made a point of getting to know Pfeiffer's wife, Sarah Feinberg, a top aide to Emanuel. "If you're used to a corporate setting, and you walk into the West Wing and see people sitting outside an office, they look like secretaries. You don't understand that person is making a lot of stuff happen," said one Treasury official. "Sarah is someone Tim talked to quite a bit."[7]

Geithner was, in effect, a master diplomat, highly adept at reading the rhythms and rituals of a foreign culture and then rapidly assimilating. And there was perhaps no one whose rhythms and rituals he grasped better than the president's. Longtime members of Obama's inner circle knew of the president's deep aversion to blather, for example. They could see the exasperation in his eyes when Washington wise men would pontificate. But Geithner, it was quickly noted, would stay scrupulously silent during meetings, his obvious expertise notwithstanding. "The smartest thing to do in a meeting with the president is not say anything. He comes to you," said an administration official. "Geithner's whole m.o. is he speaks very little, but makes what he says be of consequence. I thought he got the president really well." [8]

If there was one vocation life had prepared Tim Geithner to excel at, it was adapting to foreign environments. When he was six years old, Geithner's father, Peter, moved the family to India, where he helped oversee the Ford Foundation's development programs. The five years the Geithners spent in Delhi differed from the typical expatriate experience in subtle but important ways. Unlike the families of Foreign Service officers or CIA personnel, who tended to hole themselves away in the embassy compound, the Geithners lived among the locals, albeit in an affluent district called Friends Colony. "People who were there . . . for a shorter period of time—maybe living in the embassy—tended to react to the complexities of India differently," said Peter Geithner. Some of his children's classmates were intent on becoming "more Indian than the Indians." Others walled themselves off as much as possible from the daily life of the country. "Our kids saw all its virtues and vices in a more balanced way," Peter said. [9]

One American with a similarly nuanced view of Indian society was a Protestant minister named Ernie Campbell. Campbell was a second-generation missionary whose home was the social hub of American youth in Delhi. For families who were new in town, Campbell would hold a kind of orientation seminar, which the Geithners attended. "He had a wonderful way of emphasizing differences," said Peter Geithner. The typical American was aghast to see Indians empty their nose by holding one finger to a nostril and blowing. Campbell would say, "Think of how strange it is to the Indians to see Americans wrap their bodily waste neatly into a white handkerchief and stuff it back into their pocket." [10]

Ernie Campbell and Peter Geithner could hardly be more different in their politics and sensibility. Campbell had a degree from Union Theological Seminary, a hotbed of radical social teaching when he attended in the 1940s. He would share cigarettes with teenagers, unbeknownst to their more uptight parents, and had a habit of taking in lost souls. Peter Geithner, by contrast, was a Dartmouth alumnus who'd spent nearly four years in the Navy after graduation. He voted Republican and wore an air of high seriousness. The Geithners, one fellow expat later recalled, were the "quintessential preppy family," with a golden retriever named Buff and leisure interests that skewed toward tennis and touch football. For all their globe-trotting, they still summered in Cape Cod. [11]

But Campbell and Geithner had rather similar views on questions of cultural sensitivity and economic development. Both believed that outsiders must scrupulously defer to local custom.

The 1970s were a time of progressive experimentation within the Ford Foundation. The organization was on the cutting edge of creating local institutions—indigenous training facilities, think tanks, farmer associations—and Geithner, despite his more conservative politics, was a leading proponent of the grassroots approach. Colleagues recall him constantly traveling to the most remote parts of the country to cultivate relationships with Indian officials and to vacuum up intelligence from his staff. [12] The father's cultural humility would make a lasting impression on the son. "My father . . . is a deep believer in institution-building," Tim Geithner said years later. "You're finding talent and supporting it. You're not going to tell them the right thing to do." [13]

Geithner spent his teenage years in Thailand, where his father also held a top Ford Foundation job, then returned to the United States to attend Dartmouth, the family finishing school. But he continued to nurture his interest in Asia. While at Dartmouth he enrolled in Thai- and Chinese-language classes and spent two summers studying in Beijing.[14]

Geithner's time in China came only a few years after the two countries had reestablished relations, and the Chinese were invariably stunned to see pale-faced Americans roaming through their capital. Their reflex was to point and gawk liberally. Geithner had a trademark technique for approaching the gawkers: he would bob his head while swaying his hips and shoulders, like something out of a Steve Martin sketch on *Saturday Night Live*. "It was almost like a wild-and-crazy-guy-type dance move," said Justin Rudelson, Geithner's roommate in Beijing. "He had a really warm, funny way about him. . . . Within seconds, he'd break through." One minute Geithner would meet ordinary Chinese, the next he'd be helping them buy some household appliance at a nearby "friendship store," which catered exclusively to foreigners with hard currency (the Chinese had to spend months on a waiting list). In this way, Geithner collected invitations to Chinese dinner tables, where he'd field-test his Mandarin over a homemade meal.[15]

One day in Beijing, Rudelson and Geithner went out for ice cream and began discussing their career plans. Rudelson had assumed his friend aspired to become a China specialist. Geithner relieved him of this notion: "I don't want to be a China hand. I don't want to be . . . pigeonholed, just focusing on Chinese." Instead, he said, he hoped for a career with more breadth—a U.S. government job focused on the entire international system.

But there was also a more emotional explanation at work. Having grown up overseas, Geithner had seen more than his share of expatriates caught up in the romance of becoming the "other." He was sophisticated enough to understand the folly, even arrogance, of this exercise. Or, as Rudelson distilled Geithner's thoughts, "What do you call an American brain surgeon who goes to China and learns Chinese? You call them a dumb American. They're never going to be seen [by the Chinese] as breaking through totally." [16] Throughout his career, Geithner would relate well to foreigners, but he wouldn't pretend to be something he wasn't. He preferred to feel at home in one society—the United States—rather than an outsider in two.

After college, Geithner earned a master's degree at the Johns Hopkins School of Advanced International Studies (SAIS), then filled out his résumé as a researcher at Kissinger Associates, the former secretary of state's consulting firm.[17] To his fellow SAIS alumni, the Kissinger gig heralded Geithner's arrival. "We thought that was a pretty cool job," recalled Brewer Stone, a friend and former classmate.[18] But Geithner was soon restless. He had more interest in shaping policy than in writing about it or advising corporate clients. When he asked around, he learned that Treasury was a place where he could win meaty assignments at a young age. He landed a position there as a junior trade official in 1988.

Within two years, Geithner's bosses recommended him for an assistant attaché job that had opened up in Japan. Such postings were considered a stepping-stone for up-and-comers, and Geithner fit the profile. "He was smart, self-assured, well-traveled . . . had a certain strength of character that I could see," said Bob Fauver, one of his early supervisors.[19] In the spring of 1990, Geithner and his wife Carol packed up the contents of their Capitol Hill apartment, gave away their wine collection, and set off for the U.S. Embassy in Tokyo.[20]

Much of Geithner's work in Japan entailed bona fide diplomacy, which he executed ably. The ambassador at the time, Mike Armacost, recalled that Geithner played a key role in persuading the Japanese to increase their financial contribution to the first Gulf War, part of a U.S. government effort dubbed "Operation Tin Cup." Geithner recognized that success meant appealing to the middle ranks of Japan's powerful Ministry of Finance (MOF), and he cultivated them assiduously. "It's important in their bureaucracy, where the minister can't make decisions of that magnitude without support down underneath," Armacost said. "Policy bubbles up rather than trickles down." [21]

Geithner was deft at sizing up his MOF counterparts. He understood the constraints they operated under and the nationalistic pride they derived from being Japan's best and brightest. But he never succumbed to the malady that often plagues talented diplomats—a kind of clientitis, in which the envoy associates himself more with the interests of the foreign government than the interests of the government he serves. "The quality that I found appealing in Tim was that he had that capacity to have empathy for the host country, yet analytic detachment about it," said Armacost.[22]

If anything, Geithner seemed a bit partisan on behalf of the United States. It was as if, having grown up abroad, he was determined to adopt his native country.

While serving in Japan, Geithner was in regular contact with a number of American expatriates, mostly financiers and journalists, and often debated economics with them. "He could always talk very interestingly about what the implications of different policy options were," said one, "why a leader piece in *The Economist* didn't make sense." The conversations were normally relaxed and candid. But if someone criticized U.S. policy—complaining, say, that the Japanese had cleaned our clocks in an auto-import dispute—Geithner would become unyielding. "He was not the kind of guy who would say, 'That sucks. We just got fucked on that,'" this person recalled. "If I was pooh-poohing the U.S. trade debate—saying, 'We're not getting anything'—he became more like an attorney with one client": the U.S. government.[23]

Treasury was a highly establishmentarian institution in those days, from its political leadership down to an elite corps of bureaucrats that thought of itself as well-bred and high-minded, the aristocracy of the civil ranks. In its noblesse oblige sensibility it rivaled the Foreign Service, albeit with a more pro-business bent.[24]

Geithner blended easily into this world with his overseas background, his Ivy League pedigree, and the family ethos of public service. He even had an insider's sense of humor—a knack for jokes that identify both teller and listener as part of an exclusive club. In 1992, Treasury Secretary Nicholas Brady arrived in Tokyo to consult with the Ministry of Finance. The Japanese supplied Brady's entourage with a police escort, which, after the local fashion, rode ahead of his caravan and screamed at drivers to move aside. Before long, a top Brady aide turned to Geithner and asked what the police were saying. "They're saying, 'Get the fuck out of the way!' " he quipped. The aide later raved about Geithner to the secretary on the strength of this well-deployed F-bomb.

By the spring of 1992, Geithner was back in Washington, where Larry Summers would soon discover him. Geithner had been serving as an aide to a top Bush Treasury official, and Summers kept him in the role until 1994, when he made him a deputy assistant secretary. Geithner's first major task after his big promotion was to take over a negotiation with the Japanese government that had been ongoing in one form or another since the early 1980s. For decades, the Japanese had placed numerous restrictions on the kinds of financial services that foreign banks and securities firms could offer in the country. For example, the Japanese invested a portion of their version of the Social Security trust fund in the stock market. But only a small cartel of Japanese firms was entrusted with these transactions. Further, foreign companies couldn't operate mutual funds in Japan, or serve as the main underwriter for offerings of stocks and bonds.

Neither the Reagan nor the Bush Treasury Department had made much headway on this front despite an enormous investment of effort. By the time Geithner inherited the portfolio under Clinton, it had become an assignment fit for a young official with little stature. Anyone else would recognize it for the dog it was and beg off.

Geithner was a shrewd choice. There was, for one thing, his knowledge of Japanese negotiating strategy. At each meeting, a small number of senior Ministry of Finance officials would be accompanied by several rows of "Munchkins," junior aides whose job it was to take notes and report back to Tokyo. This forced the higher-ranking officials to, in effect, perform. They were constantly taking a much harder line than they could plausibly hope to enforce. Then it would be the Americans' turn to appear implacable, so that the Munchkins could describe the barriers the Japanese were up against. With these lines drawn, the top negotiators could then engage one another off to the side of the discussion and work out an understanding.

Geithner was expert at tacking back and forth between the performance elements of the ritual and the actual bargaining— approaching the former with the appropriate amount of winking and nodding. "He would sprinkle humor," recalled a colleague. For example: "You're not going to believe what I'm about to say, Mr. Saito. This is totally indefensible what you're doing here." [25]

But just as important as his procedural know-how were his substantive insights. Geithner's time as attaché had helped him forge ties to the four big American firms operating in Japan—Goldman Sachs, Morgan Stanley, Merrill Lynch, and Salomon Brothers—whose executives he often pumped for financial intelligence. This proved to be an enormous asset throughout the negotiations.

The biggest asset of all was a Morgan Stanley lawyer named

Robin Radin. Radin had once been a graduate student at Berkeley and Kyoto University, where he'd researched a thesis on Japan's 1918 rice riots; he had then earned a law degree at Harvard. He spoke and read Japanese. "The MOF was scared of Radin," said Jack Wadsworth, then the head of Morgan Stanley in Japan. "He knew more about the MOF than anyone in the MOF." [26]

Geithner had met Radin during his embassy days and leaned on him for strategic advice. The upshot was a document Radin produced called "Negotiating Principles for Opening Japan's Financial Markets," in which he unearthed a secret weapon: a recent Japanese statute called the Administrative Procedure Act. The law officially gave foreigners the right to enter all the businesses the big U.S. securities firms were desperate to enter. Only it was constantly flouted. Radin proposed negotiating a deal to make sure the law would be enforced. "This was like the Trojan horse. How could they refuse to agree to their own law?" Radin recalled. "The trick was to use that." [27]

Geithner loved the idea and made it the basis for the negotiation. "Robin gets a lot of credit for pointing us in that direction. But Tim was a very quick student," said a colleague involved. When Geithner mentioned the law to the Japanese, they were surprised the Americans even knew about it. They played for time and later offered a tortured explanation for why it didn't allow in practice what it seemed to allow in principle. Months of back-and-forth ensued, but Treasury had real leverage. A few hours before the New Year came in, the Japanese agreed to give the American side most of what it wanted.

In February 1995, the new secretary, Robert Rubin, and the Japanese ambassador to Washington officially signed the agreement. Geithner's star at Treasury had never been higher. "The bottom line is that's what really got Tim started on his ascent, that negotiation," said the Treasury colleague. [28]

• • •

For Geithner, the agreement was something to be unambiguously proud of. The Japanese treatment of American firms *had* been blatantly unfair. The arguments the U.S. firms made were completely legitimate. That Geithner was able to redress their grievances where so many of his predecessors had failed was a patriotic achievement.

But there was a risk to overempathizing with big American investment banks even if they happened to be right in this instance. The risk was that Geithner would identify their success too closely with the country's success—that he would be too quick to associate their view of public policy with the right view of public policy.

In fact, the episode highlighted the extent to which the Treasury Department—indeed, much of the economic apparatus of the U.S. government—had an ongoing symbiosis with Wall Street. By assimilating so thoroughly into the Treasury bureaucracy, by swallowing up its ethos so eagerly, Geithner was to some extent swallowing up the ethos of the financial world, too. There was a risk of clientitis after all. For Geithner, it came at home rather than abroad.

Over the next fifteen years, there were very few instances of a big public policy question when he stood on the opposite side from the largest financial institutions. One major debate during the financial crises of the 1990s was whether to impose "haircuts" (aka losses) on lenders when foreign countries or foreign corporations could no longer keep up with their debts. The U.S. Treasury tended to frown on this idea, arguing that losses could panic financial markets and cause lenders—banks and other investors—to withdraw credit from even perfectly healthy economies. Washington generally favored large bailout packages to reassure the markets that investors would be made whole.

For their part, many European governments, the Germans chief among them, argued that the lenders had no God-given right to repayment in full. They'd lent money knowing there was a risk of getting stiffed—that was the point of charging different interest rates based on how reliable each country appeared. If a country could afford to pay its creditors only 70 cents on the dollar, then there was no reason the international community should have to make up the other 30 cents. The lenders should eat part or all of the loss themselves. Worse, protecting lenders through bailouts would only weaken their incentive to vet these risks in the future. That was the so-called moral hazard problem.

The conflict played out in crisis after crisis: In 1995, in a rare diplomatic slight, the Germans pointedly abstained from the IMF vote approving Mexico's $18 billion bailout, because they worried it would lead to more careless lending elsewhere. In 1997, when Thailand, Indonesia, and Korea all careered toward default after borrowing heavily for years, the Germans partly blamed the Mexican precedent. By the time Russia flirted with default in 1998, the Germans refused to support another bailout and Russia's foreign creditors took a bath.[29]

Geithner faithfully planted himself on the Treasury side of this divide and remained there after accepting a job in 2001 as head of policy development for the IMF, essentially the organization's third-ranking official. The question of haircuts and moral hazard had split the IMF during the nineties and took on new urgency with the arrival of Geithner's immediate superior, a prominent American economist named Anne Krueger, around the time Geithner assumed his post.

Like the Germans, Krueger opposed assuring lenders of repayment when a country ran out of cash. On November 26, 2001, she gave a speech proposing a formal bankruptcy process for countries, which would open the lenders to losses.[30] A coalition of banks, investors, and their Washington front men soon mobilized to strangle the idea in its infancy. Charles Dallara, a former Treasury assistant secretary (and Geithner's onetime boss) whose company represented Wall Street's biggest foreign lenders, derided the proposal as "a nuclear-bomb solution that could really backfire." The lenders warned that they'd sooner stop investing overseas than take their chances with a global bankruptcy court.[31]

Geithner was too savvy a bureaucratic player to fight Krueger head-on, but his reservations were well known to IMF colleagues. "Tim was concerned that if the proposal was pushed too hard by the Managing Director and Anne Krueger, it would inject uncertainty into the market," said one.[32] Even if the bankruptcy process was desirable in some cases, Geithner worried, a hard-and-fast rule forcing countries into it would tie Washington's hands at moments when it needed maximum flexibility. Over time, he threw his weight behind a weaker counterproposal, which undermined support for Krueger's idea but went nowhere itself.[33]

In the fall of 2003, Geithner left the IMF to become president of the Federal Reserve Bank of New York, a job for which he had few obvious qualifications. Officially, the New York Fed regulates some of the country's largest banks, and Geithner had never worked as a regulator—or, for that matter, at a bank.

But, unofficially, the New York Fed is the Federal Reserve System's embassy on Wall Street, collecting market intelligence and transmitting it to the mother ship in Washington. Geithner was in some ways a perfect fit for this second task, having spent much of his career as a financial diplomat. When the two leading candidates for the job withdrew from consideration, Rubin recommended him to the New York Fed's board of directors, who were impressed by his experience at Treasury and the IMF.[34]

The New York Fed's dual mandate makes it a strange hybrid. In principle, regulating banks implies an adversarial relationship. The banks must be taken to task if their supply of capital dwindles or if their risk-taking becomes reckless. They must be fined if they run afoul of laws barring predatory or discriminatory lending. But the

New York Fed's ambassadorial function makes collaboration essential. In fact, the mandate to collaborate is built right into the institution's architecture: it is officially owned by the banks it regulates, and Wall Street executives traditionally hold several seats on the board that hires and fires the president. It wasn't a stretch to argue that Geithner was as much Wall Street's man at the Fed as he was the Fed's man on Wall Street.

Geithner worked hard to understand the institution he was now running. Unlike the presidents of the other regional Fed banks, the New York Fed has a permanent vote on the Federal Open Market Committee (FOMC)—the clique of Federal Reserve big shots that normally meets every six to eight weeks to set interest rates. Geithner convened a weekly meeting of the top research economists in his building to bring himself up to speed on monetary policy. He also met frequently with the titans of finance. "He would often have lunches with leaders of Wall Street and would be penetrating in his questions," said Pete Peterson, the chairman of the board of directors at the New York Fed at the time it hired Geithner. "Whatever he didn't know was quickly learned. . . . My impression is that he was in constant touch with Wall Street." [35]

Among Geithner's regular dining companions during his five-year tenure were several top executives at Citigroup. He became friendly with Sandy Weill, the Citigroup founder, who was another member of the board that brought him on at the Fed. He met often with Chuck Prince, Weill's successor as CEO. The interactions bled into activities other than banking. In 2007, he joined the board of the National Academy Foundation, a charity Weill founded to help disadvantaged teenagers.[36] "The structure of the Fed system is very good against the reality of conflict of interest. The CEOs who sit on the board of directors have no role in supervision or lending decisions. The structure of the Fed system is less good against the perception of conflict of interest," Geithner later said in an interview.[37]

But Geithner was intent on expanding his circle beyond the most identifiable faces on Wall Street. He made a special effort to engage the less recognizable but equally powerful insiders—the lawyers, consiglieri, and trusted lieutenants—with whom the secrets of the financial world often reside.

No one better fitted this profile than a courtly, almost elfin, securities lawyer named Rodgin Cohen. Cohen ran Sullivan & Cromwell, the whitest of white-shoe corporate firms, and his command of the legal arcana behind Wall Street deal making was second to none. Of particular relevance to Geithner was that he was often said to know more about the powers of the New York Fed than anyone who happened to work there.[38]

Not long after taking the job, Geithner invited the legal eminence to lunch in his personal dining room. The two men talked about how, even though the Fed primarily regulated commercial banks (actually, their parent companies, called bank holding companies), its purview often expanded during a crisis, when it suddenly became the de facto firefighter for the entire financial system. Investment banks, hedge funds, insurance companies—they all came calling at the first sign of smoke. In these moments, both men agreed, the Fed president must do whatever it takes to douse the fire, however unorthodox, no matter the political consequences.

All of these relationships proved enormously valuable to Geithner once the crisis flared up in 2008. Cohen's firm represented Bear Stearns, whose sale to JP Morgan Geithner brokered and sealed with a $29 billion Fed loan. Cohen also represented Lehman Brothers and advised AIG in the final stages of its near-death ordeal.

AIG was an instructive example. Its CEO at the time, Robert Willumstad, arrived at Geithner's door on a Sunday night in mid-September, just as the rescue of Lehman was coming apart, to announce that the company would need more than $50 billion within days to avoid collapse. By the next morning Geithner had leaned on the CEOs of JP Morgan and Goldman Sachs to dispatch teams of bankers to stitch together a private sector bailout for the firm. The following day, the bankers told him it wasn't possible: AIG needed more like $80 billion or $90 billion, and the banks could lend only $50 billion. But by this point it was clear that losing AIG would be catastrophic. And so Geithner effectively took the JP Morgan–Goldman plan, supersized it to match AIG's needs, and had the New York Fed step in to execute it.

Geithner's willingness to set aside concern for appearances and keep kicking dirt on the fire until he smothered it probably saved the financial system. Extrapolating from the nasty effects of the failure of Lehman, hardly the biggest firm on Wall Street, the U.S. economy would almost certainly have collapsed without the numerous bailouts, dispensations, and arranged marriages Geithner helped orchestrate. Beyond AIG, these interventions also saved Citigroup, Bank of America, Merrill Lynch, Goldman Sachs, and Morgan Stanley. It was Geithner's proximity to these firms that helped make the actions possible. Ben Bernanke later told the *New York Times* that Geithner's Wall Street Rolodex was an "invaluable" weapon in defeating the crisis.[39]

But the hatching of these bailout schemes was also an incestuous, cringe-inducing affair. And Geithner made it even more incestuous and cringe-inducing than necessary. One consequence of the AIG bailout, for example, was to pay the companies on the other side of its real estate bets—called "counterparties"—every cent of what AIG owed them, over $20 billion in all. The beneficiaries were massive financial firms like Goldman Sachs and Deutsche Bank.[40] Given that the money flowed to them from the New York Fed after only briefly passing through AIG's hands, Geithner could have insisted that they accept less than 100 cents on the dollar. This would have reflected the reality that the counterparties were the lucky beneficiaries of a bailout and therefore hardly entitled to every penny they sought.

Indeed, when a company goes bankrupt, its counterparties typically make do with a mere 60 or 70 percent of what they're owed.[41] But Geithner approved the full repayment. He contended that he had no leverage to demand a haircut because, having committed to saving AIG, he couldn't credibly threaten an outcome associated with bankruptcy.

In many ways, Geithner's performance during the darkest days of the financial crisis echoed his performance during the negotiations with the Japanese fifteen years earlier. In both cases, Geithner leaned heavily on the financial sector to guide his actions. In both cases, the benefits—preventing a financial catastrophe and opening up a major foreign market—outweighed the costs of the collaboration, however unappealing it was.

So while Geithner's bias was to see the world through the eyes of large financial institutions, this was forgivable during a crisis, when it could save the country from economic doom. The real problem was that he applied the same approach to the daily hustle of minding the banks. It was this second instance in which it became much more ominous.

The case of Citigroup was instructive. After barring Citi from acquiring companies in 2005, partly because of its failure to properly monitor its existing subsidiaries, New York Fed reversed the ban the following year, citing "significant progress" in the way Citi managed risk. At the time, the bank was piling into subprime mortgage securities, on which it would suffer more than $17 billion in losses in late 2007.

In response, many outside analysts began calling on Citi to issue large amounts of new stock. This would raise money as a buffer against future losses. To Geithner's credit, he did urge the company in this direction.[42] In fact, according to an internal report dated April 2008, the Fed also considered Citi's capital buffer a matter of concern.[43] But these efforts were always too feeble and too late. Citi consistently lowballed its issuance of new stock, thereby hurting existing shareholders (many of them Citi executives) by diluting the value of their shares. In the fall of 2008, it received the first install-ment of what would be a $45 billion bailout and $300 billion in government insurance.

In principle, shareholders are supposed to bear the brunt of a firm's missteps. But, after Geithner brought several aides from New York to Washington to assist with his transition at Treasury, one administration economic official noticed that "anytime you did any-thing that was perceived as threatening even to [shareholders], the New York Fed [aides] were extremely concerned."[44]

When it came to regulation, the ethos of the New York Fed was that it must be done in collaboration with the banks involved, not antagonistically. As president, Geithner generally hewed to this dictum, and never more so than on the question of derivatives. In 2004, Geithner gave a generally prescient speech about the risks that were building up in the financial system.[45] Not long afterward, Gerald Corrigan, a former New York Fed president cum Goldman Sachs partner, approached Geithner about the specific risks posed by derivatives. Geithner soon asked Corrigan to explore ways to defuse the threat.[46]

Corrigan's report came out in July 2005 and included several useful proposals. At the time, derivatives contracts were breathtak-ingly casual arrangements. The betting partners would commit terms to a piece of paper that they typically faxed to one another and promptly misplaced in some file cabinet or closet. If there was ever a need to quickly identify who owed whom what—when, say, a major betting partner like Lehman or AIG careered toward failure—it would be utterly hopeless. Panic and chaos would ensue. Corrigan proposed a standard template for derivatives contracts and a set of procedures for filing and cataloging them, basic infrastructure that would help the market survive a crisis.[47] He suggested that the industry adopt it voluntarily.

A few months later, in the musty tenth-floor dining room of the New York Fed, Geithner convened a meeting of representatives from some fourteen derivatives dealers—the "fourteen families," as they're known in downtown Manhattan—along with other regulators from Washington (like the SEC) and Europe. He encouraged the banks to come up with an "action plan" for whittling away their backlog of unfiled contracts. He set deadlines and nudged the banks to meet them. He even appeared at two bank conferences to tout the importance of the exercise.[48]

The efforts were important. The dealers had more or less eliminated the clutter by the time of the crisis, saving the financial world from far greater devastation. But these efforts were also utterly uncontroversial. A Goldman Sachs partner had proposed them. And though the benefits would spill across the financial system, the biggest beneficiaries would be the banks that carried them out. The chief obstacle was simple inertia, which Geithner could defeat with mere prodding.[49]

By contrast, on the subject of reforms that wouldn't have just eased the crisis but prevented it in the first place—the kinds of reforms Gary Gensler would later insist on, which would have cost the banks real money—Geithner had little to say.

As ever, Geithner was a diplomat through and through. He excelled at understanding a subculture and integrating himself into it, qualities that served him and the country exceptionally well during the crisis. But, like most diplomats, he was rarely capable of challenging the system, much less transcending it.

13

THE SURRENDER

Gary Gensler wasn't the only would-be reformer with a knack for moving the administration to places it never expected to be. A few weeks before Treasury released its plans for cleaning up Wall Street in June 2009, the president invited Paul Volcker, the legendary former Fed chairman, to a meeting of his economic team. Volcker was then serving as Obama's top outside economic adviser and the president wanted to know what he thought of Treasury's handiwork. The former chairman said that there were a number of features he liked, but that he had a few serious reservations. Above all, he said, he was troubled to see that banks that bought and sold stocks and bonds for their own accounts, rather than strictly on behalf of customers, would have access to government deposit insurance and cheap loans from the Fed. If a bank wanted to engage in this risky practice, known as "proprietary trading," that was fine. But if it did, it should have to forfeit government backing so that it wouldn't be gambling with taxpayers' money. He proposed banning proprietary trading at any federally supported bank, from Citigroup and Bank of America to Goldman Sachs and Morgan Stanley.

Geithner was unmoved. He didn't believe proprietary trading had caused the crisis, but said he'd have his department look into the idea if the president was interested. Obama seemed satisfied with this and moved on.

Before long, though, Volcker got the distinct impression he was being ignored. From the outside, there was no sign the administration was weighing a ban on proprietary trading at federally backed banks. He had trouble even scheduling a meeting to discuss the issue with top Obama economic officials. One day in late July, he turned up unannounced at the Senate Dirksen Building and asked an aide to cold-call staffers on the Banking Committee. When he finally corralled three of them, Volcker complained bitterly about being frozen out. "The White House is not listening to me on [financial] reform," he said. "I'm trying to make a difference here, and they won't even give me the time of day." He urged the staffers to write his ban into their legislation.

Like Gensler, the eighty-one-year-old Volcker was someone with whom Geithner had a history. In 2004, after Geithner had levied a $70 million fine on Citigroup, Volcker called him up to offer an unsolicited attaboy. "That's exactly the kind of thing I want to see you doing," he said. Four years later, on the frantic March weekend when Geithner married off Bear Stearns to JP Morgan with a generous dowry from the government, he paid the older man a visit to apprise him of the Fed's role. "You're going to find it repugnant," Geithner confessed, but he added that the move had been necessary to save the financial system. Not long after, Volcker groused in a speech that the Fed had operated at the "very edge" of its legal authority.[1]

Volcker was a famous curmudgeon, who'd been skeptical of the great Wall Street debt machine long before it went haywire. He warned as early as 2005 of a real estate bubble, noting in a speech, "We are buying a lot of housing at rising prices, but home ownership has become a vehicle for borrowing as much as a source of financial security."[2] In the March 2008 speech about Bear, he acidly complained that our "bright new financial system . . . has failed the test of the marketplace," having produced "unimaginable wealth for some, while repeatedly risking cascading breakdown." Now, in the postcrisis debate over the banks, Volcker loomed as a rumpled, six-foot-seven-inch paragon of financial virtue.

Over the course of the summer of 2009, Volcker's evangelizing had begun to sway people normally resistant to populist-sounding arguments. Nicholas Brady, the former George H.W. Bush Treasury secretary, warmed to the proprietary trading ban, as did John Reed, the former CEO of Citibank. In August, Stan Fischer, who'd worked closely with Summers and Geithner as the number two official at the IMF in the 1990s, gave a high-profile speech questioning whether government-backed banks should be allowed to speculate.[3]

By the fall, with the public craving rough justice for the banks, the president had also begun to fixate on proprietary trading. He summoned Geithner and Summers for another meeting with Volcker, this time in the Oval Office. Geithner raised a number of skeptical questions about how the proposal would work, but promised again that Treasury would look into it. Only this time he could tell from the president's demeanor that he'd have to follow through. "It was clear [Obama] was taking the idea seriously," said one official at the meeting.[4]

Geithner had always had a pragmatic side, a gift for co-opting opponents when the alternative was defeat. A few weeks later, when he was satisfied the proposal could be put in place without too much indigestion, he returned to the president. He said he still didn't believe the provision was necessary, but if embracing it would win over Volcker and defuse criticism from the left, he was open to it.[5]

On January 19, 2010, Republican Scott Brown stunned more or less every licensed operative in national politics by winning the Massachusetts Senate seat that Ted Kennedy's death had left vacant. Two days later, the White House unveiled the so-called Volcker Rule. Brown had benefited from populist anger over Wall Street and the economy, as well as a backlash against Obama's health care push.[6] The White House, unsure about whether to moderate the latter, seemed keen to redouble its efforts on the former. "When banks benefit from the safety net that taxpayers provide," the president said, "it is not appropriate for them to turn around and use that cheap money to trade for profit." He went on to denounce the "soaring profits and obscene bonuses" at banks that claimed they couldn't afford to increase lending.[7]

Two months later, when Congress finally passed the much overdue health care bill, the White House was eager to throw its full weight behind financial reform, an issue where it could align itself with the populist fervor rather than tack against it.

The unofficial start of the legislative endgame was March 22, when Senator Chris Dodd would open the committee debate on his bill. Heading into this showdown, the Republicans had filed hundreds of amendments with which they'd intended to tie up Dodd's bill for days if not weeks. So as to make this opposition as uncomfortable as possible, Geithner had prepared an uncharacteristically harsh speech, timed for the first day of proceedings. "Listen less to those whose judgments brought us this crisis," Geithner planned to say. "Instead, listen to the families and businesses still suffering from this crisis."[8]

Not for the last time, the administration underestimated the political forces propelling reform forward. On the way back from

Geithner's event, a member of the secretary's entourage got an e-mail from one of the wonks Treasury had dispatched to Dodd's committee room. "It's done," the e-mail said. "They just voted on it. We're going to the W for drinks." To the astonishment of everyone in Geithner's car, the Republicans had withdrawn every last amendment, having calculated that there was little percentage in fighting guerrilla-style on behalf of the banks.[9] The public mood was just too ornery. After a mere twenty-one minutes of back-and-forth, dizzying speed by Senate standards, the bill passed Dodd's committee in an anticlimactic party-line vote.

Nowhere was the public crankiness toward Wall Street more evident than on derivatives. Ever since Dodd had written his bill in the fall of 2009, the industry had dismissed its relatively tough stance toward derivatives as a mere "placeholder." Lobbyists predicted with sublime confidence that the provision would disappear once Senate Agriculture Committee chair Blanche Lincoln negotiated a compromise with the top Republican on her panel and merged it into Dodd's broader bill.[10] (The Agriculture Committee shares jurisdiction with the Banking Committee over derivatives for obscure historical reasons.) "If they try to push the Dodd bill as currently written on derivatives, it can't fly," one industry lawyer predicted even after the rout in Dodd's committee.[11]

The banks were counting on a dynamic that almost always favors the deep-pocketed opponents of reform: the simple passage of time. The more complicated the issue, the tougher it is to sustain the public's attention, without which there are endless opportunities for mischief. But in this case time actually favored the reformers: the more weeks and months that passed without the banks suffering consequences for their reckless risk taking, the angrier the public became.

Derivatives proved to be the chief victim of this new reality, partly because of a tactical decision by Republicans. Following the advice of the party's all-purpose rhetorical guru, Frank Luntz, the

GOP labeled portions of the Democratic plan a recipe for "permanent bailouts." This, in turn, prompted the White House to scout out more favorable terrain. And derivatives, which could be neatly summarized as the cause of AIG's collapse, looked uniquely promising. "Rahm's view is: 'I like the derivatives issue,'" said one administration official at the time. "'We're on better ground on that than talking about bailouts. If they talk bailouts, we talk derivatives.'" [12] In March, Obama concluded a statement on financial reform with the demand, "All derivatives must be regulated." [13]

On April 8, two and a half weeks after Dodd's bill sailed through his committee, Senator Lincoln finally sent the administration a draft of her compromise. The deal would have represented a retreat, since it did not require any derivatives to trade on an exchange and exempted others from key regulations. Treasury quickly concluded there was no way the president could bless it, and senior White House officials—Emanuel, Axelrod, Summers—agreed. A few days later, Michael Barr, an assistant secretary who served as one of Geithner's envoys to Congress, called Lincoln's top committee aide, Robert Holifield, and told him the administration would fight the compromise if she pursued it.

The industry's logic had momentarily failed. Less clear was whether the administration had truly converted to the populist cause, or was just co-opting public opinion.

Inside Lincoln's camp, the administration's rebuff went down about as well as a criminal indictment. Holifield refused to let Barr off the phone while he argued the merits of the Lincoln approach, then made Barr promise to double-check with his administration colleagues before handing down a final verdict. (Barr did; it was unchanged.) But there was at least one member of Lincoln's staff who wasn't displeased by the turn of events: a longtime financial services regulator and lawyer named Pat McCarty.

McCarty had first crossed paths with Geithner back in 2005, on the day the New York Fed president, flanked by regulators from agencies like the SEC and FDIC, gathered executives from the fourteen big Wall Street firms in his cavernous dining room and advised them to clean up their act on derivatives. At the time, McCarty was serving as the general counsel for the Commodity Futures Trading Commission, the agency Gensler later took over, so he had no formal authority over the banks. He'd been invited as a mere observer. But that didn't mean McCarty lacked opinions. In fact, while he agreed that the action was necessary, he didn't think much of the voluntary approach Geithner and Wall Street preferred. The way to get the banks' attention, McCarty liked to say, was to "take the first big guy out and make an example of him." If it were up to him, the Fed would have picked out an offending bank, ordered it to cease and desist, slapped it with a $100 million fine, and given it forty-five days to get its books in order. If its competitors still didn't get the message, he'd have made examples of them, too. He believed Wall Street was operating in an "unsafe and unsound" manner—a legal term for "dangerous"—and so time was of the essence.

After the CFTC, McCarty had moved to a hedge fund that failed, then helped start a derivatives clearinghouse before landing at the SEC. Finally, in December 2009, he went to work for Blanche Lincoln, who'd become a key player in financial reform after taking over as chair of the Senate Agriculture Committee a few months earlier.

When the administration rejected Lincoln's bill, McCarty's boss asked him to draw up a replacement that lurched in the opposite direction. It was a measure that instantly inspired fear and loathing in the minds of bankers. The centerpiece of the new-look Lincoln bill would forbid federally backed banks from dealing in derivatives, period. If the banks wanted federal support, they would have to push out their derivatives businesses to a separate affiliate, which they'd have to infuse with ample helpings of capital, so as to absorb any losses that might arise. McCarty was, in effect, homing in on the same principle Volcker had put forth: no bank should be able to use taxpayer funds to subsidize its riskiest activities—dealing and trading derivatives, in this case. Except that McCarty was applying the principle on a scale that Volcker himself had never contemplated.

Blanche Lincoln, for one, was intrigued. A few weeks earlier, she'd suddenly found herself in a bitter primary campaign against Arkansas's lieutenant governor, who'd styled himself an enemy of big banks. Having spent her twelve years in the Senate cultivating a reputation as a business-friendly Democrat, she had depressingly few options for reinventing herself as a populist. McCarty's rewrite just might be her lifeline.

The yowling from Wall Street commenced almost immediately. Lincoln argued that betting on the future value of corporate bonds or mortgage securities, or on swings in interest rates and foreign currencies—that is, all the bets and hedges derivatives allow people to make—was not a "core" banking activity. Certainly it was not one that merited government backing. The banks argued that this was simplistic: a bank that makes a loan should be able to insure it with a derivative that pays off if the value of the loan declines or if interest rates change. But these arguments were strained. In 2009, the New York State insurance commissioner estimated that 80 percent of the $25 trillion market for credit default swaps, or bets on the value of bonds and other debt securities, were "naked." [14] That is to say, the purchaser didn't own a piece of the loan or bond it was ostensibly insuring. The banks were running taxpayer-backed casinos.

Never ones to be compelled by intellectual rigor, the bank lobbyists promised total war against the Lincoln measure. And with a handful of conservative Democrats on her committee, the threat was credible, at least for the first forty-eight hours. On day three, the SEC announced it was suing Goldman Sachs for defrauding investors to whom it had sold subprime mortgage securities. The mere suggestion of fraud by the most detested name on Wall Street transformed the public's mild hostility toward the banks into pickax-wielding blood-lust.

The measure soon passed Lincoln's committee, garnering a Re-publican vote in the process. The push-out provision then survived the merger of Lincoln's bill with Dodd's. And it sat unmolested in the legislation that passed the full Senate in late May. There are a million ways for a senator to squelch an inconvenient regulation on behalf of a powerful industry, from stripping it out by brute force (i.e., amendment) to mandating studies and reports that delay it indefi-nitely. Wall Street couldn't find a single Democratic taker for even the kindest and gentlest of these methods.[15]

Treasury now had a problem. It vehemently opposed Lincoln's push-out idea, which Geithner argued would make derivatives even riskier by placing them out of the reach of bank regulators. (He neglected to mention that they would move into the reach of the CFTC, which could do no worse than the regulators who'd fallen asleep before the crisis, and perhaps could do better.) But like dozens of anxious Democrats in the U.S. Senate, he could see the futility of waging his counterinsurgency in front of a wild-eyed public. In a let-ter he sent to Lincoln greeting her second stab at reform, he didn't so much as mention her controversial brainchild.[16]

The last chance for the powers that be to solve their problem would be the conference committee, whose job it was to combine the House and Senate bills into a single piece of legislation. Having failed to defeat the Lincoln proposal before this, Geithner did what any pragmatist would: he sued for peace. Treasury opened up a ne-gotiation with Lincoln's legislative aides; the White House, led by deputy chief of staff Jim Messina, opened up parallel negotiations with her political team. Treasury proposed that the banks push out roughly 10 percent of their derivatives business—like those dealing with commodities, certain metals, and agricultural products—while leaving the most profitable derivatives in house. It was mostly the status quo, in other words. But it was the status quo pitched so that Lincoln could save face.

In early June, Lincoln survived her primary challenge; presumably, she was now free to bargain. But before long, Treasury noticed a curious pattern. An understanding would be reached with Lincoln or Holifield. Then, within a couple of days, Treasury staffers would be back to haggling over the same familiar details. Geithner began to suspect the hidden hand of Pat McCarty, who he worried was scuppering the deals behind closed doors. (In fact, Lincoln had her own concerns about these compromises.) Over at the White House, meanwhile, Rahm Emanuel had another culprit in mind: Gary Gensler. The issue was threatening to hold up the entire financial reform bill, since Wall Street–friendly New Democrats, like Representatives Melissa Bean of Illinois and Joseph Crowley of New York, had labeled it an absolute deal-breaker. Emanuel believed Gensler had the stature to make the problem go away by coming out against the Lincoln provision. But instead of weighing in unequivocally, the CFTC chairman was ducking the debate. Emanuel was going out of his mind. "Get that cocksucker in here so I can rip him a new one," he roared to aides.

Fewer than forty-eight hours out from closing the books on a bill that was over a year in the making, a few administration officials met with Lincoln's staff in the Senate to make one last stab at winning her over. To their surprise, the Lincolnites brought Gensler as a kind of expert witness. A smile came over the face of Neal Wolin, the deputy secretary. The administration team had a chance to pin down the Treasury gadfly at long last. Wolin laid out the compromise and asked Gensler if he supported it. Gensler hemmed and hawed for several minutes, raising a handful of questions and points of clarification. Finally, he said he thought it would achieve enough of what Lincoln wanted that she should support it. The drama was over.

Senator Lincoln's surrender on the push-out idea was probably inevitable given the idea's unlikely provenance and the fanatical opposition it kicked up on Wall Street. But in a way, the episode epitomized the reform bill's last days—the restoration of order that the industry had long expected.

The banks won major concessions on nearly every element they'd fiercely resisted. Dodd's original bill required banks to trade their derivatives on exchanges, or at least through electronic terminals that performed a similar function, so that anyone could see what it cost to buy and sell a derivative contract. By the time the ink had dried on the final financial reform bill, the definition of the exchange alternative was so vague that a future regulator could extend it to include a private phone call between dealer and buyer. Lincoln's version of the bill had assigned the dealers a "fiduciary" obligation to look out for pension funds and municipalities, which would have made it easier to win a lawsuit after a derivatives-related loss. This provision went mysteriously missing from the final bill, replaced by a weaker obligation to such clients.

The real culprits tended to be the New Democrats in the House.[17] Bean and Crowley opposed the "fiduciary" language, for example. (Bean supported requiring municipalities to hire financial advisers who would serve as their fiduciaries.) These members used the cover of the closed-door conference committee to let their powerful donors off the hook. In many instances, the administration's biggest sin was a kind of passive complicity that could be rationalized as a tactical retreat. But Geithner also worked behind the scenes to ensure that some of the same reforms he'd endorsed publicly turned out weaker than advertised.

The Volcker Rule was a prime example. The rule's two biggest champions in the Senate, Democrats Carl Levin of Michigan and Jeff Merkley of Oregon, sought to spell out, in the text of the bill, which types of speculative bets would be off-limits to government-backed banks. Geithner preferred to let the regulators come up with this standard. At first blush, this sounded like a trivial difference. But Congress's impartial research arm, the Congressional Research Service (CRS), worried that neglecting to write the rule into law, as Levin and Merkley proposed to do, could allow a future regulator to disregard it entirely. As one Senate aide involved in the back-and-forth observed, "If a strong restriction is put in place this year, and twenty years from now a regulator guts it, they [CRS] think it's possible that a court could uphold the gutting of it." [18] And that's assuming that the regulators wrote a tough rule in the first place. There was no guarantee this would happen.

The trouble with investing so much power in regulators is that they're far more insulated from public opinion, and therefore susceptible to the blandishments of industry officials, than even the most out-of-touch congressperson. Often the corruption is psychological rather than literal. During boom times, it's easy to believe that the captains of industry are uniquely enlightened, or that they at least know what they're doing. But the heady days of a boom are when the industry is most likely to ignore basic standards of prudence and good behavior. This was a reasonably good description of the run-up to the financial crisis.

Yet Geithner rejected the idea that the regulators were destined to blow it. In his preferred narrative, the regulators had often succeeded when they had had the right tools and the proper jurisdiction. Though Geithner conceded that regulators had made mistakes, the problems arose where they hadn't had these advantages. "The failures in the financial system that made this crisis so devastating were largely failures . . . where the Fed had no authority" and no other regulator knew who was in charge, he said.[19]

Geithner's narrative was a bit of a stretch. It was true that Bear and Lehman and AIG had fallen through some regulatory cracks. But a giant like Citigroup had done the impressive work of immolating itself right under the New York Fed's nose. Still if, like Geithner, you blamed the obstacles the regulators faced rather than the regulators themselves, then the solution was as simple as removing the obstacles. In fact, if you happened to see the world the way Geithner did, then the hollowing of the Lincoln proposal was completely defensible. After all, most of what Lincoln hoped to accomplish could in principle be accomplished by tougher regulators. Lincoln believed that placing a bank's derivatives in a sister company would force the bank to back them with more capital—that is, a bigger financial buffer against losses—since, under the status quo, the banks sometimes used the same capital for two or three different purposes. Geithner believed the way to end this double- and triple-counting was simply to require more capital for derivatives and have regulators enforce the new standard.

Lincoln's idea was, in effect, a hedge against the risk that regulators would fall back into the same see-no-evil stupor that afflicted them before the crisis. But having been a bank regulator himself, Geithner had trouble admitting that regulators would fail. His faith in them was unbroken.

How much trust to place in regulators was really the central question of financial reform. If, unlike Geithner, you couldn't bring yourself to trust them again, then the implications were enormous. In that case, it wouldn't do to give regulators new powers. It might not even do to outlaw a few dubious practices, as Volcker proposed, or spin off certain functions, as Lincoln had done. In a world where regulators were unlikely to rein in reckless megabanks, and where the consequences of that recklessness were either bailouts worth hundreds of billions of dollars (to save the banks) or an apocalyptic crisis, then the solution was to make the system less dependent on regulators. The solution was to make banks small enough to fail.

Ted Kaufman was increasingly of this persuasion. Kaufman was a onetime aide to Joe Biden who'd rejoined the Biden entourage during the vice-presidential campaign and then served out his term in the Senate. From the beginning, Kaufman had no plans to run for reelection. He and his chief of staff, Jeff Connaughton, decided they preferred throwing themselves into the task of legislating rather than spending their days mouthing platitudes and their nights hunting cash. And the legislative task they deemed most urgent was taming Wall Street.

Their first attempt was a bill known as FERA, the Fraud Enforcement and Recovery Act, which Kaufman helped pass in the spring of 2009. The law made it easier for the Justice Department to target mortgage-related fraud. But Kaufman soon realized that sending prosecutors to mop up after the crisis was close to useless. To make an indictment stick, the FBI must typically catch a suspect perpetrating a fraud in real time. By the time Congress passed FERA and Obama's appointees had settled in at the Justice Department, most of the fraudsters were out of business. Any wires they might have tapped had long since run dry.

Meanwhile, as financial reform moved through Congress, Kaufman couldn't help noticing how brazenly the big banks were undermining it. It started to occur to him that the problem wasn't so much individual bankers as the institutions themselves. He began to muse about cutting them down to size.

This did not much endear him to the megabanks and their lobbyists. The lobbyists argued that, even after all the crisis-related mergers—Bear and JP Morgan, Wachovia and Wells Fargo, Merrill Lynch and Bank of America—the U.S. banking system wasn't especially concentrated relative to those of other countries, where a smaller number of banks controlled a bigger share of the industry. Kaufman observed that this failed a basic test of intuition. "There was a moment in time when they were too big to fail," he said, referring to the crisis. "Now they're bigger."

One day he'd just finished a speech on the Senate floor when a colleague asked him to respond to the claim, attributed to the CEO of a major Wall Street firm, that "only small banks failed [during the crisis]. None of the big banks did." It took all Kaufman had to suppress a smile. *That's right*, Kaufman thought. *None did—because the Fed bailed them out.* He returned to the microphone to point this out.[20]

The more Kaufman looked into the question of bigness, the more alarmed he became. He discovered that if you tallied up all the assets of the six largest banks—loans, mortgage securities, derivatives, etc.—the figure would have equaled 17 percent of GDP as recently as the mid-1990s. After the crisis, it was 63 percent.[21]

The impression you got from listening to Wall Street was that competition was driving the growth. The banks said they needed to be sprawling behemoths to keep pace with their overseas rivals and serve global clients. But the numbers said otherwise. In early 2010, Andrew Haldane, a senior official at the Bank of England, reviewed the available evidence and concluded that once a bank's balance sheet topped $100 billion, about one fifteenth the size of the biggest U.S. banks, it became no more efficient as it grew, and often less so.[22]

Haldane noted a relatively straightforward explanation for these findings: beyond a point, an organization simply becomes too large and complicated to manage. He pointed to a phenomenon known as Dunbar's Law, the proposition that humans are incapable of juggling more than 150 bona fide relationships at once. "Large banks grew to comprise several thousand distinct legal entities," Haldane observed. "Whatever the technology budget, it is questionable whether any man's mind or memory could cope with such complexity."[23]

There were only two real advantages to being a megabank. The first was that no government in its right mind would ever let you fail. When investors know this, they will lend you money at lower interest rates than they demand from smaller banks, thus encouraging you to borrow heavily to take big risks. Treasury's answer to this was the so-called resolution authority, the power to neatly dismantle a troubled megabank rather than bail it out or let it collapse chaotically. The government had lacked this during the crisis. But as Kaufman pointed out, there was no reason to believe the government could step in and fold up a $1.5 trillion bank like some sort of Murphy bed. One obvious problem was that most megabanks are multinational corporations, whereas Treasury would have the power to dismantle only their U.S. operations. That meant the government would be likely to end up bailing out the banks all over again, so as not to create a global panic.[24]

The second advantage to being a megabank was vaguer but perhaps more insidious. It had to do with power. In a nutshell, there were good reasons to think that a huge bank with $100 billion in annual revenue could effectively resist regulation, either by cowing regulators with its political clout or by going over their heads to Congress. Such banks have vast lobbying operations, after all, and scores of wealthy executives who donate to campaigns. Certainly it would be hard to imagine such a bank meekly submitting to dismemberment during a crisis. In addition to the other political weapons, a megabank can always tell a sob story about the tens of thousands of jobs that would be lost if it were liquidated. In 2010, Bank of America alone had almost 300,000 employees.[25]

In April 2010, Kaufman teamed up with his Ohio colleague Sherrod Brown to craft a bill that would cap the amount of money banks could borrow, other than deposits, to 2 percent of GDP, or about $300 billion at the time. The measure would have forced three of the biggest banks in the country to shrink by roughly half. For a brief moment in early May, it looked as though it just might pass as part of the broader financial reform package. The Senate's top two Democrats—majority leader Harry Reid and his lieutenant, Dick Durbin—proclaimed their support, and Reid vowed to bring it to a vote as an amendment. But when all the votes were tallied, it was clear that the fix had been in. Chris Dodd, the powerful Banking Committee chairman, opposed the measure and brought ten of the twelve other Democrats on his committee with him.

The week before, Geithner had stopped by Kaufman's office to talk banks. It was a courtesy call, really. Geithner knew he had the votes to kill the amendment. As one Treasury official later boasted to a reporter, "If we'd been for it, it probably would have happened. But we weren't." [26] Geithner was a man made magnanimous by the prospect of imminent victory.

"I'm really impressed with your passion and depth on these issues," Geithner told Kaufman. "Is it okay with you if I try to talk you out of it?" Geithner went on to explain that regulators would write rules forcing banks to hold more capital, so they'd never again get close to the point of collapse. Kaufman did not conceal his skepticism. I trust you, he said, but "what happens when we get a president who says, 'no regulation'?"—"President Kudlow," Kaufman liked to joke, after the right-wing cable commentator. Geithner laughed and brushed off the question. "It'll be hard for them to reverse the rules we put in place," he said.

In the end, what Geithner accomplished with financial reform was similar to the reforms he enacted as president of the New York Fed: an improvement over the status quo, but one whose benefits came mostly at the margins. There was little in the bill to prompt a fundamental rethinking of industry, none of the breakups or spin-offs reformers refer to as "structural" change. With the exception of the Volcker Rule and a new agency to protect consumers from abusive financial products, the legislation adopted very few ideas over the banks' objections. And in the case of the Volcker Rule, countless details were left to the regulators' imaginations, so the banks would have a big say over its final shape. As a package, the reforms might mitigate whatever crisis strikes in the next five to ten years. But they will not prevent it.

Given the enormous complexity involved, public opinion is hardly the best judge of the financial system's recent weatherproofing. On the other hand, at least part of the mandate was political—to put the country more at ease with Wall Street—and by that standard the project was a failure. A poll by Bloomberg shortly after Congress passed the bill found that nearly 80 percent of the public doubted it would offer much protection against a future crisis.[27] By a 47–38 margin, the public predicted the bill would be a bigger help to Wall Street than to consumers. At least part of the skepticism flowed from the absence of structural change: more than two-thirds of respondents expected the banks to make minor alterations to the way they do business.

Geithner made no apologies for preserving the system's basic contours. It was, after all, a system he'd spent a career promoting and defending. Suggestions that the crisis revealed a need for, say, a smaller financial sector left him utterly cold. To the contrary, he believed the financial sector should be a source of strength for the economy, a matter of national pride. In Geithner's view, the rise of countries like China and India created a global land grab: as these economies matured, they would demand more sophisticated financial services the same way they demanded cars for their middle classes and information technology for their corporations. In that case, we should want to help U.S. banks win their business.[28]

"I don't have any enthusiasm for ... trying to shrink the relative importance of the financial system in our economy as a test of reform, because we have to think about the fact that we operate in the broader world," he said in an interview. "It's the same thing for Microsoft or anything else. We want U.S. firms to benefit from that"—at least so long as they're well regulated. In effect, Geithner believed we should be as comfortable linking the fate of our economy to Wall Street as to automakers or Silicon Valley.[29]

There was a historical moment when this vision held genuine appeal, but the financial crisis revealed its flaw. During the crisis, Geithner believed with every ounce of his being that big financial firms were *different*: they were unlike GM or Microsoft because you couldn't ask their debt holders to endure even modest losses without making the global panic vastly worse; you certainly couldn't let these companies fail. But if the megabanks are different from GM or Microsoft during a crisis—if their failure would be far more dangerous—then the differences don't disappear when the sun comes back out. They remain just as dangerous, so they are a much riskier foundation for the economy. It was Geithner's blindness to this fact that put him out of step with public opinion, and that denied the administration's financial policies the legitimacy they badly needed.

14

UNDERWATER

From the outside, the spring of 2010 looked like the moment the president recovered some of the swagger he'd lost shortly after taking office and enacting the stimulus. On March 23, he finally signed health care reform into law. Two months later, the Senate passed financial reform, putting it on track to become law in July. The economy was still dicey. But with two of Obama's three landmark goals in hand (the third being climate change legislation), the administration would at least have a record to tout in the upcoming congressional elections.

In reality, the late spring of 2010 kicked off a period of drift that would extend past Election Day. And no issue better epitomized this than the fate of the trillions of dollars in tax cuts scheduled to expire at the end of the year.

George W. Bush had originally passed the tax cuts in two unsightly helpings between 2001 and 2003, claiming all manner of dubious rationales, from preventing the budget surplus from growing too large to eliminating unnecessary drag on the economy. The first round had lowered income tax rates for all workers, but of course showered the biggest benefits on the high earners, who saw the rate on much of their earnings drop from 39.6 percent to 35 percent. It also cut taxes on large estates. The second round of cuts slashed taxes on income from investments. This once again concentrated the lucre on the rich, who earn far more money (both in absolute terms and as a share of their income) from financial assets like stocks.

As always in these matters, Warren Buffett captured the lunacy best. Buffett took to *The Washington Post* to point out that, under plausible circumstances, the dividend tax cut could save him $300 million each year and lower his overall tax rate to 3 percent, while benefiting his receptionist not a lick.[1]

Thanks to the various machinations of Bush and Congress, both rounds of tax cuts were scheduled to expire at the end of 2010.[2] The question of how to handle this looming phaseout had been a preoccupation of Team Obama since the campaign, when the candidate vowed to renew the tax cuts for families making under $250,000 per year while allowing them to lapse for the truly affluent. Thereafter, the urgency of ending the upper-income cuts, which would cost $700 billion over ten years but provide almost no boost to the economy, only grew as the recession made a hash of the deficit picture. But, of course, no politician likes to open himself to the charge of raising taxes, even if only on the wealthy. Not surprisingly, the time just never seemed right for the White House to tidy up this particular Bush-era mess.

In the spring of 2010, after several false starts, the economic team finally managed a rare display of unity and counseled action. During a meeting with the president in the Roosevelt Room, wonk after wonk—Tim Geithner, Jason Furman, Gene Sperling—spoke in favor of nudging the House to pass a bill that extended only the tax cuts for those making under $250,000 per year, thereby leaving the upper-income cuts for dead. If Republicans voted against the bill, they'd be voting against middle-class tax cuts. But if they voted for it, they'd be stiffing the wealthy, their most prized constituency. Whatever the case, it wasn't likely that Republicans could stop the legislation, since Democrats had the votes to muscle it through the House and, with the help of a single Republican defector, the Senate as well.

The president's political advisers opposed the idea. The most outspoken was Phil Schiliro, the president's chief congressional liaison. Though a strong advocate of repealing the tax cuts in principle, Schiliro worried that Congress was in no mood to flirt with tax increases. According to one participant, he posited a nightmare scenario in which Democratic congressmen were berated at town hall meetings during the August recess, much as they had been over health care the previous summer. If the administration was intent on such a vote, it should push to schedule one in September or October, Schiliro counseled. "They view it through the class warfare stuff— Kerry in 2004, Gore in 2000," said one administration official of the hesitation in the West Wing. "They worry that they'll get painted as lefties, tax-raisers."[3] (Alas, Congress would prove even less interested in the matter as the election loomed in the fall.)

As the summer went on, the economic team grew increasingly anguished over this White House neglect. If Democrats couldn't drive a stake through Bush's most noxious tax cuts when they comfortably controlled the House and Senate, they reckoned, it was hard to believe they'd succeed after the midterm elections, when Republicans were sure to make big gains.

Eventually, Geithner took it upon himself to prosecute the issue, delivering a series of speeches and popping up everywhere from *Good Morning America* to the Fox Business Channel to urge action.

Treasury figured it might goad the White House into following its lead.[4] But, except for one forceful speech in September, the president was AWOL. The wonks began to morbidly joke that there was, in fact, no White House strategy on the tax cuts, just an "approach."[5]

Alas, the Bush tax cuts were hardly the only missed opportunity during this period. On Thursday, August 19, 2010, the president embarked on a ten-day getaway to Martha's Vineyard. By the following week, the administration would learn that home sales had plummeted 27 percent in July, the biggest one-month drop since 1968. Worse, this came on the heels of a nine-month peak in unemployment claims. The president abruptly arranged a conference call with Geithner, Summers, and Romer, all of whom were also on vacation, to solicit ideas for bolstering the shaky recovery. "It was the second phase of 'uh-oh,'" recalled a Treasury official.[6] As if to underscore the malaise, the president could barely hear his advisers—the phone connection was as dodgy as the economy.

The call, which the White House quickly leaked to the press, looked like the beginning of a furious policy response. Upon closer examination, it was more a statement of impotence than a sign of initiative; the sort of stunt an administration resorts to when it's out of ammunition, not when it's on the verge of bold action.

The economy had actually been weakening since the spring, when the Greek debt crisis unsettled the global financial markets. In mid-July, Emanuel charged his policy shop with brainstorming ways to reverse the slide. But even then it was clear that any proposal for boosting growth would go nowhere in Congress without a focused PR campaign to press members into action. When administration aides made inquiries on Capitol Hill, the Republicans responded with their usual intransigence. More frustratingly, Democrats were just as dismissive, complaining that the measures couldn't possibly help the economy in time to save them from a midterm rout. "By the summer of 2010, the [congressional] Democrats—I won't say they were finished with us," said the Treasury official, "but there wasn't a lot of confidence." [7]

The more realistic hope was to ready plans that might get a hearing in Congress during the lame-duck period following the 2010 election, or in the January 2011 State of the Union address. But after the gruesome-looking August data, the White House decided it needed policies it could tout immediately. This set off a scramble in Washington, where only a rump force of administration economists was manning the spreadsheets thanks to the late summer break. For the better part of a week, the task of fleshing out ideas that had been floating around at various stages of gestation fell mostly to Brian Deese and David Kamin, two obscure Summers aides at the NEC. Summers himself barely had time to read the memo before signing his name to it.

Once the senior White House staff returned to Washington the week before Labor Day—many of them shortening vacations to focus on the sudden economic relapse—Rahm Emanuel hosted a series of meetings to finalize the list of proposals. There would be three proposals in all: allowing companies to deduct the entire cost of new investments in the year they made them, rather than over several years, at a price tag of about $30 billion; $50 billion worth of transportation infrastructure projects; and making permanent a beefed-up research and development tax credit for business, which would run $100 billion over ten years.[8]

The package resembled a big-budget Hollywood script, both for good and for ill. On the plus side, there was something for every constituency. The tax deduction would strike a centrist note, no trivial benefit for a White House often maligned as antibusiness. The research and development credit would underscore the president's focus on the long term. The infrastructure money would please the left, while also producing tangible evidence of government action and passing muster with business groups, which complained about the nation's deteriorating roads and airports.

Still, one couldn't shake the feeling that the aim was to make a splashy debut rather than a lasting impression—that the emphasis was on "concept" over plot development, in the vernacular of the movie business. Emanuel loved the R&D and infrastructure proposals in particular, but he seemed more taken with their imagery than their substantive merits. "I won't say it was all marketing. But these proposals weren't designed to break new policy ground," said the same Treasury official.[9]

Even as a marketing proposition, the effort seemed halfhearted. Toward the end of September, Geithner asked his economists to produce a series of reports on potential benefits that the White House could flog in public. The infrastructure report did come out within two weeks, in time for a presidential event on Columbus Day.[10] The tax deduction report came out at the end of October,[11] too late to be much use before the election, but potentially helpful for the lame-duck period. And the report on research and development— ostensibly Emanuel's baby—wouldn't be completed until the following March.[12]

It was housing that was perhaps the biggest casualty of this period of policy-making languor. Late June 2010 saw the expiration of a major real estate subsidy Congress had enacted the previous year— the homebuyer tax credit—removing one of the few forces propping up the market. This explained the abrupt collapse of home sales that had caught the administration's attention in August. It also explained why, after several months of moderate increases during the winter and spring, home prices stalled out and then began to tumble in the summer and fall.

Diagnosing the problems with the housing market was relatively straightforward: millions of Americans had bought homes at inflated prices during the previous decade. These were homes the buyers could afford only at artificially low "teaser" interest rates, which were typically adjusted upward during the first year or two of ownership, boosting their monthly payments dramatically. As long as home prices rose at a similar pace, as they did until 2006, the borrowers could always refinance at another low introductory rate. But once the market lost altitude, the refinancing escape hatch slammed shut. There's basically no way to refinance a house worth less than the original mortgage. This sent millions of people into foreclosure, which depressed prices further and accelerated the vicious circle.

Upon taking office, the administration estimated that the millions of people in this situation—so-called underwater borrowers—collectively owed $500 billion more than their homes were worth. That left essentially two options. First, the government could eat the full $500 billion itself, an enormous cost at a time when it was already on the hook for the stimulus and the bank bailout. The second option was to ignore the 10 million people in this situation who managed to stay current on their mortgages even though they couldn't refinance. If, instead, you focused on the 3 million to 4 million people at risk of foreclosure, many but not all of them underwater, the cost would be a small fraction of the original $500 billion. The catch was that the politics would be brutal. The homeowners making payments would rage that only the deadbeats got bailed out.[13]

It was essentially the second option that Team Obama embraced, but with one major caveat designed to insulate itself politically. The program the administration designed for at-risk borrowers—called the Home Affordable Modification Program, or HAMP—would itself be modest in nature. Even the goodies the deadbeats got wouldn't be that good. (The 3–4 million figure included some troubled homeowners who weren't underwater and neglected some homeowners who were underwater but too far behind to be helped.)

Under HAMP, the government and the banks would split the cost of trimming a borrower's monthly payments to roughly one third of that borrower's income. Almost from the get-go, it was clear that the program was weak brew. The big banks deployed laughably few workers to process requests, and the result was a nightmare of endless delays, false starts, and dead ends for struggling homeowners.

At one point, the Treasury Department held a public event where foreclosure candidates could submit HAMP applications to be filed on their behalf. Over three hundred homeowners jumped at the chance to enlist Treasury's help, thinking surely the U.S. government could make more headway than they could on their own. But not long after Treasury faxed off the applications, the servicer—a major U.S. bank—confessed that it had lost them. Under pressure, the bank eventually excavated eighty of the applications, but it could never explain what had happened to the rest. It came as no surprise, in other words, that only 200,000 people had seen their mortgages permanently modified one year into the program, against the administration's announced goal of helping 3 million to 4 million overall.[14]

Still, the bigger issue was that even if HAMP had worked entirely as expected, it simply didn't have the juice to fix the problem. Borrowers facing foreclosure might jump at the chance to lower their monthly payment from half their income to one third. But even one third often proved unaffordable. And, indeed, of the roughly 400,000 who received modifications in the program, nearly 120,000 were no longer current on their mortgages by mid-2011.[15]

The truth was that the administration never intended for HAMP to solve the housing problem. (It was Emanuel who had pushed for the goal of 3 million to 4 million people, against the better judgment of the economists at Treasury and in the White House.) Instead, many in the administration, especially in Larry Summers's orbit, viewed it as a simple play for time. "It was pretty clear that all it was going to do was at best kick the defaults down the road," said one White House economist.[16]

In theory, that in itself could be helpful. If a world without HAMP might see 3 million foreclosures in 2009 and 3 million in 2010, then HAMP might spread those foreclosures out, so that the numbers were more like 2 million in each of those years and another 2 million in 2011. That would prevent the housing market from collapsing in 2009 or 2010. By 2011, the economy might be stronger, and unemployment a lot lower, so that even the final 2 million foreclosures wouldn't come to pass.

It was a reasonable gamble, in any case. It just didn't end up working. The economy never bounced back the way the administration hoped, a problem that had become obvious by August 2010. In fact, not only was the economy not appreciably stronger than it had been one year earlier; it was on the verge of getting worse.

At this point, another troubling thought reared its head: what if it wasn't the economy that was hurting the housing market, but the housing market that was killing the economy?

Since the beginning of the recession, economists had generally assumed that, as workers lost their jobs, even those who had borrowed responsibly would struggle to make their mortgage payments, and that this situation would create a glut of foreclosures. When the banks tried to unload all the foreclosed houses, they would drive down prices for the entire market. The longer unemployment lingered above 9 percent, the longer housing would get squeezed.

But there was one school of economists who believed that this logic, while not necessarily wrong, missed the real story. The group's godfather was a Japanese economist named Richard Koo, who laid out the theory in a book modestly titled *The Holy Grail of Macroeconomics*.[17] Koo's insight, drawn from the experience of Japan's "lost decade," was that consumers and businesses who heap on debt during a bubble reverse course once the bubble bursts, paying back old loans and begging off new ones. The reason is partly economic:

the collapse has pummeled the values of their homes and their stock portfolios, but leaves their mortgages and credit card bills intact. This means they have a lot less wealth supporting the same pile of loans. But the deeper reason is psychological. The crash creates a kind of emotional trauma that impels them to pay off debt before they can think of borrowing again.[18]

Unfortunately, people busy paying down debt tend to spend very little, whereas the economy depends heavily on spending by consumers. Growth slows to a crawl, or worse. Moreover, this stinginess lasts until workers winnow their debt to a manageable level, a process that can drag on for years. In the case of Japan, whose real estate and stock markets collapsed in the early nineties, this took over a decade.[19] In early 2009, a little-noticed paper by economists at the San Francisco Fed suggested it could take nearly as long in the United States.[20] The only hope for speeding up the process would be if someone or something—say, the U.S. government—came along and wiped away a big chunk of consumers' debts. All those underwater mortgages would be a natural place to start.

Not every economist sympathetic to Koo agreed with every detail of his story. In principle, if the problem was too little wealth supporting too much debt, then you could also solve it by boosting wealth—that is, with policies aimed at driving up stock and housing prices, like low interest rates. Some economists put more emphasis on this as a possible solution. Others believed that people might spend a bit more than Koo assumed even while they paid off their debts. As evidence, they noted that the saving rate had leveled off between 5 and 6 percent in 2010 and 2011: high by recent historical standards, but not so ascetic as to be monklike.[21] Even so, by the summer of 2010, with spending weak and the saving rate more than twice its prerecession level, it wasn't hard to see that debt was a massive, lingering problem.

Larry Summers was familiar with Koo's work, and with similar

work by Carmen Reinhart and Ken Rogoff, two former IMF economists who'd studied the history of recessions following a financial
crisis.[22] Though Summers was among the fellow travelers who didn't
embrace the Koo doctrine in all its particulars, he was perhaps the
administration's biggest proponent of a more aggressive assault on
the housing morass—and, therefore, the last best hope for all the
Koovians kibitzing from the outside. Anytime a respected economist
penned an op-ed touting an ambitious housing plan, Summers would
dispatch an aide to get the writer on the phone. He would convene
the economic team members every two or three months to make sure
they hadn't overlooked a promising fix.

In the back of his mind, Summers couldn't shake the anxiety that
the only way to solve the problem once and for all was to bite the
bullet and spend $500 billion or $1 trillion bailing out homeowners.
But anytime such a plan came up, the defects became so glaring he
quickly thought better of it. There were, for one thing, the nagging
technical issues, which the op-ed writers invariably overlooked. Then
there was Treasury, which objected to any major course correction
because it believed that, with enough time, HAMP could eventually
solve the problem on its own. "Treasury was always claiming that,
with one more tweak, HAMP was going to start to move money in
substantial quantities," said a White House economic aide.

And, of course, there was the matter of the mind-blowing cost.
Austan Goolsbee, a Romer deputy who took the lead on housing,
just didn't see how the administration could pay what he believed
was a $750 billion price tag to fully address the problem. Even if you
forced the banks to eat half the losses themselves, that would leave
$375 billion, and in that case you might have a bunch of belly-up
banks on your hands, too.

This was a real concern. As it happened, though, there had been
a way to pay for a massive homeowner bailout. When the government took over the two mortgage-buying giants, Fannie Mae and

Freddie Mac, back in September 2008, it gave them each a $100 billion line of credit with the U.S. Treasury, which it could (and did) increase as it pleased. Using Fannie and Freddie, the government could in principle spend as much money as it wanted paying down Americans' mortgages.[23] Though this would have required the assent of the two agencies' independent regulator, the Federal Housing Finance Agency, the FHFA had been open to large-scale interventions through most of 2009.[24]

But in the end, there was no bailout, through Fannie and Freddie or any other channel. Nor was there much of any change of course when it came to housing. The administration was too worried about the dreadful politics—that those who hadn't made an ill-advised housing purchase would rightly protest about anything that looked like a bailout for those who had. Yet as terrible as a trillion-dollar housing bailout was politically, it wasn't as bad as 9 percent unemployment and a stagnant economy for the rest of the president's term.

On Tuesday, November 2, an ornery electorate tossed six Democrats from the Senate and sixty-three from the House of Representatives, snatching the Speaker's gavel from Nancy Pelosi and handing it to John Boehner. Boehner owed his speakership to the dozens of new representatives who'd drawn money and energy from the right-wing Tea Party movement, which denounced what it considered an explosion of government under Barack Obama.

By this point, however, liberal activists nearly matched the Tea Partiers on the right in their frustration with the president—a development that had memorably reared its head back in August, when White House press secretary Robert Gibbs derided the "professional left" for its persistent bellyaching. Now the West Wing, belatedly recognizing that liberal angst had hurt its cause by weighing down turnout in the midterms, was eager to avoid repeating the mistake. Three days after the election, it invited representatives of several dozen progressive groups to a White House conclave to remind them that "we love you, we've all got to work together," as one participant summed up the message.[25]

The only problem was that the mistake hadn't been corrected after all, at least judging from the demeanor of the aide who presided—a senior official named Tina Tchen. Tchen was then serving as the director of the White House Office of Public Engagement, meaning she'd had occasion to interact with key constituencies before. And yet one of the first comments out of her mouth was a warning that the meeting would have to move quickly, since there was another event scheduled in the same room for the top of the hour. "The White House is having a meeting with all its important allies, and the initial message is, 'We couldn't get a room for more than an hour,'" said the participant. "You've got to be shitting me."[26]

It wasn't just Tchen. Everyone from the president on down was out of sorts following the midterm massacre. Obama turned in a less than resolute performance at a press conference the following afternoon, lamenting that the pounding "feels bad," and wondering, "Could I have done something differently or done something more?"[27] Then he set off on a ten-day trip to Asia.

Shortly after the president left, Axelrod roused the ire of pretty much every Democratic voter in America when he hinted to a reporter about a retreat on the Bush tax cuts. This was to be the key debate of the so-called lame-duck period—in itself a consequence of administration dithering earlier in the year. But the White House seemed woefully unprepared to engage it.

Eventually, Obama and his top advisers greeted the defeat as a chance at a new start, beginning with personnel. Peter Orszag had already left over the summer, defeated by the twin frustrations of his protracted stalemate with Summers and his increasingly tense relations with the politicos in the West Wing. Christy Romer had been frustrated by the constant struggle to find her place on a team composed of Washington insiders. She, too, had partly worn out her welcome among the operatives, who considered her an overly shrill presence. "She went in and said, 'Well, maybe I should leave,'" said a White House colleague. "We said, 'Let's announce it.' . . . I think she ended up feeling pushed."[28] Romer left in September, having initially planned to stay through the end of the year.

Meanwhile, the top operatives were also rotating out. Despite intending to stay on as chief of staff until mid-2011, Rahm Emanuel decamped for Chicago to run for mayor in October, after the incumbent, Richard Daley, announced his retirement. He was followed by David Axelrod, who'd long intended to wrap up his White House tour after two years.

Larry Summers, for his part, had impressed no one with his skills as a policy broker. Instead, he had watched Geithner firm up his position as the administration's preeminent economic voice and found himself increasingly at the margins of internal debates. Particularly demoralizing was the outcome of the Volcker Rule, the ban on speculative trading at government-backed banks. Summers had opposed the idea along with Geithner, only to watch the Treasury secretary peel off in late 2009 and accommodate the president's political needs, to the everlasting gratitude of the West Wing.[29] By the summer of 2010, it was clear that the Republicans would retake one chamber of Congress, and he did not relish the looming face-off against them. The Fed chairmanship was out of Summers's reach and he had no higher job to aspire to, so the timing for his departure seemed right. He would leave in December 2010.

Though the president wouldn't decide on some of their replacements until January, there was one new hire that had been arranged well in advance. For as long as any White House staffer could remember, Obama had intended to enlist David Plouffe, his presidential campaign manager, as the chief White House strategist when Axelrod returned to Chicago. Once Obama began to revisit his 2008 campaign themes of transcending partisanship within a few weeks of the midterm election, it was a sign that Plouffe was already positioning him to work with the new Republican House, perhaps on a deal to deflate the ballooning budget deficit.

As in early 2009, the White House believed heading into 2011 that Republicans would have to meet the president halfway, albeit for different reasons this time around. Back then, it had been because the country had demanded "change" from Washington when it elected Barack Obama. Now, it was because the GOP shared a "responsibility" to govern. "[W]e're probably in a better position now than if we'd barely held control of the House," said one strategist close to the White House.[30]

And so, as with Tina Tchen's misbegotten efforts to bury the hatchet with liberals, it looked as if the strategic lessons of the first two years—not least the futility of earnestly courting Republicans—would go less than fully learned, at least by the person whose education mattered most.

By the time the White House turned to strategizing for the Bush tax cut showdown that began later in November, almost the entire political and economic team had concluded that the way to proceed was with an aggressive opening bid: say, insisting that the upper-income tax cuts expire while all the middle-class cuts stay in place. This would put pressure on Republicans and give Democrats leverage in striking the eventual deal. Only the president disagreed, opting to go straight to the negotiation without the political salesmanship beforehand. "His argument was, look, if we've already decided that we've got to get a deal—that we're not willing to [let taxes go up for everyone]—then we ought to actually try to engage in something serious," said a top White House aide.[31]

To their credit, Geithner, Sperling, and the rest of the administration's negotiators managed to extract key concessions from Republicans nonetheless, including a temporary payroll tax cut worth more than $100 billion over the following year and an extension of government benefits for the long-term unemployed. Still, these victories came at a bitter cost: not just the $60 billion for the upper-income Bush tax cuts over two years, but also $70 billion in cuts to the estate tax that only the country's millionaires and billionaires paid.

Against all evidence to the contrary, the president was still determined to show that Republicans could be reasoned with. It would be a troubling omen of things to come.

15

SNOOKERED

By January 2011, it had long been clear that Obama's reelection chances would hinge on the economy. The challenge for the West Wing was to determine which economic issue would loom larger: the trillion-dollar budget deficit or the stubbornly high unemployment rate.

The president's new political team concluded from the recent midterm elections that the deficit was the higher priority. Bill Daley, a former Commerce secretary and JP Morgan executive who had replaced Emanuel as chief of staff, considered the administration so out of touch with the public on matters of government spending that large cuts could only bring political benefits. "Part of the reason [Daley] took the job was that he felt an imperative to get the presidency back toward to the middle," said an administration colleague.[1]

David Plouffe, too, thought Obama needed to establish himself as a budget cutter to regain credibility with voters. The polls increasingly showed the deficit to be a major concern for independent voters, many of whom had soured on big-ticket spending items like the stimulus and health care reform. "Plouffe specifically said, 'We're going to need a period of ugliness'—he meant with the left—'so that people in the center understand that we're not wasting their tax dollars,'" one administration official said.[2]

Though the names had changed, the West Wing's preoccupation with the deficit was hardly new. In fact, it was almost as old as the administration itself. Since the spring of 2009, White House political aides like Rahm Emanuel and David Axelrod had worried that the deficit was repelling independent voters. "They [Emanuel and Axelrod] would be like, 'We've got to fucking do something on the deficit, we've got to fucking do something on the deficit,'" recalled one economic official.[3] The angst intensified in the fall of 2009, when Democrats lost governorships they'd controlled in Virginia and New Jersey. "After an election that demonstrates that the left-leaning thing isn't working so well, you respond," said the official.[4]

The lone force restraining this impulse back then was the economy, which wasn't yet strong enough to withstand deep cuts in government spending. But after the White House finagled some $200 billion to $250 billion of additional stimulus in exchange for extending the upper-income Bush tax cuts in December 2010, it felt confident that the recovery was finally irreversible. "Remember the holiday season—consumer spending was better than the year prior, there was reasonable hiring over Christmas. We kind of all thought we'd turned a corner," said a White House economic aide. "We thought the Bush tax cut [deal] pushed us over."[5]

Which meant the only questions to sort out for 2011 were tactical, and Plouffe and Daley settled them quickly. First, they decided, the White House would negotiate the long-overdue 2011 budget with Republicans in the House of Representatives, where Democrats had failed to pass a budget the previous fall. The newly elected Tea Partiers were demanding tens of billions of dollars in cuts, and the White House believed it could settle the impasse quickly by accepting a measure of austerity. Then it would turn to a much more consequential matter—the long-term deficit—and seek a deal with Republicans to cut trillions over the coming decade. Meanwhile, even as he sought to cut, the president would vow to protect the spending that mattered most for the long term: education, science research, infrastructure. "[Plouffe's] view was that you had to demonstrate you were willing to cut spending, live within your means" in order to invest later on, said one White House official.[6]

Within the White House, there was only one prominent dissenter from this plan: Gene Sperling, the successor to Larry Summers as director of the National Economic Council. Sperling believed the Republican demands for budget cuts were simply too extreme, and that the administration could win a public fight on the issue. While voters were telling pollsters they wanted the belt-tightening to begin straightaway, they typically lost their enthusiasm once you spelled out what that meant in terms of specific programs. Sperling favored a campaign that would spell it all out.

Sperling spoke with some authority, having worked as a top White House aide when Clinton had prevailed in his stand-off with Republicans. He was also the man most responsible for the biggest economic policy success of the last year: the $120 billion payroll tax cut Obama had won from Republicans in December. While Summers, Geithner, Romer, and Orszag had spent much of 2009 and 2010 feuding over the question of additional stimulus, Sperling was the one Obama official who'd gone out and made it happen.

But when it came to a showdown over spending cuts, Sperling encountered resistance from Plouffe and the political brass. They insisted the stakes were too small to launch a counteroffensive—would the public really get worked up over a few billion dollars here or there? They felt the president couldn't count on Senate Democrats, who would be skittish over their own reelection prospects. If nothing else, they hoped to ease away the president's partisan edges and dreaded a confrontation that would have the opposite effect. "In order to try to do everything he could to help the party in the election, the president got much more partisan, much more political, than he had been to date," said one White House aide. "So getting him back to first principles was an important thing." [7]

But, underlying it all, Plouffe waved off such pleas because, unlike Sperling, he didn't want a fight on spending. The whole idea was for Obama to join in the cutting so that Americans could see him hacking away at the wasteful underbrush. Then, as he turned to the longer-term deficit, the debate would no longer be about whether to cut—since the president had proved himself willing—but how: the president's judicious pruning versus the Republicans' indiscriminate slashing. " 'Cut and invest' versus 'cut everything,' " as the White House aide put it. [8] This was a debate the White House would be in a better position to win.

That was the theory, in any case. The reality turned out quite a bit different.

Far more so than Daley, whose role was more manager than grand strategist,* it was Plouffe who devised the White House master plan for 2011. Thanks to a new White House organization chart, Plouffe took over a number of functions that had sprawled across various nooks and crannies of the West Wing. Chief among them were all the communications operations, which had been fragmented among top aides like Robert Gibbs and Dan Pfeiffer during the first two years of the administration. Plouffe also took a much more direct interest than

---

*Daley had been relieved of his day-to-day management portfolio by November 2011. [9]

Axelrod, his predecessor, in outreach to liberal interest groups, which was officially run from Valerie Jarrett's public engagement operation.

Whereas the previous regime under Axelrod and Emanuel could change its focus every few days, Plouffe preferred to choreograph Obama's moves weeks in advance and stick with them no matter how great the temptation to shift course. "Pfeiffer, Axe, Gibbs—as much as they like to talk about strategy, they were still very much twenty-four-seven news-cycle guys," said an administration official. "Plouffe cultivates this aura of 'We can sacrifice a day or two [to win the larger battle].' It's much more Obama's style in terms of being cerebral, not excitable." [10]

The central question facing Plouffe was whether the playbook that had worked so well in 2008—selling Obama as a scrupulously nonpartisan problem-solver—was suited to a moment defined by 9 percent unemployment and Republican control of the House of Representatives. If so, the return to "first principles" could succeed. If not, the emphasis on deficits and independent voters would be disastrous.

On one level, it was hard to begrudge Plouffe his preoccupation with independents. He had long been attentive to their political sensibilities. His big break had come when he was twenty-eight: a New Jersey congressman named Bob Torricelli tapped him to manage his 1996 campaign for U.S. Senate. Running statewide in New Jersey is a daunting undertaking under any circumstances. Though the state isn't especially large, most of its voters watch television stations based in neighboring New York and Philadelphia, making it an outrageously expensive place to run ads. But Plouffe made it his top priority to reach the state's great mass of independent voters on television, and the strategy paid off. After polls showed the race close in the final weeks of the campaign, the congressman coasted to a ten-point victory. [11]

Still, as impressive as the win was, the race also revealed a confusion in Plouffe's thinking that would linger fifteen years later. After bringing on Plouffe to run the campaign, the candidate also enlisted the efforts of a prominent African-American political organizer named Regena Thomas to help court black voters. Three years earlier, the incumbent Democratic governor, Jim Florio, had lost reelection in one of the biggest upsets in state history, partly because he'd neglected the black vote. Torricelli wanted to avoid repeating Florio's fate.

Thomas planned to hire a group of recently unemployed cafeteria workers—SEIU Local 617—to fan out in heavily African-American neighborhoods, shaking hands, knocking on doors, and generally talking up Torricelli. But when she approached Plouffe to fund the effort, he was uninterested. He maintained that the race was all about "persuasion"—the term of art for focusing on swing voters rather than the most dependable partisans. Every few days Thomas would make her case again: "David, come on, I'm worth two to three points" on the final margin. The young manager stared back blankly. "Plouffe," she said. "We're watching Queen Latifah reruns. You're not buying ads on the stations that African-Americans watch." The manager's face barely twitched. Finally: "Since you're persuading, I need to persuade black people to come back to y'all," Thomas said. Plouffe let out a small chuckle, then went on about his business.

Plouffe seemed to divide up the electorate into "the base"—of which African-Americans were a key component, but which also included many unions, other minorities, and lower-income seniors—and independents, which included everyone else you might win. In his mind, there was little point worrying excessively about the base, since it would generally show up and vote Democratic regardless of how much attention the campaign paid it. In fact, funding such an effort was worse than useless; it was like throwing money down a sinkhole. The key was to marshal one's resources for the fight over less partisan voters.

Thomas eventually got her money by going over Plouffe's head to Torricelli's inner circle. "I am convinced Torricelli won because we were able to encourage African-Americans to come back," she said during an interview in 2008. But Plouffe never acknowledged that this had a meaningful impact on the race. "He had a plan and stuck with his plan," Thomas recalled. "He would say it was the plan" that cemented the victory.[12]

This theory of politics served Plouffe well enough in New Jersey, and later when he was the manager of Obama's presidential campaign: his attentiveness to voters who weren't loyal Democrats—young people, independents, even moderate Republicans—helped clinch the nomination over Hillary Clinton and win the general election. (The one exception in 2008 was black voters. Plouffe knew that, with an African-American candidate for president, this particular slice of the Democratic base would be a worthwhile investment and the campaign spent enormous sums turning it out.)

But at times Plouffe's preoccupation with independents and his skepticism toward the Democratic base overflowed into outright disdain for the party's traditional interest groups. "He didn't want to have a desk"—a formal outreach operation—"for every ethnic group," said one campaign colleague. "He had this thing: 'We're different.'"[13]

Plouffe even coined a name for the Democratic old guard when he'd had his fill of their unsolicited advice: "bed-wetters." The bed-wetters wanted Obama to focus on their own narrow constituency or pet issue; Plouffe wanted to run a campaign about sweeping themes like "change." The bed-wetters wanted Obama to spend more time in the usual battleground states—Ohio and Pennsylvania. Plouffe wanted to tip perennially Republican states like Indiana and North Carolina into the Obama column.

Plouffe was often proved right in these judgments. But his theory of independents—of who they were and how they voted—was flawed, a fact that became clear only in 2011. What Plouffe hadn't sufficiently appreciated is that most voters who claim to be independents aren't meaningfully different from other voters. They tend to be reliable Republicans and Democrats who simply prefer not to confess their party affiliation.[14] The upshot was that, two years into his presidency, Obama's trouble with many right-leaning independents was really the same problem he had with Republicans: though he'd won over many of them in 2008 because of their fatigue with George W. Bush, they were always likely to revert to partisan form once Bush faded from the scene.

By contrast, actual independents who swing back and forth between the two parties tend to be working-class whites, and they are far and away the most likely group of voters to base their vote on the economy above all else.[15] While these bona fide independents were indeed expressing frustration over the deficit, the stimulus, and health care reform, the biggest reason for their frustration was that none of these policies appeared to have helped the economy.[16] They didn't necessarily oppose the policies themselves.

In the same way, several polls after the 2010 midterm elections had shown that voters favored deficit reduction over government spending on jobs. But this meant only that they viewed government spending as ineffective, not that they considered the deficit more important than jobs, or even that they cared much about the deficit at all. A few days after the midterm elections a *CBS News/New York Times* poll asked voters which issue the new Congress should take up first. Fifty-six percent cited jobs and the economy. Only 4 percent volunteered the deficit.[17]

Plouffe had assumed that independents must be distinct from Democratic partisans in their concerns about the deficit: the partisans wanted to spend, whereas the independents wanted to cut. In fact, the independents who mattered most to Obama's political fate were just as concerned about the economy and jobs as traditional Democrats, if not more.

Even if cutting the deficit had been politically desirable, it was far from clear that accommodating the Republicans during the 2011 budget fight was the best way to go about it.

For one thing, the two sides began staggeringly far apart. The previous fall, after Democrats in the House had failed to pass a budget for 2011, they'd approved a series of temporary measures known as "continuing resolutions," which kept the government running until March 4 at 2010 levels of spending. Because the portion of the budget Congress controls—known as "discretionary spending"—tends to rise by billions of dollars each year, even this was effectively a cut. But with March 4 looming, the new Republican majority in the House insisted on cutting $60 billion more over a mere six months, something the Democrats considered outrageously stingy. The government faced a shutdown unless the two sides could reach agreement.

The first indication that the GOP had no interest in compromise came early in March, when Jack Lew, who had replaced Orszag as budget director, began to meet with House Republican appropriators to sort through the 2011 budget. Appropriators are the people who write the laws that fund government agencies. As such, they are normally the most pragmatic members of Congress. They have hundreds of billions of dollars to spend and not much time to spend it. Lew was a thirty-year veteran of budget stand-offs, having served as an aide to House Speaker "Tip" O'Neill in the 1980s and as Bill Clinton's budget director in the late 1990s. Even when the Republican Party was in the throes of one of its periodic conservative manias, he'd always found GOP appropriators to be levelheaded deal makers.

But now they were completely immovable. When Lew contacted Bob Inglee, the top Republican appropriations aide, to flesh out an understanding he'd reached with the GOP leadership, Inglee refused to budge from his party's official line of $60 billion in cuts. "It became much more challenging," recalled one person who participated in the discussions. "You'd go meet with the appropriators, and they would be more Catholic than the Pope." The appropriators knew their Tea Party brethren considered them ideologically suspect, and so they were determined to prove their mettle.[18]

The second sign came not long after. In order to keep the government running while Democrats and Republicans negotiated, Congress needed to pass two more short-term funding measures over the next few weeks. Such measures are normally routine affairs. But, in both cases, the Republicans demanded spending cuts as the price of approving the extension—the "toll road" approach, administration officials dubbed it. And yet even after Democrats paid the toll, fifty-four conservative House Republicans still refused to approve the second extension because they took a dim view of any deal Democrats might agree to.

The White House faced a choice. It could declare its differences with Republicans too big to bridge through negotiation and argue that the only way to resolve them was to shut the government down and let the public decide whom to blame. Or it could simply accept that the burden of compromising would fall almost entirely on Democrats. The administration chose the latter course. "The problem with the shutdown advocates is that you want to make sure you emerge in a stronger position, with an outcome that would not have been available but for the shutdown," Geithner later said in an interview. "It was hard to know with confidence."[19]

Republicans soon seized on this display of weakness. During a meeting between the two sides on March 22, GOP negotiators insisted on using their own budget, which featured $60 billion in cuts below the 2010 funding level, as the basis for the talks. The previous "baseline" had been the 2010 level itself, so this switch massively skewed the conversation in the Republicans' favor. Lew was so upset by this tactic that he abruptly ended the meeting.[20] But within a few days, Daley had essentially conceded the point to House Speaker John Boehner. In conversations with Boehner's staff, Daley offered to meet Republicans more than halfway, offering $33 billion in cuts.

This pattern repeated itself again and again. By Monday, April 4, the White House believed it had reached a deal with Boehner on the $33 billion figure. The next day, Boehner announced that $40 billion was the minimum he could accept. The president decided he could go $5 billion further. According to a strategy he and Lew had settled on at the outset of the negotiations, the extra savings would come from money that had been assigned to certain programs, like children's health insurance, but was unlikely to be spent in 2011. This would give Boehner a higher number to throw out to his fevered rank and file without squeezing the budget much harder.

By Thursday night, the White House believed it had a deal with Boehner for $38 billion in cuts. But Boehner kept issuing demands— many of them bizarrely off-point, such as depriving Planned Parenthood, the family planning services provider, of federal funds. It was only after the White House accepted a more modest ban on public funding for abortion in the District of Columbia that Boehner finally accepted. His Republican colleagues approved the deal late on the night of April 8, minutes before the looming government shutdown.

Privately, the White House congratulated itself on having bested Boehner with its wily budget maneuvering, which limited the effects of the cuts. "Boehner and his guys got snookered," said one White House aide. "We protected what we wanted to protect."[21]

But this reading of events missed the importance of what had happened. The White House had hoped to wrap up the unfinished 2011 budget quickly so it could move on to the long-term deficit and usher in a debate over who could cut *the smartest*. At that point, it assumed, the Democrats' approach—protecting investments in science, education, and infrastructure even as they cut the deficit—would compare favorably with the GOP's nihilism. Instead, Obama had stumbled into a quagmire of a debate over who could cut *the most*, which favored the GOP. It was the Republican obsession with cuts, cuts, and more cuts that now dominated the conversation in Washington. "Inside a few months, an ascendant Republican Party has managed to impose its small-government agenda on a town still largely controlled by Democrats," proclaimed *The Washington Post*.[22]

The president himself advanced this narrative when he hailed the agreement from the White House. While announcing that he'd pre-served the "investments we need to win the future," he twice made the peculiarly Republican-sounding claim to having secured "the largest annual spending cut in our history."[23]

With the 2011 budget finally on the books, Plouffe relished the chance to turn to the long-term deficit. Since the beginning of the year, the president had contemplated an ambitious deal—not just the usual nips and tucks, but one that took aim at his party's most sacred pro-grams: Medicare, Medicaid, and Social Security. Plouffe urged the president to give it a shot. "I said he [Obama] should be big on enti-tlements," Plouffe told one former administration official, by which he meant reining in these budgetary elephants.[24] Sure, this would enrage the party's base. But the political upside with the rest of the country would more than make up for it. In any case, the stubborn resistance to reforming Medicare and Social Security was just another instance of old-school special pleading. "Plouffe is pretty big on accomplish-ments trump normal politics," said one White House colleague. "Plouffe's view is that big trumps the little."[25]

The unknown variable was whether Republicans would make

the first move. The White House had been stung by the recent midterm campaign, when the GOP seized on cost savings in Obama's health care bill and labeled Democrats hostile to seniors. If the White House was going to propose far bigger cuts, it wanted to be sure it wasn't simply serving up fodder for future GOP attacks. "Our plan was always to roll out our deficit plan after [the 2011 budget fight] was over," said one White House aide. "The reason to wait was to let the Republicans go first. . . . Otherwise they'll just want to whale away on our thing." [26]

A few weeks before Obama and Boehner finalized their agreement on spending for 2011, Representative Paul Ryan of Wisconsin, the resident Republican sage on budgetary matters, made it known that he would soon release a ten-year, $4 trillion deficit-cutting proposal. The White House expected Ryan to tackle the big three entitlement programs and greeted his forthcoming plan as a major opportunity—the political cover it was looking for. Obama directed Sperling, his economic adviser, to begin drawing up an alternative to what Ryan was likely to propose.

Plouffe was feeling confident. He believed the budget negotiations in March and April had established a rapport between Obama and Boehner that could be leveraged into a long-term agreement. "A very important predicate has been made here that the speaker, the president, the vice president and the Senate majority leader can do business together," he told the *New York Times* the day after the two sides averted a government shutdown. "The trust was increased." [27]

But this judgment—really the basis for the entire forthcoming negotiation—was deeply misguided. In practice, it didn't matter whether or not the springtime negotiation had built trust between Boehner and Obama. Boehner presided over a roster of House members who subscribed to a radically antigovernment ideology and deemed even the smallest compromise with the president an act of betrayal. The question wasn't whether Obama and Boehner could do business. The question was whether Obama and the Tea Partiers could do business. And the answer to that was almost certainly no.

Even the Ryan plan had been a cause for concern in this respect. When the congressman finally unveiled it in early April, the details were immediately identifiable as right-wing lunacy. The way Ryan reduced the deficit was first to cut taxes for the wealthy by $2.4 trillion relative to the president's budget—which is to say, to *worsen* the deficit by that amount—and then cut spending by $6.2 trillion, so that the net effect was roughly $4 trillion in savings. From the perspective of lowering the deficit, it was as nonsensical as trying to get to Boston from New York by first driving south to Philadelphia. But Ryan was playing to conservative colleagues upset that the president was choking down only $38 billion in cuts for 2011. And, as a play for conservatives, it made perfect sense: Ryan was promising both $2 trillion more in tax cuts and $2 trillion more in spending cuts than anyone else in Washington was talking about.

The White House may have missed the significance of this pressure from the Tea Party, but Boehner and his aides lugged it around with them everywhere they went. After Rob Nabors, the White House congressional liaison, confronted Barry Jackson, Boehner's chief of staff, over the Republicans' insistence on Planned Parenthood restrictions, Jackson was utterly bereft. "Boehner could lose his speakership over Planned Parenthood," he moaned. To keep his job, Jackson said, Boehner needed some kind of abortion restriction as part of the final deal.

Perhaps if the president had stood up to the machete-wielding Republicans and rallied the public to his side, as Gene Sperling had recommended, he might have convinced them that their zealotry had a cost. Perhaps then they could have done business. But in his willingness to accept large cuts, Obama had only affirmed their conviction that they spoke for the country. He had allowed conservatives to conclude that, if anything, voters were demanding even deeper cuts. "While I respect that some of my Republican colleagues will ultimately support this spending deal, I believe voters are asking us to set our sights higher," said Representative Jim Jordan of Ohio, head of the House conservative faction, in explaining his vote against the Obama-Boehner package.[28]

Plouffe believed that the initial round of budget cutting had put Obama in a better position to hammer out a long-term deficit agreement. That was the thinking behind the entire White House strategy in March and April. Instead, the April 8 deal left House conservatives feeling even more righteous, more entitled, and more empowered than ever. As long as those feelings persisted, there would be no more bargains between Obama and Republicans, or at least none a Democrat could support.

16

THE WRONG WAR

The president planned to unfurl his vision for cutting the deficit in a speech at George Washington University on April 13, 2011. For several weeks leading up to the speech, the economic team met almost daily in Gene Sperling's office to hash out the details. Among the key questions were what to do about Medicare and Medicaid, the government health insurance programs for the elderly and the poor, which top officials like Lew and Geithner favored streamlining.

Medicare and Medicaid loomed large for Geithner because they created most of the government's cash flow problems in the coming decades. It would be hard to take seriously any deficit plan that didn't cut them. But, especially given their sacred status within the party, a Democrat who proposed such cuts would win needed credibility in the financial markets.

To Geithner, credibility was king. He believed that the deficit piling up over the coming decade—mostly the work of a deep recession and various Bush-era policies, like tax cuts, a Medicare prescription drug benefit, and two expensive wars—posed risks to the economy. Without a credible plan to narrow it, investors might start to doubt that the government would repay its debts, in which case they would dump their holdings of U.S. bonds and send interest rates into the stratosphere. He felt that Democrats in Congress and some of his administration colleagues were irresponsible in trying to keep spending levels high, even though the increase was supposed to be temporary under emergency programs like the stimulus. "We just had the worst crisis," he would say. "Things are hard after crises."

But to Geithner, Medicare and Medicaid were even more important than such shorter-term spending: even if you generally preferred to reduce the deficit through tax increases rather than spending cuts, you couldn't raise taxes enough to pay for all the government's commitments under these programs. They would have to be scaled back.

Nevertheless, the idea of cuts to Medicaid and Medicare encountered internal resistance. The leader of the rejectionist faction was the head of the White House health care office, Jeanne Lambrew, who argued that cutting the iconic programs was not just overly punitive; it would also cede a political issue that had boosted the party's standing among seniors for decades—no small point given that the aging baby boomers were swelling the ranks of the country's elderly voters. When Sperling asked Lambrew to array the proposals for major cuts to Medicare and Medicaid from most to least acceptable, Lambrew protested that the president had just made cuts to Medicare while enacting health care reform two years earlier. Now wasn't the time to revisit the issue, she felt.

But the order had come from the president, and Lambrew grudgingly assented. Eventually, Sperling and his deputy, Jason Furman, collected the proposals and presented them to Obama and his senior political advisers: Plouffe, Daley, and deputy chief of staff Nancy Ann DeParle. DeParle had preceded Lambrew as head of the White House health care office before becoming Daley's deputy. Like Lambrew, she was concerned about ceding too much ground on Medicare. But she accepted the Geithner-Lew view that the administration had to propose *something* on this front, and eventually endorsed a compromise: The president would commit to a total of $500 billion in savings, but without releasing specific proposals for how to achieve them.[1] (The two programs cost the federal government just over $750 billion in 2010.)

When it came to the overall amount of deficit reduction to aim for, there was less disagreement. The day that Sperling convened the economic team to discuss the matter, everyone in the room immediately agreed that $4 trillion was the "gold standard," as several participants recalled—the number bandied about by every budget-monger in Washington's deficit-industrial complex. Four trillion dollars was roughly the amount of savings it would take to stabilize the government's debt as a share of the economy.[2]

The only real debate was over how quickly to arrive at that goal. Geithner favored achieving it in ten years. Sperling felt that paring the deficit so quickly would put too much pressure on core Democratic programs. He and Bruce Reed, the vice president's chief of staff, proposed aiming for thirteen or fourteen years instead. Both men had been top advisers to Bill Clinton when he sparred with the Republican Congress in the mid-nineties. They remembered how well Clinton had been served by proposing a ten-year timetable to balance the budget when the GOP insisted on seven.

On one level, the Sperling-Reed approach was encouraging, a more humane alternative to Geithner's schedule. And yet the exercise was still misguided. Implicit in Geithner's theory of postcrisis retrenchment was that the crisis had actually passed. But, at the time, the economy was growing at a rate of less than 1 percent per year—

perilously close to recession territory. As a matter of economics, the administration was adopting precisely the wrong approach, whether it favored cutting trillions over ten years or fourteen.

In fairness, Geithner preferred that most of the cuts take place during the second half of the decade, when the economy might be stronger. But the economy was so weak in early 2011 that it needed active government support, not just a reprieve from harsh cuts. As the Nobel Prize–winning economist Joseph Stiglitz pointed out, even announcing future cuts to Medicare and Medicaid can hurt the economy immediately by prompting the poor and middle class to spend less in anticipation of a costlier retirement.[3]

Several days before the George Washington University speech, the economic team met with the president in the White House to finalize the details of its plan. The crucial question of the time-table was still unresolved, and so Sperling ran through the options. "Mr. President, there's no way consistent with your values that we can do $4 trillion over ten years," he said when he'd finished. "But you could do it easily over fourteen. And we should be able to get there in thirteen." The president took it all in. Though he'd entered office with an activist agenda, he had always been a deficit hawk at heart. Now, he felt, it was time to put the budget back on solid foot-ing. When he finally spoke, he said he liked the idea of extending the time horizon, but that thirteen or fourteen years was simply too long. "Try harder," he instructed his aides. Then, with his trademark clipped tone: "Get there in twelve."

In retrospect, then, the White House had made a variety of mistakes heading into the spring of 2011. It had based its strategy for the year on the political and economic imperative to cut the deficit, when in fact the imperative was to boost the economy. It had passively ac-cepted large cuts to the 2011 budget believing they would help the president's deficit-cutting credibility with voters, when in fact these cuts only emboldened the GOP to seek even larger cuts later on. And it had opened the door to scaling back Medicare and Medicaid in a way that could undermine the traditional Democratic political advantage on these programs while further weakening the economy in the short term.

Many of these decisions were defensible at the moment they were made. It had been far from clear in early 2011 that the economy was still so weak. The Republicans' determination to shrink the government seemed almost impossible to withstand following the party's landslide victory in November 2010. At the same time, elite opinion had congealed around the urgency of lopping trillions off the deficit. After a commission of presidential appointees had released recommendations for reducing the deficit, the columnists and cable chatterers questioned Obama's seriousness for not instantly adopting its recommendations.

But there was one last mistake that was harder to forgive. It had to do with the debt ceiling, an obscure procedural hurdle the White House would soon have to clear.

The debt ceiling is a cap on the total amount of debt the federal government can run up at any given time, a legal anachronism that dates back to World War I. For decades, raising the ceiling had been an unappetizing and occasionally contentious chore. But the majority party in Congress generally herded up the votes without too much suspense in the end. In late 1995, perhaps the most famous earlier episode, House Republicans vowed to block the debt-limit increase, effectively threatening to either default on the debt or defund the government unless Bill Clinton negotiated over their plan to balance the budget by cutting Medicare and Medicaid.[4] They also tried to extract social policy concessions, like limiting death-row appeals. But Clinton rejected the link between the debt ceiling and these other issues, and the Republicans eventually backed down.

In late 2010, the importance of raising the debt ceiling was little understood outside a few rarefied precincts of Washington. Fortunately for the Obama administration, one of those precincts was the Treasury Department, where Geithner's chief of staff, Mark Patterson, was a veteran of past debt ceiling fights thanks to his former life as a Senate aide. In the weeks after the midterm elections, Patterson worried that the incoming Tea Partiers would issue threats similar to those of their predecessors in the mid-nineties, only they'd be even less prone to backing down. Many had campaigned on their opposition to raising the limit. And while most economists believed that hitting the debt ceiling could trigger a run on U.S. Treasury bonds by raising doubts about the government's creditworthiness, the Tea Partiers blithely asserted that refusing to raise the debt ceiling would simply force Congress to spend less money, a desirable outcome from their perspective.

Patterson thought the administration should try to defuse the debt-limit issue once and for all as part of its year-end compromise with Republicans over the Bush tax cuts. He drafted a law giving the president the authority to raise the debt ceiling unilaterally and sent it to the White House. To sell it politically, the president could simply explain that renewing the upper-income tax cuts, as Republicans were demanding, would cost the government $700 billion over ten years, forcing it to take on more debt and hit the debt ceiling sooner. One Treasury aide recalled: "Imagine the alternative reality where the president comes out in December and says, 'I understand you want to increase the high-end tax cuts. But that will make the deficit go up. . . . I am willing to do some of what you want to do, but you have to pay for it by raising the debt ceiling.'"[5]

The White House was interested, but dropped the idea once Republicans made clear they wouldn't part with their debt-ceiling fantasies before the Tea Partiers even took office.[6] In any case, the president's aides doubted that the House and Senate could get much done during the late-fall lame-duck session. "They're just going to come in and check their mail," was the popular refrain around the West Wing, which chose to prioritize a deal on the expiring Bush tax cuts instead. Still, there was another explanation at work: the White House simply didn't have the appetite for going to war so soon after its midterm rout. "The feeling [at the White House] was, 'Let's go home, lick our wounds, sort it out.' There wasn't a lot of fight in folks," said the Treasury aide. "We [at Treasury] were a little bit obsessed. They were, 'Yeah, yeah, yeah, we'll deal with it later.'" [7]

By January 2011, the drawbacks of this posture were becoming clear. As Patterson had feared, the Republicans began to claim they would raise the debt ceiling only if Democrats agreed to cut trillions from the deficit—essentially threatening the country with financial collapse unless they got their way on the budget. The proper way to deal with such a threat is simply to refuse to negotiate under duress, and for a few months the White House gamely toed this line. It insisted that Congress send it a "clean" debt ceiling increase unconnected to budget cuts. But the effort was halfhearted: the White House wanted to strike a deficit deal, too, after all. And, as Daley argued, it was hard to believe wealthy Republican donors on Wall Street would let the party seriously threaten financial turmoil. Meanwhile, even some conservative Democrats in Congress agreed that spending cuts should accompany any increase in the debt ceiling, making the White House position harder to defend.

Nonetheless, Treasury pleaded with the White House to hold the line. It worried that Daley was overstating the corporate world's power over conservative Republicans. "I would note with some degree of respect that Mr. Daley's estimation of the politics of the business community and the GOP were not spot on," said a second Treasury official.[8] But the White House dismissed the Treasury view as naive. "It was clear that we couldn't hold Democrats on the Hill for a clean debt ceiling [vote]. We couldn't win the argument with the public," said a White House official. "It was more, 'How long do we act is if it could happen?' And we knew that we'd be in a stronger position in the debate if we were debating how to reduce the debt."[9] In mid-April, the White House folded on the clean debt-limit increase, as Plouffe publicly said deficit reduction could be a part of the deal.[10] (Ironically, public opinion on the debt ceiling would later shift dramatically in the direction of raising it.)

Obama had not only entered into an ill-advised negotiation. Thanks to the risk of default now hanging over his head, he'd entered into an ill-advised negotiation with zero leverage.

Fortunately, as of April, there was still a way out before taking the final, fateful turn into an economic dead end. The White House could have shelved the idea of earnestly engaging with Republicans to reach a big deal and instead assailed them over their maximalist demands.

Within the White House, there was anxiety that the president's deficit plan was too reasonable. The Republican proposal—the extreme right-wing Ryan plan—was a classic opening bid, leaving ample room for concessions. But the White House had started substantively where it basically hoped to end up. It proposed to hit the $4 trillion deficit reduction target with roughly $3 in spending cuts for every $1 of tax increases, a heavy tilt in the direction of smaller government. The $500 billion in cuts to Medicare and Medicaid would be especially hard for liberals to swallow.

To compensate for this imbalance, the president and his advisers decided they had to be blistering in their criticism of Ryan. Otherwise, both left and right would assume they intended to compromise even further. "The entire economic team was of the view that [the president] had to be pretty tough at a more values level," recalled one economic aide. "We were now making a decision to go pretty close to the center [substantively]. . . . We had to convince both our side and their side this was our position, that we were not going to split the difference." [11]

When Obama stepped to the podium at George Washington University to give his address, he was uncharacteristically withering. The Republican plan "paints a vision of our future that's deeply pessimistic . . . a vision that says up to 50 million Americans have to lose their health insurance in order for us to reduce the deficit," he said. "I don't think there's anything courageous about asking for sacrifice from those who can least afford it." [12]

The speech could have served as the opening shot in a communications offensive against the Republicans. In fact, the White House had readied plans for hammering away at each galling detail of Ryan's proposal. There were plans to highlight the way Ryan would force retirees to pay $6,000 more per year for their Medicare benefits by 2022, and to point out how this would require the average senior to come up with some $200,000 more in retirement. The Ryan plan also cut trillions in taxes for the affluent as it slashed benefits for middle-income seniors. The administration intended to show how this would shower billions of dollars on the country's four hundred wealthiest people, who'd already seen their tax rates fall dramatically the previous decade. To illustrate these points, the White House had even filmed a series of "White Board" videos featuring Austan Goolsbee, who now chaired the Council of Economic Advisers, and whose lucid monologues on economic policy had won widespread media attention.

The upshot of this campaign would have been two possible scenarios: Either it would have sabotaged the negotiations over a grand bargain and set the stage for a much smaller deficit deal. The White House could have then delegated these negotiations to Democrats in Congress while the president went out and talked about jobs and the economy. Or it would have struck fear into the hearts of the suddenly exposed Republicans, giving the administration some badly needed leverage. But shortly after the president's speech, the White House unilaterally disarmed. There would be no hearts-and-minds campaign while the negotiators huddled around their conference tables.

The order to stand down came directly from Biden, Geithner, Lew, Sperling, and Reed—the administration envoys to the deficit talks that began in early May with Eric Cantor and Jon Kyl, the second-ranking Republicans in the House and Senate. When Biden and the rest of the group trooped back from their first few meetings, they were convinced they had a chance at success. Cantor in particular was serious, pragmatic, and strikingly well prepared. "The view from the negotiators in the room was that publicly attacking the Republicans would blow up the negotiations," recalled one White House colleague. "They thought the negotiations were going well. No one was leaking out details to the press. They thought they could do it." [13]

Jack Lew, Gene Sperling, and Bruce Reed were the three members of the Obama economic team most thoroughly steeped in the ways of Washington. All three had served for eight years in the Clinton administration: Lew toiled as deputy budget director, then took over the agency's top job; Sperling had a similar trajectory at the NEC, as did Reed at Clinton's Domestic Policy Council. Throughout 1997, while Summers, Geithner, and Rubin circled the globe dousing the flames of one foreign crisis or another, Lew and Sperling were seated side by side in some caucus room on Capitol Hill, haggling over budget details with Congression Republicans. Reed swooped in at the end of those dealings to manage the implications for welfare reform, one of his pet issues.

Whereas Summers spent much of the Bush administration at Harvard, and Geithner running the New York Fed, Sperling and

Reed stayed put in Washington. Reed became head of the Democratic Leadership Council, the centrist policy group. Sperling secured a perch pondering domestic policy at a succession of Washington think tanks—the Brookings Institution, the Center for American Progress, the DC Council on Foreign Relations. (Even his big payday, nearly a million dollars from Goldman Sachs, came from designing a philanthropic education program.) Mostly, the two former Clinton hands spent their days advising Democratic politicians and producing book-length policy manifestos with titles like "The Pro-Growth Progressive" (Sperling) and "The Plan: Big Idea for America" (Reed). Even Lew, who joined Rubin at Citigroup in 2006, never quite shed his Washington habits long enough to assimilate on Wall Street. "He was not commercial," said one former Citi colleague, using the Wall Street term of art for "business-minded." "You'd trust him with your life, but he was not commercial." [14]

Heading into the confrontation with Republicans in 2011, these extensive Washington résumés—and especially the experience of the mid-nineties—informed the three men's judgment in ways large and small. In the nineties, for example, they'd learned the art of conceding an imposing-sounding budget cut while rigging the details to be much more forgiving, a skill Lew deployed during the budget showdown of March and April 2011. More broadly, they'd learned that if you wanted to win a budget stand-off with Republicans, you couldn't ignore their demands. You had to produce a kinder, gentler, Democratic alternative. "If Clinton's reaction to Republican plans to balance the budget had just been, 'No, we can't do it,'" said one Clinton veteran working for Obama, "he never would have won the argument. . . . Our own side would have attacked us for not being serious."

As much as they invoked the nineties, they weren't prisoners of the experience. They were quick to recognize differences between the modern-day Tea Partiers and their antecedents in Newt Gingrich's Republican revolution. "We never had a doubt with Gingrich and company that if we reached agreement with [them], we could make it stick," said this person. "These guys [Cantor and Boehner] were—I'm not faulting them—too new to the jobs to have proved that." [15]

Still, the nineties had left them with a basic optimism that a deal was at least possible. They remembered the way John Kasich, the Budget Committee chairman under Gingrich, had come off like a Neanderthal in public but became eminently reasonable behind closed doors. It didn't seem like a stretch to see Eric Cantor playing the same role. "We believed that it was ultimately in any elected official's interest to solve problems rather than fail at solving them," said the Clinton veteran. "The experience we had with the Republican Congress in the mid-nineties was that they came in and didn't want to reach agreement. But by mid-1996 they were pleading with us to agree with them on something." [16] Even then, it had taken another full year to consummate the agreement, and the press remained dismissive until the end. But the deal had gotten done.

In itself, this optimism was a highly attractive quality—what president wouldn't want his aides to believe they can succeed against long odds, after all? In this case, though, it blinded the group to another key difference between the 1990s and the present. In 1995, the economy was accelerating. The country could afford a two-and-a-half-year debate over the deficit. In fact, the longer the debate went on, the easier it became to balance the budget. The economy was producing so much tax revenue that the budget was on track to balance itself without sacrifice from either side. [17] (The eventual deal called for balancing the budget over five years; it ended up balanced the very next year.)

In 2011, on the other hand, the economy was distressingly fragile. Cutting the deficit would require brutal concessions, and the country couldn't afford a prolonged debate over how many each side would accept.

· · ·

The negotiations between the administration and the Republicans formally began on May 5, 2011. By early June, the group had reached provisional agreement on over $1 trillion in cuts, and the Obama contingent had begun to believe a much larger deal was in sight. Such a deal, they assumed, would involve cuts to Medicare and an end to a few narrow tax breaks, like those benefiting oil companies and corporate jet owners.

Around this time, the president convened a meeting to be briefed on the talks' progress. The negotiating team was in good spirits. "Biden and Sperling and Lew were pretty enthusiastic about where this is going," said one White House official in attendance.[18] They wanted to know how far the president was authorizing them to go now that they were treading into the most sensitive terrain.

The president turned to Nancy Ann DeParle, the health care expert who was his deputy chief of staff, and asked how much the proposed Medicare cuts would cost the average senior affected by them. DeParle said it would mean an increase of a few hundred dollars each year. The president then asked his negotiators what someone in his income bracket would have to fork over in tax increases as a result of the deal they were working on. "The answer was nothing," said the White House official. "Unless you own a corporate jet or you're an oil company, you're not going to have to pay anything more."[19]

The president frowned. "How can I ask seniors to pay $500 more and I don't have to pay a nickel? I can't do that." He told the group to return to the bargaining table and insist on more sacrifice from the wealthy.

The problem was that the team was actually presenting an optimistic view of what was possible—what it had assumed would be the *best-case* scenario. They hadn't yet broached the idea of ending tax breaks of any kind with Cantor and Kyl, and the two Republicans certainly hadn't said they would be open to raising taxes at any point during the negotiations. At the beginning of each meeting since May 5, the vice president had made a habit of stating—in his clearest Scranton, Pennsylvania, locution—that there would be no deal unless the Republicans accepted tax hikes. But Cantor and Kyl never signed off on this, even in principle. "They understood we were proceeding on the assumption that we'd have a balanced package," said one person in the room. "But they never conceded the point." [20] And considering that the Republicans were willing to breach the debt ceiling, a prospect that terrified the White House, it was hard to see why they ever would concede it.

The third group at the negotiating table was a four-man detachment of congressional Democrats, who would have to sell their colleagues in the House and Senate on whatever deal emerged. These were men acutely aware of the backlash any Democratic representative or senator would court by even contemplating Medicare cuts. As the conversation drifted in this direction, they became adamant that it was time to discuss tax increases. "Medicare beneficiaries have a median income of $23,000 a year," one of the Democrats told Cantor and Kyl. "Why should we be engaged in a conversation asking them to pay more unless you're talking about closing corporate tax loopholes and special breaks for corporate jets?"

At this, Cantor and Kyl became visibly flustered, according to several observers. They groused that it would be far more productive to stay focused on the spending cuts all sides could support, at least in theory, rather than get bogged down talking tax increases, which the Republicans opposed. Their strategy, the Democrats eventually concluded, was to resist tax increases and simply pocket whatever spending cuts everyone in the room would accept.

"Let me get this right," Kyl finally said to Lew and Sperling as the discussion became tense. "You're saying there are Medicare savings you think would be good policy. But you won't do them unless we agree to raise taxes?" Lew and Sperling looked back at him stone-faced and simply said: "Yes." A few days later, on June 23, Cantor and Kyl withdrew from the negotiations.

Even as Biden and his team tried against all hope to squeeze money out of the Republicans, the president was steadily losing interest in their work. The most optimistic outcome for the Biden talks involved reducing the deficit by just over $2 trillion. But as the president saw it, there was no percentage for him in this sort of mid-range deal, assuming it could even be achieved. The left would kvetch about even the smallest cuts to Medicare. The right would scream about modest tax increases. And no one in the middle would think Democrats and Republicans had done much of consequence to tamp down the deficit. "The middle deal does not work politically," said one White House official, channeling the president's thinking. "It's not worth the political cost to dip your toe into entitlements and revenue if you're not going to do something big." [21]

For Obama, of course, the presidency had always been about big achievements. He'd entered office with ambitious plans to reform health care and stop global warming. Now all anyone could talk about was cutting spending. Well, he figured, as long as you're taking on spending, you might as well do that ambitiously, too.

And so, in late June, a few days after the two men met for a much-hyped bipartisan golf game, the president opened a back channel with House Speaker John Boehner to sniff around the edges of a so-called grand bargain that would save $4 trillion. Obama said he could entertain serious cuts to Medicare and Social Security; Boehner said he might be able to come up with $800 billion in revenue in return. The president had Lew and Nabors meet with Boehner's staff, which offered to produce the money either by reforming the tax code or, failing that, by canceling the Bush tax cuts for the highest income earners—the same tax cuts Obama had failed to bury the previous December.

The offer notwithstanding, Republicans' opposition to tax increases was so ironclad it was hard to believe they'd go along in the end, even for the sake of hacking away at the welfare state. But Team Obama believed there were reasons to take the offer seriously. The biggest was the GOP's sudden angst over its political vulnerability on Medicare. In May, the Democrats had won a special election in a safely Republican district of upstate New York. The winning candidate had tied her opponent to Paul Ryan's plan for dismantling the program, which the Republican House had approved several weeks earlier. Now Republican senators were concerned that the Ryan plan could wipe them out in 2012 unless they did something to defuse future Democratic attacks. That something looked increasingly like a deal in which Democrats also agreed to Medicare cuts, thereby neutralizing the issue. "We knew as soon as we heard the [special election] results that Republicans would be more eager for a deal," said one White House official. "Every conversation we had [with Republicans] confirmed that." [22]

Meanwhile, even though the Biden talks had broken down, it was possible to view them hopefully. Biden himself had always believed the point was to resolve whatever could be resolved, then hand the work-in-progress to Obama and Boehner. It would be up to the two leading men to settle the hardest questions—entitlements and taxes—and ink a final deal. One participant summarized the strategy as follows: "Build trust by getting accomplishments on what you can agree to and put off the hard things till the end." [23] The feeling was that trust had manifestly been built.

Before long, Lew and Nabors briefed the rest of the economic team on Boehner's offer. The downside was that the $800 billion was money Obama could get in principle even without a deal. All of the Bush tax cuts were scheduled to expire in 2013. Assuming he was reelected, Obama could simply veto any extension for the affluent. The deal also put almost four times as much of the burden for narrowing the deficit on spending cuts as it did on tax increases. To the average Democrat, it would sound very far from "balanced," in the vernacular of the moment. Nonetheless, Geithner, Sperling, and Bruce Reed agreed that the deal would be worth doing. The White House staff began to negotiate with Boehner's office.

For the entire month that followed, the two sides went back and forth at frequent intervals. But while the buzz of activity mimicked a high-stakes negotiation, there was never anything to show for it. At one point, over the Fourth of July weekend, the president called back his entire economic team from vacation because it looked as if the talks were ripening. But by the following weekend, after Boehner had sent the White House a detailed list of negotiating principles and the White House had sent back its own "paper"—a key step that would open the door to the actual horse trading—Boehner's office went silent with no explanation. The White House only learned Boehner was bowing out of the talks as Boehner was issuing a press release.

A week later, Boehner returned to the bargaining table, this time with Cantor at his right flank. A week after that, both men were gone, again with no explanation. Sperling began cracking that he "wouldn't want to date these guys. They don't say, 'We're having problems, can we take a break, see other people?' They just leave."

To his credit, Obama finally dispensed with the caution of his economic advisers and shed his reluctance to call out his negotiating partners. He spent much of July criticizing Republicans for their aversion to "shared sacrifice." Obama's tough stance helped shift public opinion in his direction, but the Republican position had long since hardened. By late July, it was blindingly obvious that Boehner was simply incapable of bringing his party with him on any deal involving taxes, however minuscule the amount. The GOP leaders may have feared their vulnerability on Medicare, but not as much as they feared crossing the most rabid antitax jihadis in the Conservative political establishment, to say nothing of their own restive rank and file in the House. The two sides may have built the trust they needed to agree to spending cuts, but getting the GOP to raise taxes by more than a token amount wasn't a matter of trust. It was a matter of freeing a party from the grip of ideological fanaticism, which is not the sort of thing that happens over coffee in a Senate meeting room. And, finally, even if Boehner could somehow persuade his troops to trade tax increases for Medicare cuts, winning their blessing for making the deal with Barack Obama, whom they regarded as a socialist menace, was another matter entirely.

In retrospect, the encouraging signs from the Biden-Cantor talks weren't actually that encouraging. "We began by talking about specific [spending] cuts," said one person involved. "And so it wasn't surprising that Republicans were willing to engage. I don't know why they [the White House] concluded that was an indication we were going to get a deal." [24] In fact, Cantor and Kyl had made it abundantly clear that they would *not* be raising taxes. The White House just hadn't entirely believed them.

Under normal circumstances, the logical response to a negotiation in which one's counterpart walks away from increasingly attractive offers is simply to give up. Alas, this was no longer an option by late July 2011. At the time, there were less than two weeks before the government's mounting pile of IOUs ran smack into the debt ceiling, potentially triggering a global financial calamity. After three and a half months of largely fruitless negotiation, the White House still had to reach agreement with the Republican House.

Not surprisingly, given that Obama was determined to avoid a debt ceiling catastrophe while many Republicans believed hitting the limit might actually do the country some good—it might be akin to depriving a compulsive shopper of his or her credit card—the eventual deal skewed heavily toward Republican priorities. It cut $900 billion over a decade from the pot of money Congress doles out each year and instructed a special "supercommittee" of congressmen and senators, the Joint Select Committee on Deficit Reduction, to find at least $1.2 trillion more in cuts. Were the committee to fail at this task, then the deal called for automatic cuts totaling $1.2 trillion over a decade, with roughly half to come from defense spending and half from domestic programs, including Medicare. The deal raised not a cent of taxes.

In effect, the Republicans had maneuvered Obama into a position in which he granted them a large concession (raising the debt ceiling, which became necessary thanks to the Bush tax cuts they insisted on extending). In return for allowing Obama to grant them this concession, they demanded many more concessions—in the form of large cuts to spending.[25] If it weren't so tragic, it might be an entertaining plot for a David Mamet movie.

The irony is that, had the Obama administration not been so preoccupied with striking a grand bargain, it might have negotiated a better deal, and months earlier. Cantor had repeatedly suggested he would be open to inking a "cuts-only" deal in the neighborhood of $2 trillion, while throwing in some economic stimulus that Democrats favored, like extending the temporary payroll tax cut through the end of 2012. The Cantor deal wasn't great on its own terms. But it was preferable to the eventual agreement.

Instead, the president and his economic team spent another two months chasing a deal premised on tax increases that the Republicans were never going to accept. In the meantime, the economy continued to limp along, creating a mere 20,000 jobs in June and just over 100,000 in July—barely enough to hold the unemployment rate steady as the population grows.

Worse, in trying to lay the groundwork for a deficit deal, the president primed the country with rhetoric that made it much harder to return to the jobs crisis. "Now every family knows that a little credit card debt is manageable," Obama said in a speech in late July. "But if we stay on the current path, our growing debt could cost us jobs and do serious damage to the economy."[26] In fact, the opposite was the case. It was the failure to spend more money in the short term that was costing jobs and damaging the economy. By agreeing that deficits were the biggest threat to the economy, the president lent credence to the fallacious argument that cutting breeds prosperity, which Republicans wielded against his efforts to secure more stimulus. (The IMF, among other authorities, has found that a country facing similar circumstances will only sabotage its economy, at least in the short term, by cutting government spending.)[27]

On Friday, August 5, 2011, Standard & Poor's downgraded U.S. government debt from triple-A to double-A plus, having been proved right in its April prediction that Democrats and Republicans would be unable to agree to $4 trillion in budget savings. When the bell rang on Wall Street the following Monday, August 8, the Dow Jones plunged 634 points, capping off two weeks of harrowing losses.

At first blush, the stock market bloodletting seemed to vindicate the scolds inside and outside the administration who'd warned that the untamed deficit would one day precipitate an economic crisis. But, upon closer examination, the markets were sending precisely the opposite message. While stock prices tumbled, interest rates on U.S. bonds began to drop as well. They kept dropping until they reached record lows. The most plausible interpretation of these two figures, as the economist Paul Krugman pointed out,[28] was that investors craved the safety and security of U.S. debt (hence falling interest rates) because they feared another bout of deep economic malaise (hence the stock market declines).

EPILOGUE

It wasn't lost on Team Obama that the economy was wilting during the spring and summer of 2011. At a retreat with senior White House personnel in June 2011, chief of staff Bill Daley gave Gene Sperling an hour longer to brief the group than he gave Tom Donilon, the national security adviser, because the circumstances looked so dire. Thereafter, the march of lousy data was a constant anxiety on Pennsylvania Avenue. By the time the debt ceiling negotiations reached their messy climax the following month, the president was well aware that he'd have to refocus on jobs and growth, if for no other reason than to persuade Americans he wasn't out of touch.

The semiofficial return to those nagging questions came in early August, when Sperling showed Obama a plan to renew the payroll tax cut Congress had okayed the previous December. Only this time the tax cut would be larger, and it would benefit both workers *and* their employers, who shoulder half the tax burden. The plan also included at least $50 billion of spending on crumbling roads and bridges and tens of billions of dollars to create jobs and ease financial hardship for the long-term unemployed.

Obama was supportive but somewhat underwhelmed. For two and a half years he'd been hatching proposals with an eye toward winning over the opposition, beginning with the first stimulus in 2009 (which included hundreds of billions of dollars in tax cuts), continuing through the late summer of 2010 (when he'd touted a number of business tax credits), and culminating with his deficit-cutting offers to the House GOP the previous month. In most cases, all it had gotten him was even more extreme demands from Republicans and not an ounce of bipartisan support. Now, after the final searing experience of the deficit deal gone bad, he still wanted reasonable, centrist policies. But he was done trying to fit them to the ever-shifting conservative zeitgeist. He told his aides not to "self-edit" so as to improve the measure's chances of passing the Republican House of Representatives. "He pushed us to make sure this was not simply a predesigned legislative compromise," one recalled.[1]

Sperling and his colleagues took the directive to heart, and by the end of the month had come up with another $100 billion worth of ideas, including $35 billion to help states pay the salaries of teachers, the police, and firefighters. The sum total of all the proposals now ran to $450 billion, and many of the political operatives worried that the sheer size of the package would be a liability. The cost was more than half the original 2009 stimulus bill, which Republicans gleefully derided as a bloated boondoggle.

The politicos urged the wonks to scale back the price tag toward $350 billion. But on September 2, the Labor Department reported that the economy added no new jobs in August. Sperling, who had been the internal voice of policy ambition all summer, seized on the distress this goose egg created (although the number was later revised up to 100,000). During an Oval Office gathering the following Monday, three days before the president planned to pitch Congress on his proposal, Sperling made the case for the full $450 billion. He argued that, in order to turn the heads of economists, the package should aspire to increase growth by close to 2 percentage points above what private forecasters were expecting, to a total of more than 4 percent. Given the abysmal economic data, he said, it was better to overshoot than undershoot.

The president agreed. The key mistake of the first stimulus—really of his entire economic agenda to date—had been to undershoot. Now he was refusing to make it again. On Thursday, September 8, Obama delivered to a joint session of Congress a speech as muscular as the American Jobs Act Sperling had crafted. Obama called it "an outrage" for the country to watch its roads and bridges decay at a time when millions of idle workers were eager to rebuild them. He reminded Congress that the unemployed didn't have "the luxury of waiting fourteen months"—until after the next election—for relief, and dared Republicans to defy him. Most important, he said he would take this message to "every corner of this country," as he proceeded to do throughout the fall with real success.[2] Obama had finally learned that there was no percentage in sweet-talking the GOP.

As public approval over his handling of the economy dropped, Obama had also learned that the nonstop commotion over the deficit was a political loser, especially when he put himself at the center of it. When the so-called supercommittee convened in September to scare up at least $1.2 trillion in budget savings, the president got nowhere near the action. As of early November, he hadn't held a single meeting with committee members to weigh in on the process, and hadn't dispatched a single representative to observe the committee's proceedings.[3] Obama left the congressional hagglers to forge ahead on their own and stuck single-mindedly to his message of jobs. It

was the strategy he should have adopted back in April, before he offered up his head for repeated banging against a wall of Republican
intransigence.

The benefits of the new approach were quickly apparent. At the
time of his speech to Congress, a *Washington Post* poll showed voters with no more faith in him than in congressional Republicans on
the question of who could create jobs. In October, one month later,
the same poll would show the public favoring Obama by 15 points
on this question.[4]

And yet, as encouraging as this evolution was, Team Obama still
hadn't corrected some basic flaws in the selling of its agenda. On
Friday, September 9, Bill Daley convened a group of top economic
and political advisers to discuss how to pay for the jobs plan Obama
had premiered the night before. Though there was consensus on
policy—everyone favored limiting tax deductions for the affluent—
the group split over tactics. Geithner and Jason Furman, Sperling's
deputy at the NEC, warned that trumpeting tax hikes as a way to
pay for the measure would detract from the discussion about jobs.
They proposed asking Congress to come up with the money instead.
But Plouffe and Jack Lew convinced the group that the bill wouldn't
be credible without a concrete plan for funding it.

When the administration submitted its recommended "pay-fors"
to Congress the following Monday, it was immediately clear that
Geithner and Furman were right. Republicans had spent the previous few days sounding their conciliatory best. "The proposals the
president outlined tonight merit consideration," Boehner announced
shortly after Obama's speech. Now they dropped the sweet talk and
lacerated Obama for peddling higher taxes. "It would be fair to say
this tax increase on job creators is the kind of proposal both parties
have opposed in the past," Boehner's spokesman said.[5] Whatever the

political merits of the bill—and they were not inconsiderable—its legislative prospects had plummeted to zero.

In retrospect, there was an obvious solution to the "pay-for" problem, which even Geithner and Furman had dismissed: the administration could have declared the jobs crisis a national emergency, thereby eluding the congressional requirement that the bill's costs be offset. But Team Obama was still too cowed by the political perils of deepening the deficit to entertain this idea seriously. "The fact that it was paid for was a huge part of public acceptance of this," said a White House official.[6]

The episode was instructive in a variety of ways. First, it highlighted a fallacy that had gripped the economic team—and the president himself—since the summer of 2009: that the only path to procuring more stimulus was to "pay for it" with future tax hikes or budget savings. Orszag in particular had spent much of his tenure evangelizing on this point. But, as the Jobs Act showed, taking on these two tasks at once was an act of self-sabotage. The practical effect was to shift the political debate from a place where Republicans felt vulnerable (blocking legislation that might produce jobs) to a place where they felt comfortable (attacking the administration for raising taxes or for proposing wimpy budget cuts). And that was setting aside the rhetorical contortions involved in saying the government should simultaneously spend and scrimp.

Second, the Jobs Act punctuated the chronic confusion about the connection between politics and governing. Too often, the two activities were treated as an either-or proposition in the West Wing. Obama generally believed the way to pass his program was to engage earnestly with the opposition, not take his case public. A president never has more leverage with Congress than when he's riling up voters, but Obama rarely exploited the massive stature of his office as a tool for influencing legislation. During the making of the original stimulus in 2009, during the initial push for health care reform that spring and summer, during the bargaining over the Bush tax cuts in late 2010, and during much of the deficit dalliance in 2011, Obama did little to make life uncomfortable for the Republicans he was negotiating with. Only in the final few weeks of the debt ceiling negotiations did he take his case public—with encouraging results. But by then the GOP was dug in.

In general, Obama seemed to think a president should hit the hustings only if the point *wasn't* to pass legislation. In September 2011, when he did finally launch a tour long enough to impress the average roadie, he was unprepared to reap the benefits in Congress. He had done little to line up Democratic support for his jobs bill and the corresponding tax hikes. As a result, there were stories about disarray among supposed allies.

Finally, the Jobs Act revealed that the Obama White House never grasped quite how closely its fate was tied to the labor market. This misunderstanding dated all the way back to the transition, when the president-elect stuck with his otherwise noble ambitions on health care and the environment rather than switching his focus to jobs. The misunderstanding continued during the fall of 2009, when Obama took his first fateful step into the no-man's-land of deficit cutting and shortchanged additional stimulus. After the president made penny-pinching the cause of his third year in office, the White House rejoiced when polls showed that voters favored Obama's approach to budget cuts over the Republicans'. It seemed tragically unaware that, however impressive Obama's margins on these questions were, they were also mostly irrelevant because truly up-for-grabs voters base their views of the president on the availability of work.

By the time it turned to the jobs issue, the White House did recognize that the politics of jobs closely mirror the reality of jobs. "We've got to understand what it is from a public relations standpoint we're trying to achieve here," Plouffe told his colleagues, according to one of them. "The president's approval rating on the economy is tied to the economy itself."[7] Still, Plouffe believed that the Jobs Act could improve Obama's performance on two related measures: the extent to which voters believed he had a plan for fixing the economy; and whether they believed he was sufficiently focused on the issue. In this way, devising a bold jobs plan was plainly helpful to Obama. But it was still a poor substitute for *enacting* a jobs plan, at least as time went by. The same *Washington Post* poll that showed voters favoring Obama over the GOP on job creation in early October showed the two sides dead even by early November— exactly where they had been when the effort began.

Obama may well win reelection. His vision of government is vastly more humane than that of his GOP foils, and his recipe for boosting the economy is much more plausible. Moreover, as the president's reelection campaign understands well, the public genuinely likes Obama personally. Voters consistently deem him to be a smart, honest man who simply hasn't succeeded the way they'd hoped.

The public may give him credit for these advantages on Election Day. But, if so, it will be grudging credit, and the reelection will be distressingly close for his supporters—much more so than if he'd devoted his presidency to delivering jobs.

In fairness, cataloging the administration's missteps in late 2011 can be a detour into academic quibbling. With the Republicans in control of the House of Representatives, a conservative mob peering over their shoulders, and a presidential election looming, there may have been no way to pass the jobs bill even if the administration had executed a well-laid plan flawlessly.

In fact, Obama had faced obstacles beyond his control throughout his presidency, and these obstacles help explain the sluggish recovery. There was, for one thing, a recession of unusual depth and force, for which Obama is entirely blameless, and which would have challenged policy makers of preternatural wisdom. Beyond that, it's fair to single out conservative Democrats in Congress, who seemed to come by their notions of loyalty from watching the townsfolk in *High Noon*. These Democrats constantly undermined Obama's legislative prospects by fleeing at the first sign of adversity. Finally, there was the brutal procession of shocks to the economy as it struggled to recover: the debt crisis in Europe, the economic fallout from a massive Japanese earthquake, the spike in oil prices amid revolution in the Muslim world.

Against this backdrop, the governing experience of Obama's economic advisers was a real asset, especially as the new president took office. "Your first budget is impossible. You have to do in four weeks what you normally do in six months," said one Clinton veteran who returned under Obama. "We had to do that and save the economy, rescue the financial system. . . . The reason we pulled off decent policy out of all this was that everyone on the team had done it before."[8]

That Team Obama helped avert catastrophe is indeed beyond question. The economy was losing a breathtaking 700,000 jobs per month in the winter of 2008. In the fourth quarter of that year, it shrank at an annual rate of nearly 9 percent. These were depression-sized numbers. By the summer of 2009, however, the economy was growing again. As the economists Mark Zandi and Alan Blinder have documented, the combination of Obama's stimulus, Bush's $700 billion bank bailout, and trillions of dollars of loans and subsidies from the Federal Reserve almost certainly averted a 1930s-style economic black hole.[9]

Despite these heroic efforts, the Obamans nonetheless failed at the task they set for themselves—of restoring the economy to something resembling its precrisis vitality. "It's going to take some time to achieve a complete recovery," Obama said in September 2009. "But

I want you all to know, I will not rest until anybody who's looking for a job can find one." [10] Yet almost three years after Obama took office, unemployment hovered around 9 percent. The economy spent much of 2011 flirting with a recessionary double-dip.

Though the challenges facing it were indeed enormous, the administration resorted to shoulder-shrugging professions of futility too often during Obama's first term. The president still had enormous power to affect the economy for the better. Suppose, for example, that Obama had proposed his September 2011 jobs plan in the spring of 2010 and sold it just as relentlessly. At the time, Democrats still comfortably ruled both houses of Congress. Given that the unemployment rate was even higher (9.5 versus 9.1 percent), and that the economy was visibly deteriorating as Europe devolved into turmoil, it's hard to believe the popular reception would have been less enthusiastic. Assuming that conservative Democrats eventually fell in line—a plausible assumption given their worship of polls, if less than airtight—Obama would have needed to pick off a single Republican senator, something his determined barnstorming might well have accomplished.

The reason Obama didn't seize this opportunity is that he deferred too much to the members of his economic team, chiefly Orszag and Geithner, who considered the deficit a higher priority, and to the members of his political team, like Emanuel, who assumed the public wouldn't stand for another jolt of spending. He didn't give enough credence to the views of dissident advisers like Christy Romer. And the one aide who had both correctly diagnosed the problem by late 2009 and still enjoyed influence with the president, Larry Summers, was incapable of brokering agreement internally, even with natural allies.

Peter Orszag looms as an especially tragic figure, in some ways a perfect reflection of Obama himself. Orszag was analytically brilliant and as able as anyone in government. Moreover, he had a capacity for self-reflection that he was not afraid to exercise. Orszag had a habit of fessing up to the data points he'd overlooked and the arguments he'd minimized. "In fairness, it's true," he later said, conceding that Team Obama had missed the implications of Americans' towering piles of debt for the recovery. "There were people out there saying [this] in 2009. That view was not given very much weight at all." [11] Tim Geithner, though nearly as smart and able, was less reflective. Larry Summers was brilliant and thoughtful, but with limited skill as a bureaucrat. Only Orszag combined all these qualities. But he'd come under the spell of a dubious political-economic theory—one that elevated deficits above all else—and so the upshot of his considerable talents was to nudge Obama in the wrong direction.

Still, it was, finally, Obama's decision not to demand bold action sooner, at least not on the economic front. The president spent 2009 waging a historically important and ultimately successful campaign for health care reform. Given the circumstances, however, the effort might have been better spent fast-tracking tough-minded financial reform. This would have satisfied the country's legitimate hunger for change on Wall Street. And, by defusing some of the populist anger that voters soon trained on the government, the strategy also might have improved Obama's chances of delivering another major course of stimulus.

But, then, it's not clear Obama would have seized the opportunity to pass another large stimulus. He spent much of his first term more taken with the case against deficits than with the case for jobs. Thus a president who had run for office as a genuine outsider, who had campaigned against the most destructive practices and preoccupations of the nation's capital, embraced the hoariest of Washington's old saws: that the American people are so offended by out-of-control government that they would insist on scaling it back even at a cost to their own livelihoods in a time of deep economic unease. This was an article of faith among the city's grayest estab-lishmentarians—the editorialists and the think-tank denizens, the people who largely dismissed Barack Obama when he took his first halting steps toward the White House. That it came to define the Obama administration is the most dispiriting irony of his presidency.

ACKNOWLEDGMENTS

This book grew out of several conversations with my former *New Republic* editor and colleague, Frank Foer, in the fall of 2008. At the time, I had spent over a year covering the presidential campaign. I was intrigued by the phenom who was about to enter the White House. But the thought of covering the Obama operation head-on, as I'd been covering him and the other candidates, filled me with a certain amount of dread. I'd had my fill of political journalism for the moment.

Frank suggested I come at the new administration differently, by focusing on the biggest challenge it faced. Given my background in economics, which I'd written about on and off since joining *TNR* in 2000, he figured it would be a natural fit. He thought there might even be a book in it.

That I would entertain an assignment like this is first and foremost the doing of my parents, Dalia and Howard Scheiber, who have been encouraging me as a writer since I could hold a pencil. My father probably read every draft of every composition I wrote between the ages of six and seventeen. When he wasn't busy doing this, he was plying me with the collected works of some obscure British novelist, or indulging me in a game of wordplay.

My mother was the source of my interest in politics and government. I was probably the only elementary school student in El Paso, Texas, on a first-name basis with "Mort" and "Fred," two of my illustrious *New Republic* predecessors. This was entirely my mother's influence.

It was, not surprisingly, a lifelong dream to work at the magazine that employed them, and pretty much every minute of my time at *TNR* has lived up to expectation. I owe special thanks to my first boss, Peter Beinart, for hiring me, and for letting me opine at cover length at the ripe age of twenty-five. Whether this was an act of discernment or profound misjudgment I will leave to readers to decide.

My time at *TNR* has been a running conversation with some of the smartest, most creative people on the planet. In addition to Frank, whose editorial guidance and big-brother wisdom has been indispensable, I've benefited endlessly from my interactions with current and former colleagues: Jon Chait, John Judis, Leon Wieseltier, Jonathan Cohn, Michelle Cottle, Chris Orr, Peter and Sacha Scoblic, Jason Zengerle, Ryan Lizza, Michael Crowley, Ruth Franklin, Kate Marsh, Sarah Blustain, Ben Wasserstein, Greg Veis, Isaac Chotiner, Chloe Schama, Tom Frank, Brad Plumer, Eve Fairbanks, Seyward Darby, Barron YoungSmith, and Jeremy Kahn. Our current editors, Richard Just and Rachel Morris, are worthy heirs to the *TNR* tradition and have been beyond understanding with my ever-lengthening book leave. Alec MacGillis and Tim Noah are new office mates, but writers whose work I've admired for years. Henry Riggs and Bruce Steinke have somehow never clocked me despite the many ways I've complicated their lives during *The New Republic* production process. Marty Peretz and Larry Grafstein have humbled me with their generous support of my work and the institution. I am especially grateful to the colleagues who read portions of my manuscript. Rachel Morris was kind enough to read from start to finish.

Outside *TNR*, I owe thanks to a handful of friends who've endured more discussion of my writing than is fair to ask of any civilian. Justin Driver always obliged with penetrating observations about my subjects and much-needed feedback on my copy, including this book. Jake Sullivan was generous with his insights on the way politics and policy actually work. Chris Suellentrop and Bryan Curtis never let me forget that being a journalist is the best job in the world. Adeel Qalbani showed me what it means to live in the financial markets. Roy Bahat taught me how to ask a real question. I learned how to be a writer, and occasionally even how to write, through close observation of Daniel Max.

This book would not have come about without the relentless efforts of my agent, Elyse Cheney, and my editor at Simon & Schuster, Priscilla Painton. Beyond their otherworldly wisdom, they deserve hardship pay for putting up with my cascading authorial neuroses. Jon Karp, who took over as publisher of Simon & Schuster midway through this project, flattered me with his enthusiasm. Priscilla's assistant, Mike Szczerban, was a font of practical knowledge and sound judgment. Lisa Healy and her production team were heroic in shepherding the book to completion despite my best efforts to knock them off course. Ann Adelman's copyediting was breathtaking in its thoroughness. I benefited from the research assistance of Alex Hart and Matt Zeitlin far more than I could afford to pay them for it.

Outside *The New Republic* and Simon & Schuster, the New America Foundation was a critical source of institutional support. I owe Steve Coll and Andrés Martinez much gratitude for their interest in this book, and for their input and advice along the way. Faith Smith and Caroline Esser helped translate their commitment into logistical reality. Marie Lawrence was a scrupulous researcher in her own right.

Aside from my sources, to whom I am eternally grateful, I really learned how to think about the financial crisis and the recession from the work of other writers. Among those I read most closely and often were Liaquat Ahamed, Edmund Andrews, Binyamin Appelbaum, Ryan Avent, Dean Baker, Jackie Calmes, John Cassidy, Sewell Chan, David Cho, Eric Dash, Justin Fox, James Galbraith, Neil Irwin, Phil Izzo, Simon Johnson, Ezra Klein, Mike Konczal, Paul Krugman, James Kwak, Devin Leonard, David Leonhardt, Michael Lewis, Roger Lowenstein, Lori Montgomery, Megan McArdle, Joe Nocera, Damian Paletta, Steve Pearlstein, Sudeep Reddy, Felix Salmon, Deborah Solomon, Andrew Ross Sorkin, James Surowiecki, David Wessel, Ben White, Martin Wolf, and Matt Yglesias. Ryan Lizza wrote an important early piece about the Obama economic team in *The New Yorker*. Josh Green wrote an important early profile of Tim Geithner in *The Atlantic*.

My biggest regret in writing this book has been the time away from my family. One of the lucky breaks that made it easier to pull off was the support of my father- and mother-in-law, Mick and Nancy Sullivan, who were a frequent, stabilizing presence in our household, as were my sister-in-law, Katie Sullivan, and her husband, Kwasi Mitchell. My parents were also gracious and tireless in pitching in with child care.

Above all, there were two people who sustained me through the process: my beautiful infant daughter Finoula, whose bath I looked forward to every evening, and whose complete lack of interest in this book was a needed source of perspective. And my wife, Amy Sullivan. There is no doubt my manuscript benefited from Amy's editorial eye. But writing a book is as much an emotional endurance test as an intellectual exercise. I'm quite certain I could not have survived it without her love, empathy, and unyielding faith. She has always been the believer in our family. I fear it might be contagious.

AUTHOR'S NOTE ON SOURCES

When I began this project in the fall of 2008, I had no idea whether the administration would surmount the worst financial crisis in eighty years or the recession that coincided with it. What I did know was twofold: That I wanted to chronicle the efforts of the men and women the president-elect had put on the problem. And that the only way to understand the decisions they made was to understand the experiences that had shaped them. In that spirit, the goal for this project was not only to tell the central story of this administration. It was also to probe the biographies of the remarkable public officials thrust into the middle of it.

This turned out to be a daunting challenge. Over the next three years, I interviewed more than 250 people, many of them five or six times each. A small, unfortunate handful indulged me for over a dozen conversations. Inevitably, the range of sources sprawled across place and time—from Larry Summers's second-grade teacher in sub-urban Philadelphia in the early 1960s to Tim Geithner's colleagues at the U.S. Embassy in Tokyo during the early 1990s. I spoke with officials in Congress and independent federal agencies, and with nu-merous executives at banks and hedge funds.

Still, the vast plurality, if not the majority, of my sources were people who worked in the Obama administration, primarily the White House and the Treasury Department. These relationships came about almost entirely through my work for *The New Republic* magazine in Washington, where I've written about politics and eco-nomics for the past eleven years. It was on a *New Republic* assign-ment that I first met Barack Obama in May 2004, not long after the young legislator won his U.S. Senate primary. I distinctly remember trailing Obama through a caucus room in Springfield, Illinois, look-ing down at my feet while he told curious colleagues where I'd come from. It was like being an American music critic who stumbled across the Beatles in Liverpool in 1962.

I spoke with Obama a few times for that piece, then not again until November 2007, on the eve of the primary victories that pro-pelled him to the presidency. Perhaps more important for the sake of this book, covering the presidential campaign helped me get to know many of Obama's key advisers, both policy wonks and politi-cal aides. Those contacts proved invaluable as I tried to make sense of the incoming administration's economic agenda.

Most of the events and conversations re-created in this book are the product of interviews with multiple firsthand sources, especially when I have described the event or conversation at some length. For example, I spoke with six people present for the scene that opens this book. In several cases, the sources provided notes, e-mails, tran-scripts, and memos to corroborate their claims and supplement their memories.

Fortunately, a surprising number of sources were willing to be quoted on the record, and I have inserted their comments where relevant. Still, the pressures of working in contemporary Washington are such that many more were reluctant to go public. Often we spoke under an arrangement known as "deep background," meaning that I could use the information they provided so long as I didn't quote them or cite them, even generically. In these cases, I have described the events and discussions they conveyed using an omniscient narrative voice. The absence of citation or attribution indicates that the information comes from one or more of these deep background conversations.

Many other people were willing to speak with me "on background," meaning that I could quote them and attribute their comments to a generic source, such as "administration official." With only a few exceptions, I have tried to dispense with modifiers like "senior" to amplify these titles. There are hundreds of people who work for the White House and Treasury who can legitimately claim such honorifics. In all but the tiniest handful of cases, the people I interviewed hailed from this group.

Finally, I'm indebted to the vast and impressive work of my fellow journalists, without which it would be impossible to construct a narrative like this. I have tried to cite their contributions copiously, especially when they were the first to report a detail that I included in my text and had not known beforehand. Nonetheless, I am responsible for any views and mistakes contained in this book. In some cases, the previously published work I have drawn on is my own, and I've indicated this as well. I owe special thanks to the editors at *The New Republic* who helped me construct these pieces.

NOTES

PROLOGUE

1. For the best account of the rating agencies' role in the financial crisis, see Michael Lewis, *The Big Short: Inside the Doomsday Machine* (New York: W. W. Norton and Company, 2010). Lewis explains how the big Wall Street firms essentially devised the models by which the rating agencies evaluated mortgage securities, then proceeded to game the models.

2. Megan Murphy and Sharlene Goff, "Bank chiefs' pay rises by 36%," *Financial Times,* June 14, 2011; available at www.ft.com/intl/cms/s/0/77431a66-96b0-11e0-baca-00144feab49a.html-axzz1g3W1din9.

3. Administration official, interview with the author, September 28, 2011.

4. Second administration official, interview with the author, October 26, 2011.

CHAPTER 1: THE REUNION

1. Noam Scheiber, "The Audacity of Data," *The New Republic*, March 12, 2008; available at www.tnr.com/article/the-audacity-data.

2. Remarks by Senator Barack Obama at Cooper Union, New York, NY, March 28, 2008; transcript available at www.nytimes.com/2008/03/27/us/politics/27text-obama.html?pagewanted=print.

3. Robert Rubin, interview with the author, March 14, 2011.

4. Noam Scheiber, "Moneyball," *The New Republic,* October 12, 2009. Available at www.tnr.com/article/politics/moneyball.

5. Senior Obama transition official, memo read verbatim by official during an interview with the author, July 19, 2011.

6. Academic who advised Barack Obama during 2008 campaign, interview with the author, February 15, 2008.

7. Senior Obama adviser who attended the meeting on November 12, interview with the author, May 27, 2011.

8. Daniel J. Hemel, "Summers's Comments on Women and Science Draw Ire," *Harvard Crimson,* January 14, 2005; available at www.the crimson.com/article/2005/1/14/summers-comments-on-women-and -science/.

9. Timothy Geithner, interview with the author, January 25, 2011.

10. Unnamed Democratic senator, interview with the author, May 3, 2011.

CHAPTER 2: THE BIG IDEAS PROJECT

1. Remarks by Senator Barack Obama at the Iowa State Democratic Party Jefferson-Jackson Day Dinner, Des Moines, Iowa, November 10, 2007. Transcript available at http://blogs.suntimes.com/sweet/2007/11/sweet_blog_extra_text_of_obama.html.

2. Pete Giangreco, interview with the author, August 2, 2010.

3. Obama campaign aide, interview with the author, March 18, 2011.

4. Remarks by Senator Barack Obama, presidential campaign speech in Newport News, Virginia, October 4, 2008; available at www.asksam.com/ebooks/releases.asp?file=Obama-Speeches.ask&dn=Health%20Care.

5. Senior Obama campaign aide, interview with the author, May 27, 2011.

6. Larry Summers, interview with the author, June 29, 2011.

7. Remarks by Senator Barack Obama, nomination victory speech, St. Paul, Minnesota, June 3, 2008. Transcript available at www.huffington post.com/2008/06/03/obamas-nomination-victory_n_105028.html?

8. Jim Cauley, interview with the author, July 23, 2010.

9. Ibid.

10. Remarks by Senator Barack Obama, presidential campaign announcement speech, Springfield, Illinois, February 10, 2007. Transcript avail-

able at www.nytimes.com/2007/02/10/us/politics/11obama-text.html? ref=politics.

11. Remarks by Senator Barack Obama at the Iowa State Democratic Party Jefferson-Jackson Day dinner.

12. David Axelrod, interview with Matt Lauer, NBC's *Today Show*, August 1, 2008. Transcript available at www.msnbc.msn.com/id/26010577/ ns/msnbc_tv-the_ed_show/t/race-white-house-david-gregory-friday -august#.TpiOwpuImU8.

13. Remarks by Senator Barack Obama, presidential campaign rally in Henderson, Nevada, November 1, 2008. Transcript available at www .newsreview.com/reno/newsview/blogs?date=2008-11-01.

14. Senator Barack Obama, interview with the author, November 19, 2007.

15. David Leonhardt, "Obamanomics," *New York Times Magazine*, August 20, 2008; available at www.nytimes.com/2008/08/24/magazine/ 24Obamanomics-t.html.

16. Senator Barack Obama, interview with *Reno Gazette Journal*, January 15, 2008.

17. See, e.g., Sam Stein, "Obama Compares Himself to Reagan, JFK . . . But Not Bill Clinton," *The Huffington Post*, January 16, 2008; available at www.huffingtonpost.com/2008/01/16/obama-compares-himself-to_n_ 81835.html.

18. Noam Scheiber, "Cruel Intentions," *The New Republic*, May 28, 2008; available at www.tnr.com/article/cruel-intentions.

19. Rick Pearson and Bob Secter, "Obama and Daley Political Allies Now, But They're Hardly Cronies," *Chicago Tribune*, November 16, 2008; available at www.chicagotribune.com/news/local/chi-obama -daley17nov17,0,3006937,print.story.

20. Jonathan Alter, *The Promise: President Obama, Year One* (New York: Simon & Schuster, 2010), pp. 67–68.

21. Ted Kaufman, interview with the author, July 12, 2011.

CHAPTER 3: "PEOPLE WILL THINK WE DON'T GET IT"—LARRY SUMMERS

1. For more on the differences between the CEA and the NEC, see Noam Scheiber, "Numbers Game," *The New Republic*, May 6, 2002; available at www.tnr.com/article/numbers-game.

2. Draft of internal transition memo, December 2008, obtained exclusively by the author in August 2011. For the end result of this analysis, see also Christina Romer and Jared Bernstein, "The Job Impact of the

American Recovery and Reinvestment Plan," January 10, 2009. Report available at http://otrans.3cdn.net/45593e8ecbd339d074_13m6b t1te.pdf.

3. Draft of internal transition memo, December 2008.

4. Jacob Weisberg, "Keeping the Boom from Busting," *New York Times Magazine*, July 19, 1998; available at www.nytimes.com/1998/07/19/ magazine/keeping-the-boom-from-busting.html.

5. Remarks by Federal Reserve Bank of New York President Timothy Geithner at the Trends in Asian Financial Sectors Conference, San Francisco, June 20, 2007. Transcript available at www.newyorkfed .org/newsevents/speeches_archive/2007/gei070620.html.

6. Weisberg, "Keeping the Boom from Busting."

7. See, e.g., remarks by Federal Reserve Bank of New York President Timothy Geithner at the Trends in Asian Financial Sectors Conference, San Francisco, June 20, 2007.

8. Paul Blustein, *The Chastening: Inside the Crisis That Rocked the Global Financial System and Humbled the IMF* (New York: Public Affairs, 2010), pp. 121, 125.

9. See Michael Schuman, *The Miracle: The Epic Story of Asia's Quest for Wealth* (New York: HarperBusiness, 2009), p. 48.

10. Blustein, *The Chastening*, p. 121.

11. Schuman, *The Miracle*, p. 48.

12. Blustein, *The Chastening*, pp. 121–22.

13. Ibid., pp. 122–26.

14. Ibid., p. 138.

15. Ibid., pp. 138, 148.

16. Ibid., pp. 147–48.

17. Ibid., pp. 143, 145, 148–49.

18. Schuman, *The Miracle*, p. 293.

19. Robert Rubin, interview with the author, March 14, 2011.

20. Christina Romer, "What Ended the Great Depression?" *Journal of Economic History* (December 1992), pp. 757–84.

21. Peter Baker, "The White House Looks for Work," *New York Times Magazine*, January 19, 2011; available at www.nytimes.com/2011/01/23/ magazine/23Economy-t.html?_r=1&pagewanted=print.

22. Administration colleague of Larry Summers, interview with the author.

23. Remarks by Larry Summers to the Brookings Institution, Washington, DC, March 13, 2009. Transcript available at www.brookings.edu/~/ media/Files/events/2009/0313_summers/20090313_summers.pdf.

24. Draft of internal transition memo, December 2008.

25. The first to report that the memo included only the latter two numbers was Ryan Lizza, "Inside the Crisis," *The New Yorker*, October 12, 2009; available at www.newyorker.com/reporting/2009/10/12/091012fa_fact_lizza.

26. Administration colleague of Larry Summers, interview with the author, July 5, 2011.

27. Peter Orszag, interview with the author, August 20, 2010.

CHAPTER 4: THE OPERATOR

1. See, e.g., Jackie Calmes, "Obama's Economic Circle Keeps Tensions Simmering," *New York Times*, June 8, 2009; available at www.nytimes.com/2009/06/08/us/politics/08team.html?_r=1&hp=&pagewanted=print.

2. Summers White House colleague, interview with the author, March 27, 2011.

3. Summers White House colleague, interview with the author, January 27, 2009.

4. Calmes, "Obama's Economic Circle Keeps Tensions Simmering."

5. Summers aide, interview with the author, April 4, 2011.

6. Richard Bradley, *Harvard Rules: Lawrence Summers and the Battle for the World's Most Powerful University* (New York: Harper Paperbacks, 2005), p. 8.

7. Anita Cohen, interview with the author, April 3, 2010.

8. Mark Moskowitz, interview with the author, April 7, 2010.

9. Jim Weinrott, interview with the author, November 7, 2011.

10. Jim Weinrott, interview with the author, April 8, 2010.

11. Jim Weinrott, interview with the author, November 7, 2011.

12. Noam Scheiber, "Free Larry Summers," *The New Republic*, April 1, 2009; available at www.tnr.com/article/free-larry-summers.

13. Ted Belch, interview with the author, March 23, 2010.

14. Dallas Perkins, interview with the author, April 2, 2010.

15. Summers college debate teammate, interview with the author, March 26, 2010.

16. James Buchal, interview with the author, April 15, 2010.

17. David Henderson, CEA colleague, interview with the author, June 21, 2010. The anecdote also appears in Henderson's book *The Joy of Freedom: An Economist's Odyssey* (London: Financial Times/Prentice-Hall, 2001), pp. 31–32.

18. Clinton-era aide, interview with the author, March 13, 2011.

19. Summers CEA colleague, interview with the author, June 11, 2010.

20. Jeff Shafer, interview with the author, March 16, 2011.

21. Ibid.

22. Peter S. Goodman, "Taking Hard New Look at a Greenspan Legacy," *New York Times*, October 8, 2008; available at www.nytimes.com/2008/10/09/business/economy/09greenspan.html?pagewanted=all.

23. Robert Rubin and Jacob Weisberg, *In an Uncertain World: Tough Choices from Wall Street to Washington* (New York: Random House, 2004), pp. 197–98, 287–88.

24. Ted Truman, interview with the author, March 28, 2011.

25. Jeff Shafer, interview with the author, March 16, 2011.

26. Rubin and Weisberg, *In an Uncertain World*, pp. 27–28.

27. Summers White House colleague, interview with the author, June 13, 2011.

28. Mark Moskowitz, interview with the author, April 7, 2010.

29. Ted Truman, interview with the author, March 28, 2011.

30. Member of the Obama economic team, interview with the author.

31. Christina Romer, interview with the author, November 10, 2011.

32. Rahm Emanuel, interview with the author, March 15, 2011.

33. Ibid.

CHAPTER 5: WILDEBEESTS AND CHEETAHS

1. Draft of internal transition memo, December 2008, obtained by the author in August 2011.

2. Aide to Nancy Pelosi, interview with the author, May 25, 2011. A mention of the knuckle crack also appeared in Mark Leibovich, "Obama's Partisan, Profane Confidant Reins It In," *New York Times*, January 25, 2009. Available at query.nytimes.com/gst/fullpage.html?res=9E03E6D6163DF936A15752C0A96F9C8B63&scp=5&sq=Rahm+AND+Leibovich+AND+Obama&st=nyt.

3. Aide to Nancy Pelosi, interview with the author, May 25, 2011.

4. Lawrence Summers, letter to Nancy Pelosi, Harry Reid, John Boehner, and Mitch McConnell, January 12, 2009. Letter available at www.scribd.com/doc/10162101/Larry-Summers-Letter-to-Congress.

5. Treasury official familiar with memo, interview with the author, April 22, 2011.

6. Senior Senate aide, interview with the author, August 12, 2011.

7. Ibid.

8. Einhorn's discussion of the exchange is recounted in Andrew Ross Sorkin, *Too Big to Fail: The Inside Story of How Wall Street and Washington Fought to Save the Financial System—and Themselves* (New York: Viking, 2009), pp. 107–08.

9. Colleague of Larry Summers, interview with the author, March 1, 2011.

10. Ibid.

11. Louise Story, "A Rich Education for Summers (after Harvard)," *New York Times*, April 6, 2009; available at www.nytimes.com/2009/04/06/business/06summers.html.

12. William Cohan, *House of Cards: A Tale of Hubris and Wretched Excess on Wall Street* (New York: Doubleday, 2009), pp. 197, 206, 217, 225.

13. Ibid., pp. 200–1.

14. Former Bear Stearns colleague of Lee Sachs, interview with the author, June 22, 2009. This quote also appears in Noam Scheiber, "Sachs Appeal," *The New Republic*, August 12, 2009; available at www.tnr.com/article/politics/sachs-appeal.

15. Former Bear Stearns colleague of Lee Sachs, interview with the author, May 2009.

16. Aide to Larry Summers, interview with the author, July 27, 2010.

CHAPTER 6: THE SUCCESSION FIGHT

1. Witness to Sachs-Summers exchanges, interview with the author.

2. Aide to Larry Summers, interview with the author, April 11, 2011.

3. Noam Scheiber, "Obama's Choice," *The New Republic*, November 19, 2008; available at www.tnr.com/print/article/obamas-choice.

4. Former Larry Summers colleague, interview with the author, July 23, 2010.

5. Alter, *The Promise: President Obama, Year One*, pp. 52–53.

6. Former Obama economic official, interview with the author, April 11, 2011.

7. Eric Dash and Julie Creswell, "Citigroup Saw No Red Flags Even as It Made Bolder Bets," *New York Times*, November 22, 2008; available at www.nytimes.com/2008/11/23/business/23citi.html?pagewanted=print.

8. Rubin and Weisberg, *In an Uncertain World*, pp. 90–91, 111, 301, 307.

9. Weisberg, "Keeping the Boom from Busting," *New York Times Magazine*, July 19, 1998.

10. Rubin and Weisberg, *In an Uncertain World*, pp. 141, 162.

11. Weisberg, "Keeping the Boom from Busting."

12. Rubin and Weisberg, *In an Uncertain World*, pp. 114, 112–13, 115.

13. Jackie Calmes, "Rubinomics Recalculated," *New York Times*, November 23, 2008; available at www.nytimes.com/2008/11/24/us/politics/24 rubin.html?pagewanted=print.

14. Rubin and Weisberg, *In an Uncertain World*, p. 299.

15. Ibid., pp. 86–87.

16. Testimony of Robert Rubin before the Financial Crisis Inquiry Commission, Washington, DC, April 8, 2010. Transcript available at http://fcic -static.law.stanford.edu/cdn_media/fcic-testimony/2010-0408-Rubin .pdf.

17. Ibid.

18. Robert Rubin, interview with the author, July 8, 2011.

19. Robert Rubin, interview with the author, August 16, 2011.

20. Testimony of Robert Rubin before the Financial Crisis Inquiry Commission, Washington, DC, April 8, 2010.

21. Noam Scheiber, "Obama's Choice," *The New Republic*, November 19, 2008; Blustein, *The Chastening*, p. 136.

22. Scheiber, "Obama's Choice."

23. Blustein, *The Chastening*, p. 189.

24. Senior Obama campaign aide, interview with the author, May 27, 2011.

25. Many details of this meeting were originally reported in Scheiber, "Sachs Appeal," *The New Republic*, August 12, 2009.

26. Ibid.

27. Ibid.

28. Noam Scheiber, "The Escape Artist," *The New Republic*, February 10, 2011; available at www.tnr.com/print/article/economy/magazine/ 83176/timothy-geithner-treasury-secretary.

29. Participant in March 15, 2009, meeting with the president, interview with the author.

30. Rahm Emanuel, interview with the author, March 15, 2011.

CHAPTER 7: THE FALLACY

1. Originally reported in Lori Montgomery, "Obama Team Assembling $850 Billion Stimulus," *Washington Post*, December 19, 2008; available at www.washingtonpost.com/wp-dyn/content/article/2008/12/18/ AR2008121804204.html.

2. Lori Montgomery, "Obama Expands Stimulus Goals," *Washington Post*, December 21, 2008; available at www.washingtonpost.com/wp-dyn/content/article/2008/12/20/AR2008122001395.html.

3. White House aide, interview with the author, June 13, 2011.

4. Greg Hitt, "Democrats Mull $300 Billion Stimulus," *Wall Street Journal*, October 15, 2008; available at http://online.wsj.com/article/SB122402768546534409.html.

5. Laura Litvan, "Pelosi Says U.S. House Stimulus Measure May Reach $600 Billion," Bloomberg News, December 12, 2008; available at www.bloomberg.com/apps/news?pid=newsarchive&sid=atS7dFcsN1s0&refer=home.

6. Obama administration economist, interview with the author, March 15, 2011.

7. Ibid.

8. Senate leadership aide, interview with the author, April 25, 2011.

9. House leadership aide, interview with the author, May 25, 2011.

10. Originally reported in Noam Scheiber, "The Closer," *The New Republic*, December 10, 2007; available at www.tnr.com/print/article/the-closer.

11. Senator Barack Obama, interview with the author, November 19, 2007.

12. Barack Obama, *Dreams from My Father: A Story of Race and Inheritance* (New York: Kondasha America, 1996), p. 148.

13. Obama White House official, interview with the author, March 8, 2011.

14. Paul Kane, Lori Montgomery, and Shailagh Murray, "Obama Pitches Stimulus Plan," *Washington Post*, January 6, 2009; available at www.washingtonpost.com/wp-dyn/content/article/2009/01/05/AR2009010502752.html.

15. Jeff Zeleny and David Herszenhorn, "Obama Seeking Bipartisan Support on Stimulus Bill," *New York Times*, January 6, 2011; available at www.nytimes.com/2009/01/06/world/americas/06iht-transition.1.19119115.html?pagewanted=all.

16. Longtime Pelosi aide, interview with the author, May 25, 2011.

17. Kane, Montgomery, and Murray, "Obama Pitches Stimulus Plan."

18. Draft of internal transition memo, December 2008, obtained exclusively by the author in August 2011.

19. Ibid.

20. For the most complete list of tax and spending initiatives passed under the American Recovery and Reinvestment Act (aka "the stimulus"), see Farhana Hossain, Amanda Cox, John McGrath, and Stephan Weitgerg, "The Stimulus Plan: How to Spend $787 Billion," *New York Times*; feature available at http://projects.nytimes.com/44th_president/stimulus. See also Michael Grabell and Christopher Weaver, "The Stimulus Plan: A Detailed List of Spending," *ProPublica*, February 13, 2009; feature available at www.propublica.org/special/the-stimulus-plan-a-detailed-list-of-spending. And Michael Grabell and Christopher Weaver, "The Stimulus Plan: The Tax Cuts," *ProPublica*, February 13, 2009; available at www.propublica.org/special/stimulus-plan-taxcut-list.

21. Obama White House aide, interview with the author, May 18, 2011.

22. Memo from Gary Myrick, chief of staff to Senator Harry Reid, to Democratic chiefs of staffs, obtained by the author in June 2011.

23. For details of the Alternative Minimum Tax, see Katherine Lim and Jeffrey Rohaly, "The Individual Alternative Minimum Tax: Historical Data," Urban-Brookings Tax Policy Center, October 2009; available at www.urban.org/UploadedPDF/411968_AMT_update.pdf.

24. Kane, Montgomery, and Murray, "Obama Pitches Stimulus Plan."

25. Lim and Rohaly, "The Individual Alternative Minimum Tax: Historical Data."

26. Incredulous White House aide, interview with the author, July 1, 2011.

27. Ibid. Also comes from second Obama White House aide, interview with the author, June 13, 2011.

28. Second White House aide, interview with the author, June 13, 2011.

29. White House aide, interview with the author, July 1, 2011.

30. Aide to Nancy Pelosi, interview with the author, May 25, 2011.

31. White House aide, interview with the author, July 1, 2011.

32. Ibid.

33. Alison Mitchell, "After the Nicknames," *New York Times*, March 9, 2001; available at www.nytimes.com/2001/03/09/us/after-the-nicknames.html?pagewanted=all&src=pm.

34. Much of the discussion here comes from Noam Scheiber, "Nice Guys Finish Last," February 11, 2010; available at www.tnr.com/print/article/politics/nice-guys-finish-last.

35. Gerhard Peters, "Presidential Job Approval Ratings Following the First 100 Days," American Presidency Project (Santa Barbara: Uni-

versity of California, 1999–2009). Chart available at www.presidency
.ucsb.edu/data/100days_approval.php.

36. Paul Krugman, the Nobel Prize–winning *New York Times* columnist,
was among the first to make a version of this point. See Paul Krugman, "The Economic Narrative," *New York Times*, September 1,
2010; available at http://krugman.blogs.nytimes.com/2010/09/01/the
-economic-narrative/.

37. White House aide, interview with the author, June 3, 2011.

38. Rahm Emanuel, interview with the author, March 15, 2011.

39. Second White House aide, interview with the author, March 8, 2011.

CHAPTER 8: BAIT AND SWITCH

1. See Joshua Green, "Inside Man," *Atlantic Monthly* (April 2010); available at www.theatlantic.com/magazine/archive/2010/04/inside-man/
7992/.

2. David Cho and Michael D. Shear, "How the Fed Failed to Tell Obama
About the Bonuses," *Washington Post*, March 19, 2009; avail-
able at www.washingtonpost.com/wp-dyn/content/article/2009/03/18/
AR2009031804210_pf.html.

3. Treasury Secretary Tim Geithner, interview with the author, August 8,
2011.

4. Treasury Secretary Timothy Geithner, interview with Daniel Gross,
Newsweek, December 20, 2009. Transcript available at www.thedaily
beast.com/newsweek/2009/12/20/timothy-geithner.html.

5. Jackie Calmes, "At Treasury, Geithner Struggles to Escape a Past He
Never Had," *New York Times*, August 19, 2010; available at www
.nytimes.com/2010/08/20/business/20tax.html?pagewanted=print.

6. Senior House aide, interview with the author, May 25, 2011.

7. Steve Shafran, interviews with the author, October 19, 2010, and July
24, 2011.

8. Ibid.

9. Ibid.

10. Noam Scheiber, "Geithner's Top Financial-Markets Adviser to Leave,"
The New Republic, March 4, 2010. Blog post available at www.tnr.com/
blog/jonathan-chait/geithners-top-financial-markets-adviser-leave.

11. Obama economic aide, interview with the author, October 19, 2010.

12. Louise Story, "A Rich Education for Summers (after Harvard)," *New
York Times*, April 6, 2009; available at www.nytimes.com/2009/04/06/
business/06summers.html.

13. U.S. Department of the Treasury, Public-Private Investment Program description; available at www.treasury.gov/initiatives/financial -stability/programs; shCredit%20Market%20Programs/ppip/Pages/ publicprivatefund.aspx.

14. Phillip Swagel, "The Financial Crisis: An Inside View," Brookings Papers on Economic Activity, Spring 2009 conference draft; available at www .brookings.edu/economics/bpea/~/media/Files/Programs/ES/BPEA/ 2009_spring_bpea_papers/2009_spring_bpea_swagel.pdf.

15. U.S. Department of the Treasury, Public-Private Investment Program description.

16. Rachelle Younglai, "Treasury's Toxic Asset Funds Gain 27 Percent," Reuters, January 24, 2010; available at www.reuters.com/article/idUS TRE70N0U220110124.

17. One Summers aide, interview with the author, April 11, 2011.

18. Numbers come from consultation with government officials along with author's analysis of raw data in: Board of Governors of the Federal Reserve System, "The Supervisory Capital Assessment Program: Overview of Results," May 7, 2009; available at www.federalreserve.gov/ newsevents/press/bcreg/bcreg20090507a1.pdf.

19. Obama economic official, interview with the author, June 7, 2011.

20. Conference call participant, interview with the author, May 3, 2011.

21. See Board of Governors of the Federal Reserve System, "The Supervisory Capital Assessment Program: Overview of Results," May 7, 2009; available at www.federalreserve.gov/newsevents/press/bcreg/ bcreg20090507a1.pdf.

22. Obama economic official, interview with the author, June 7, 2011.

23. Exchange first reported in Noam Scheiber, "The Escape Artist," *The New Republic*, February 10, 2011.

24. See Board of Governors of the Federal Reserve System, "The Supervisory Capital Assessment Program: Overview of Results, May 7, 2009."

25. Craig Torres and Bob Ivry, "Dying Banks Kept Alive Show Secrets Fed's Data Will Reveal for First Time," Bloomberg News, March 29, 2011; available at www.bloomberg.com/news/print/2011-03-29/ dying-banks-kept-alive-show-secrets-fed-s-data-will-reveal-for-first-time .html.

26. Bradley Keoun and Phil Kuntz, "Wall Street Aristocracy Got $1.2 Trillion in Secret Loans," Bloomberg News, August 22, 2011; available at www.bloomberg.com/news/print/2011-08-21/wall-street-aristocracy -got-1-2-trillion-in-fed-s-secret-loans.html.

27. Board of Governors of the Federal Reserve System, et al., "Joint Statement by the Treasury, FDIC, OCC, OTS, and the Federal Reserve," February 23, 2009; available at www.federalreserve.gov/newsevents/press/bcreg/20090223a.htm.

28. Former Fed official, interview with the author, May 3, 2011.

CHAPTER 9: THE BIG DIVERSION

1. Council of Economic Advisers, "The Economic Impact of the American Recovery and Reinvestment Act of 2009," January 13, 2010, p. 9. Report available at www.recovery.gov/About/Documents/100113 -economic-impact-arra-second-quarterly-report.pdf

2. I originally discussed this in my article "What's Eating David Axelrod," *The New Republic*, September 27, 2010; available at www.tnr .com/print/article/politics/magazine/77880/whats-eating-david-axelrod -noam-scheiber.

3. Obama economic official, interview with the author.

4. White House aide, interview with the author, June 3, 2011.

5. See Ezra Klein, "Financial Crisis and Stimulus: Could this time be different?" *Washington Post*, October 8, 2011; available at www .washingtonpost.com/business/financial-crisis-and-stimulus-could-this -time-be-different/2011/10/04/gIQALuwdVL_print.html.

6. Christina Romer and Jared Bernstein, "The Job Impact of the American Recovery and Reinvestment Plan," January 10, 2009. Report available at http://otrans.3cdn.net/45593e8ecbd339d074_13m6bt1te.pdf.

7. U.S. Department of Labor, Bureau of Labor Statistics, "Labor Force Statistics from the Current Population Survey"; available at http:// data.bls.gov/timeseries/LNS14000000.

8. U.S. Department of Commerce, Bureau of Economic Analysis, "Why Has the Initial Estimate of Real GDP for the Fourth Quarter of 2008 Been Revised Down So Much?" Available at www.bea.gov/faq/index .cfm?faq_id=1003.

9. Ibid.

10. *NewsHour with Jim Lehrer*, "State of the Stimulus, Including Interview with Rep. Eric Cantor," PBS, July 8, 2009. Video available at www.pbs.org/newshour/video/index.html.

11. White House aide, interview with the author, July 1, 2011.

12. Jonathan Cohn, "Stayin' Alive," *The New Republic*, April 1, 2009; available at www.tnr.com/print/article/politics/stayin-alive.

13. Senior Obama campaign aide, interview with the author, June 3, 2011.

14. Axelrod colleague in Obama administration, interview with the author, June 2, 2011.

15. First reported in Alter, *The Promise*, pp. 244–45. Discussed with former administration official present for meeting on June 2, 2011.

16. Administration wonk, interview with the author, June 2, 2011.

17. White House official, interview with the author, June 3, 2011.

18. Ibid.

19. Noam Scheiber, "The Chief," *The New Republic*, March 3, 3010; available at www.tnr.com/print/article/politics/the-chief.

20. Ibid.

21. John Biemer, "Roskam Tops $1 Million in House Race," *Chicago Tribune*, January 26, 2006; available at http://articles.chicagotribune .com/2006-01-25/news/0601250188_1_duckworth-campaign-sen -peter-roskam-fundraising.

22. Naftali Bendavid, *The Thumpin': How Rahm Emanuel and the Democrats Learned to Be Ruthless and Ended the Republican Revolution* (New York: Doubleday, 2007), p. 104.

23. Scheiber, "The Chief."

24. Former Clinton White House colleague of Rahm Emanuel, interview with the author, February 11, 2010.

25. Jehl Douglas, "White House Tries to Win 8 Converts on the Crime Bill," *New York Times*, August 16, 1994; www.nytimes.com/1994/08/16/us/ white-house-tries-to-win-8-converts-on-the-crime-bill.html?page wanted=all&src=pm.

26. Former Clinton White House colleague of Rahm Emanuel, interview with the author, February 11, 2010.

27. Bendavid, *The Thumpin'*, pp. 100–2.

28. Aide to Rahm Emanuel, interview with the author, May 12, 2011.

29. White House aide, interview with the author, July 1, 2011.

30. Aide to Rahm Emanuel, interview with the author, May 12, 2011.

31. For public opinion data on health care reform in 2009, see the Henry J. Kaiser Family Foundation, Kaiser Health Tracking Poll, September 2009. Available at www.kff.org/kasierpolls/upload/7988.pdf.

32. First reported in Scheiber, "The Chief."

33. Ibid.

34. White House aide, interview with the author, July 1, 2011.

35. Meetings first reported in Jonathan Cohn, "How They Did It," *The New Republic*, May 21, 2010; available at www.tnr.com/print/article/ 75077/how-they-did-it.

36. White House aide, interview with the author, July 1, 2011.

37. Ibid.

38. Anonymous Democratic senator, interview with the author, May 3, 2011.

CHAPTER 10: THE PURIST

1. Office of Management and Budget, Save Award Email Page; available at www.whitehouse.gov/omb/save/SaveAwardEmailPage/.

2. For a discussion of this, see Ryan Lizza, "Money Talks," *The New Yorker*, May 4, 2009; available at www.newyorker.com/reporting/2009/05/04/090504fa_fact_lizza.

3. See Peter Orszag, "Another Look at IMAC," Office of Management and Budget blog, August 4, 2009; blog item available at www.whitehouse.gov/omb/blog/09/08/04/AnotherlookatIMAC/. See also Peter Orszag, "CBO and IMAC," Office of Management and Budget blog, July 25, 2009; blog item available at www.whitehouse.gov/omb/blog/09/07/25/CBOandIMAC.

4. Scheiber, "The Audacity of Data," *The New Republic*, March 12, 2008.

5. Lizza, "Money Talks."

6. Scheiber, "The Audacity of Data."

7. Christina Romer, interview with author, December 17, 2010.

8. Remarks by Senator Barack Obama to the Brookings Institution, Washington, DC, April 5, 2006. Transcript available at www.brookings.edu/comm/events/20060405obama.pdf.

9. OMB official, interview with the author, March 10, 2011.

10. Laura Meckler, "Obama's Health Expert Gets Political," *Wall Street Journal*, July 24, 2009; available at http://online.wsj.com/article/SB124839406488477649.html#mod=todays_us_page_one.

11. OMB official, interview with the author, March 10, 2011.

12. Aide to Larry Summers, interview with the author, June 13, 2011.

13. Former aide to Larry Summers, interview with the author, July 29, 2011.

14. Scheiber, "What's Eating David Axelrod?"

15. Peter Orszag, interview with the author, August 20, 2010.

16. Gabriel Sherman, "Revolver," *New York Magazine*, April 10, 2011; available at http://nymag.com/news/business/wallstreet/peter-orszag-2011-4/.

17. Robert Rubin, interview with the author, July 8, 2011.

18. Meckler, "Obama's Health Expert Gets Political."

19. Ibid.

20. See, e.g., Laura Tyson, "Why We Need a Second Stimulus," *New York Times*, August 28, 2010; available at www.nytimes.com/2010/08/29/opinion/29tyson.html.

21. Aide to Larry Summers, interview with the author, April 11, 2011.

22. White House colleague of Larry Summers, interview with the author, May 18, 2011.

23. White House economic aide, interview with the author, June 13, 2011.

24. A somewhat different account was originally reported by Alexis Simendinger, "Summers's Ego Massage," *National Journal*, March 26, 2010; available at www.nationaljournal.com/njonline/wh_20100326_8839.php.

25. Aide to Larry Summers, interview with the author, June 3, 2011.

26. Bob Woodward, "McChrystal: More Forces or 'Mission Failure,'" *Washington Post*, September 21, 2009; available at www.washingtonpost.com/wp-dyn/content/article/2009/09/20/AR2009092002920.html.

27. Senator Barack Obama, interview with the author, November 19, 2007. Transcript available at www.tnr.com/article/politics/barack-obama-the-interview.

CHAPTER 11: THE ROGUE

1. Treasury official, interview with the author, January 3, 2011.

2. Transition colleague of Tim Geithner, interview with the author, February 18, 2010.

3. See Christine Harper, Matthew Leising, and Shannon Harrington, "Wall Street Stealth Lobby Defends $35 Billion Derivatives Haul," Bloomberg News, August 30, 2009; available at www.bloomberg.com/apps/news?pid=newsarchive&sid=agFM_w6e2i00.

4. Much of this material comes from the discussion of derivatives in Noam Scheiber/The Editors, "Derivative Thinking," *The New Republic*, April 7, 2010; available at www.tnr.com/print/article/politics/derivative-thinking.

5. Ibid.

6. Noam Scheiber, "The Breakup," *The New Republic*, June 17, 2010; available at www.tnr.com/print/article/economy/75614/the-breakup.

7. See Scheiber/The Editors, "Derivative Thinking."

8. Manmohan Singh, "Collateral, Netting and Systemic Risk in the OTC Derivatives Market," IMF Working Paper 10/99; available at www.imf.org/external/pubs/ft/wp/2010/wp1099.pdf.

9. Scheiber, "The Breakup."

10. One of the lobbyists involved, interviews with the author, May 17, 2010; June 15, 2010; and August 1, 2011.

11. The *New York Times* was the first to report on the derivative dealers' plans. See Gretchen Morgenson and Don Van Natta, Jr., "Even in Crisis, Banks Dig in for Fight Against Rules," *New York Times,* June 1, 2009; available at www.nytimes.com/2009/06/01/business/01lobby.html?hp=&pagewanted=print.

12. Lobbyist who attended Roosevelt Room meeting at White House in May 2009, interview with the author, July 14, 2010.

13. Damian Paletta and David Enrich, "FDIC Pushes Purge at Citi," *Wall Street Journal*, June 5, 2009; available at http://online.wsj.com/article/SB124417114172687983.html#mod=todays_us_page_one.

14. Joe Nocera, "Sheila Bair's Bank Shot," *New York Times Magazine*, July 10, 2011; available at www.nytimes.com/2011/07/10/magazine/sheila-bairs-exit-interview.html?_r=1&pagewanted=print. See also Sorkin, *Too Big to Fail.* For "$45 billion piggy bank," Federal Deposit Insurance Corporation, "Chief Financial Officer's Report to the Board," December 15, 2008; available at www.fdic.gov/about/strategic/corporate/cfo_report_3rdqtr_08/balance.html.

15. Paletta and Enrich, "FDIC Pushes Purge at Citi."

16. Nocera, "Sheila Bair's Bank Shot."

17. Department of the Treasury, "Financial Reglatory Reform: A New Foundation," June 17, 2009; available at www.treasury.gov/initiatives/Documents/FinalReport_web.pdf.

18. The first to break this story were Damien Paletta and Deborah Solomon, "Geithner Vents at Regulators as Overhaul Stumbles," *Wall Street Journal*, August 4, 2009; available at online.wsj.com/article/SB124934399007303077.html#mod=todays_us_page_one.

19. See David Wessel, *In Fed We Trust: Ben Bernanke's War on the Great Panic* (New York: Crown Business, 2010).

20. Blustein, *The Chastening*, p. 323.

21. Noam Scheiber, "Beating the Street," *The New Republic*, May 5, 2010; available at www.tnr.com/print/article/politics/beating-the-street.

22. Ibid.

23. Industry lobbyist, interview with the author, July 14, 2011.

24. Manuel Roig-Franzia, "Credit Crisis Cassandra," *Washington Post*, May 26, 2009; available at www.washingtonpost.com/wp-dyn/content/article/2009/05/25/AR2009052502108_pf.html.

25. Peter Baker, "The Mellowing of William Jefferson Clinton," *New York Times Magazine*, May 31, 2009; available at www.nytimes.com/2009/05/31/magazine/31clinton-t.html?pagewanted=print.

26. Rubin and Weisberg, *In an Uncertain World*, pp. 387, 403.

27. Ian Katz and Robert Schmidt, "Gensler Turns Back on Wall Street to Push Derivatives Overhaul," Bloomberg News, February 12, 2010; available at www.bloomberg.com/apps/news?pid=newsarchive&sid=a3OkrdITAZtA. See also: Gary Baer and Gary Gensler, *The Great Mutual Fund Trap: An Investment Recovery Plan* (New York: Broadway Books, 2002).

28. Gary Gensler, "Nomination Hearing to Consider Gary Gensler to Be Chairman of the CFTC," Committee on Agriculture, Nutrition, and Forestry, U.S. Senate, February 25, 2009. Transcript available at www.gpo.gov/fdsys/pkg/CHRG-111shrg54564/html/CHRG-111shrg54564.htm.

29. Scheiber, "Beating the Street."

30. Congressional staffer involved in financial reform, interview with the author, July 28, 2011.

31. Scheiber, "The Breakup."

32. This quote first appeared ibid.

33. Ibid.

34. Congressional staffer involved in financial reform, interview with the author, July 28, 2011.

35. Scheiber, "Beating the Street."

36. Ibid.

37. Ibid.

38. CFTC chairman Gary Gensler, letter to senators Tom Harkin and Saxby Chambliss, August 17, 2009. Letter available at www.scribd.com/doc/18972469/081709-Gensler-Senate-Letter.

39. Scheiber, "Beating the Street."

40. Industry lobbyist, interview with the author, July 22, 2011.

41. CFTC chairman Gary Gensler, Testimony before the House Committee on Financial Services, October 7, 2009. Transcript available at www.cftc.gov/PressRoom/SpeechesTestimony/opagensler-13.

42. Michael Scherer, "An Ex-Goldman Man Goes After Derivatives," *Time* magazine, April 22, 2010; available at www.time.com/time/magazine/article/0,9171,1983877,00.html#ixzz1atZF51Gy.

43. Remarks of CFTC chairman Gary Gensler before the Consumer Federation of America Financial Services Conference, December 3, 2009. Transcript available at www.cftc.gov/PressRoom/SpeechesTestimony/opagensler-22.

44. Katz and Schmidt, "Gensler Turns Back on Wall Street to Push Derivatives Overhaul."

45. Michael Kranish and Alan Wirzbicki, "Financial Bill Under Attack over Loopholes," *Boston Globe*, October 31, 2009; available at www.boston.com/news/nation/articles/2009/10/31/financial_bill_under_attack_over_loopholes/.

46. Treasury Secretary Tim Geithner, Testimony before the Committee on Agriculture, Forestry, and Nutrition, U.S. Senate, December 2, 2009. Transcript available at www.gpo.gov/fdsys/pkg/CHRG-111shrg62722/html/CHRG-111shrg62722.htm.

CHAPTER 12: A CASE OF CLIENTITIS

1. Scheiber, "Sachs Appeal."

2. Noam Scheiber, "Goodbye to Berlin," *The New Republic*, August 30, 2010; available at www.tnr.com/print/article/politics/magazine76973/america-germany-global-finance-conflict.

3. Scheiber, "The Chief."

4. Treasury colleague of Tim Geithner, interview with the author, January 19, 2010.

5. Scheiber, "The Escape Artist."

6. Ibid.

7. Ibid.

8. Obama administration official, interview with the author, January 19, 2011.

9. Quote and details originally appeared in Scheiber, "The Escape Artist."

10. Ibid.

11. Fellow expat who knew the Geithner family, interview with the author, March 30, 2011.

12. Ford Foundation colleague of Peter Geithner, interview with the author, November 14, 2010.

13. Treasury Secretary Tim Geithner, interview with the author, January 5, 2011.

14. Noam Scheiber, "Peking Over Our Shoulder," *The New Republic*, September 15, 2009; available at www.tnr.com/print/article/economy/peking-over-our-shoulder.

15. Quote and details originally appeared ibid.

16. Justin Rudelson, interview with the author, August 11, 2009.

17. Scheiber, "Peking Over Our Shoulder."

18. Brewer Stone, interview with the author, October 26, 2010.

19. Bob Fauver, interview with the author, January 14, 2011.

20. Friend of Tim Geithner, interview with the author, January, 2011.

21. Scheiber, "The Escape Artist."

22. Ambassador Mike Armacost, interview with the author, December 14, 2010.

23. American expatriate in Japan who knew Geithner, interview with the author, January 18, 2011.

24. The best source for the sociology of the Treasury Department during this time is Joshua Green, "Inside Man," *Atlantic Monthly* (April 2010); available at www.theatlantic.com/magazine/archive/2010/04/inside-man/7992/?single_page=true.

25. Former Geithner colleague at Treasury from early 1990s, interview with the author, October 21, 2010.

26. Jack Wadsworth, interview with the author, August 23, 2010.

27. Robin Radin, interview with the author, October 12, 2010.

28. Former Geithner colleague at Treasury from early 1990s, interview with the author, October 21, 2010.

29. Blustein, *The Chastening*, pp. 172, 269, 273.

30. Remarks by IMF First Deputy Managing Director Anne Krueger before the American Enterprise Institute, Washington, DC, November 26, 2001.

31. Joseph Kahn, "Plan to Let Nations Declare Bankruptcy Gains," *New York Times*, December 25, 2001; available at www.nytimes.com/2001/12/25/world/plan-to-let-nations-declare-bankruptcy-gains.html. See also Blustein, *The Chastening*, p. 387.

32. IMF colleague of Tim Geithner, e-mail to the author, January 26, 2011.

33. Ibid.

34. Scheiber, "Obama's Choice," *The New Republic*, November 19, 2008.

35. Pete Peterson, interview with the author, November 4, 2008.

36. Jo Becker and Gretchen Morgenson, "Geithner, Member and Overseer of Finance Club," *New York Times*, April 26, 2009; available at www.nytimes.com/2009/04/27/business/27geithner.html.

37. Tim Geithner, interview by author, November 17, 2011.

38. The three news paragraphs that follow are based on Sorkin, *Too Big to Fail*, pp. 192–94, 364, 379–80, 391–92, and 401–2.

39. Becker and Morgenson, "Geithner, Member and Overseer of Finance Club."

40. AIG press release, "AIG Discloses Counterparties to CDS, GIA, and Securities Lending Transactions," March 15, 2009. Disclosure avail-

able at documents.nytimes.com/aig-bailout-disclosed-counterparties #p=1.

41. See, for example, Richard Teitelbaum and Hugh Son, "New York Fed's Secret Choice to Pay for Swaps Hits Taxpayers," October 27, 2009; available at www.bloomberg.com/apps/news?pid=newsarchive&sid=a 7T5HaOgYHpE.

42. The New York Fed downgraded its assessment of Citigroup's risk management practices in April 2008, and in May and June of that year it reached a series of agreements requiring Citi to remedy the problems. See Financial Crisis Inquiry Commission, "Financial Crisis Inquiry Report," January 2011; available at www.gpo.gov/fdsys/pkg/ GPO-FCIC/pdf/GPO-FCIC.pdf.

43. "Federal Reserve Bank of New York, "Summary of Supervisory Activity and Findings," April 15, 2008; available at www.scribd.com/ doc/49503609/NY-Fed-Citi-Annual-Report-of-Inspection-for-2007 -April-15-2008.

44. Administration economic official, interview with author, November 11, 2011.

45. Tim Geithner, "Remarks Before the Conference on Systemic Financial Crises at the Federal Reserve Bank of Chicago," October 1, 2004; available at www.ny.frb.org/newsevents/speeches_archive/2004/gei041001.html.

46. New York Fed official, interview with the author, April 12, 2011.

47. See Gillian Tett, *Fool's Gold: The Inside Story of J.P. Morgan and How Wall St. Greed Corrupted Its Bold Dream and Created a Financial Catastrophe* (New York: Free Press, 2010), pp. 158–59, 229. See also Green, "Inside Man."

48. New York Fed official, interview with the author, April 12, 2011.

49. The first to make this point was Joshua Green in "Inside Man."

CHAPTER 13: THE SURRENDER

1. Remarks by Paul Volcker to the Economic Club of New York, April 8, 2008. Transcript available at http://online.wsj.com/public/resources/ documents/volckerspeech040808.PDF.

2. Remarks by Paul Volcker at the Stanford Institute for Economic Policy Research, Palo Alto, California, February 2005. Video available at http://video.google.com/videoplay?docid=7139127094550001840.

3. Remarks by Stanley Fischer at the 33rd Annual Symposium of the Federal Reserve Bank of Kansas City, Jackson Hole, Wyoming, August

21, 2009. Transcript available at www.maths-fi.com/jackson-hole -symposium-2009/preparing-for-future-crisis-081809.pdf.

4. Obama economic official present at the meeting with Geithner and Volcker, interview with the author, February 3, 2011.

5. Scheiber, "The Escape Artist."

6. See the original discussion of this in Scheiber, "The Breakup," June 17, 2010.

7. Remarks by President Barack Obama on Financial Reform, Diplomatic Reception Room, White House, Washington, DC, January 21, 2010. Transcript available at www.whitehouse.gov/the-press-office/ remarks-president-financial-reform.

8. Remarks by Treasury Secretary Timothy Geithner before the American Enterprise Institute, Washington, DC, March 22, 2010. Transcript available at www.treasury.gov/press-center/press-releases/Pages/tg600.aspx.

9. Noam Scheiber, "Regulators, Mount Up," *The New Republic*, March 26, 2010; available at www.tnr.com/print/article/politics/regulators -mount.

10. Scheiber, "Beating the Street."

11. Quote originally appeared in Noam Scheiber, "Street Fight," *The New Republic*, April 4, 2010; available at www.tnr.com/print/article/ politics/street-fight.

12. Scheiber, "Beating the Street."

13. Statement from President Barack Obama on financial reform, White House, Washington, DC, March 15, 2010; available at www .whitehouse.gov/the-press-office/statement-president-financial-reform.

14. Dawn Kopecki and Shannon D. Harrington, "Banning 'Naked' Default Swaps May Raise Corporate Funding Costs," Bloomberg News, July 24, 2009; available at www.bloomberg.com/apps/news?pid=news archive&sid=a0W1VTiv9q2A.

15. Scheiber, "Beating the Street."

16. Treasury Secretary Timothy Geithner, letter to Senator Blanche Lincoln, April 15, 2010. Letter available at http://online.wsj.com/public/ resources/documents/geithner_letter041610.pdf.

17. Delvin Barrett and Damian Paletta, "A Fight to the Wire as Pro-Business Democrats Dig In on Derivatives," *Wall Street Journal*, June 26, 2010; available at http://online.wsj.com/article/SB1000142405274 87045692045753292222524350534.html?mod=ITP_pageone_2.

18. Senate aide involved in the Volcker Rule, interview with the author, June 1, 2010.

19. Tim Geithner, interview with the author, November 17, 2011.

20. Ted Kaufman, interview with the author, July 13, 2011.

21. Remarks by Senator Ted Kaufman, U.S. Senate, March 11, 2010; no transcript available online.

22. Remarks by Andrew Haldane before the Institute of Regulation and Risk, Hong Kong, March 30, 2010. Transcript available at www .bankofengland.co.uk/publications/speeches/2010/speech433.pdf.

23. Ibid.

24. Peter Boone and Simon Johnson, "Way Too Big to Fail," *The New Republic*, November 7, 2010; available at www.tnr.com/article/economy/ magazine/78563/way-too-big-fail. See also Kaufman remarks, March 11, 2010, and remarks by Senator Ted Kaufman, U.S. Senate, July 15, 2010. Transcript available at www.huffingtonpost.com/sen-ted -kaufman/the-wall-street-reform-bi_b_647720.html?view=print.

25. The most comprehensive discussion of the political power of large banks appears in James Kwak and Simon Johnson, *Thirteen Bankers: The Wall Street Takeover and the Next Financial Meltdown* (New York: Vintage, 2010). See also Noam Scheiber, "Can We Fix the Banks Without Shrinkage?" *The New Republic*, October 28, 2009; available at www.tnr.com/print/blog/the-stash/can-we-fix-too-big-fail-with out-shrinkage.

26. John Heilemann, "Obama Is from Mars, Wall Street Is from Venus," *New York*, May 22, 2010; available at http://nymag.com/news/ politics/66188/.

27. Rich Miller, "Wall Street Fix Seen Ineffectual by Four of Five in U.S.," Bloomberg News, July 13, 2010; available at www.bloomberg .com/news/2010-07-13/wall-street-fix-from-congress-seen-ineffectual -by-four-out-of-five-in-u-s-.html.

28. Geithner's discussion of these ideas was originally reported in Scheiber, "The Escape Artist."

29. Discussion and quotes originally reported ibid.

CHAPTER 14: UNDERWATER

1. Warren Buffett, "Dividend Voodoo," *The Washington Post*, May 20, 2003; available at www.washingtonpost.com/ac2/wp-dyn/A13113-2003 May19?language=printer.

2. The 2003 tax cuts were originally scheduled to expire in 2008. In 2005, Congress extended them two more years, so that they would expire in 2010.

3. The quote originally appeared in Noam Scheiber, "Loose Change," *The New Republic*, December 8, 2010.

4. See Scheiber, "The Escape Artist."

5. Scheiber, "Loose Change."

6. Treasury official, interview with the author, September 15, 2011.

7. Ibid.

8. For details of the proposal, see Jonathan Weisman and John D. McKinnon, "Obama to Push Tax Break," *Wall Street Journal*, September 6, 2010; available at http://online.wsj.com/article/SB10001424052748 70439210457547592086869934.html.

9. The same treasury official, interview with the author, September 15, 2011.

10. Department of the Treasury with the Council of Economic Advisers, "An Economic Analysis of Infrastructure Investment," October 11, 2010. Report available at www.treasury.gov/resource-center/economic-policy/Documents/infrastructure_investment_report.pdf.

11. U.S. Department of Treasury's Office of Tax Policy, "The Case for Temporary 100 Percent Expensing: Encouraging Business to Expand by Lowering the Cost of Investment," October 29, 2010. Report available at www.whitehouse.gov/sites/default/files/expensing_report.pdf.

12. U.S. Department of Treasury's Office of Tax Policy, "Investing in U.S. Competitiveness: The Benefits of Enhancing the Research and Experimentation (R&E) Tax Credit," March 25, 2011. Report available at www.treasury.gov/resource-center/tax-policy/Documents/Research%20and%20Experimentation%20report%20FINAL.PDF.

13. For a lucid discussion of the options facing the administration on housing, see David Leonhardt, "Bailout Likely to Focus on Most Afflicted Homeowners," *New York Times*, February 17, 2009; available at www.nytimes.com/2009/02/18/business/economy/18leonhardt.html. See also David Leonhardt, "Obama's Housing Plan: Who Will It Benefit?" *New York Times*, February 18, 2009; available at http://economix.blogs.nytimes.com/2009/02/18/OBAMAS-HOUSING-PLAN-WHO-WILL-BENEFIT/?PAGEMODE=PRINT.

14. Acting Comptroller of the United States Gene L. Dodaro, Testimony before the Committee on Oversight and Government Reform, U.S. House of Representatives, March 25, 2010. Testimony available at www.gao.gov/new.items/d10556t.pdf.

15. Comptroller of the Currency and Administrator of National Banks, "OCC Mortgage Metrics Report, Second Quarter 2011," September

2011; available at www.occ.treas.gov/publications/publications-by
-type/other-publications-reports/mortgage-metrics-q2-2011/mortgage
-metrics-q2-2011.pdf.

16. White House economist, interview with the author, March 1, 2011.

17. Richard Koo, *The Holy Grail of Macroeconomics: Lessons from Japan's Great Recession* (Hoboken, NJ: Wiley, 2009).

18. For a distillation of Koo's book, see Noam Scheiber, "Handoff or Fumble," *The New Republic*, October 20, 2010; available at www.tnr.com/article/politics/78515/could-shopping-save-the-country?page=0,0.

19. Ibid.

20. See Reuven Glick and Kevin J. Lansing, "U.S. Household Deleveraging and Future Consumption Growth," Federal Reserve Bank of San Francisco Economic Letter, May 15, 2009. Paper available at www.frbsf.org/publications/economics/letter/2009/el2009-16.html.

21. See Scheiber, "Handoff or Fumble."

22. Carmen M. Reinhart and Kenneth S. Rogoff, *This Time Is Different: Eight Centuries of Financial Folly* (Princeton, NJ: Princeton University Press, 2011).

23. Noam Scheiber, "Desperate Measures," *The New Republic*, October 29, 2010; available at www.tnr.com/article/economy/78762/desperate-obama-economy-republican-congress.

24. Zachary A. Goldfarb, "Obama's Efforts to Aid Homeowners, Boost Housing Market Fall Far Short of Goals," *Washington Post*, October 23, 2011; available at www.washingtonpost.com/business/economy/obamas-efforts-to-aid-homeowners-boost-housing-market-fall-far-short-of-goals/2011/09/22/glQAoJdeAM_print.html.

25. Participant in the White House conclave with liberal groups, interview with the author, December 3, 2010.

26. Ibid. This quote originally appeared in Scheiber, "Loose Change."

27. President Barack Obama, press conference, November 3, 2010. Transcript available at www.whitehouse.gov/blog/2010/11/03/president-obama-s-press-conference-lets-find-those-areas-where-we-can-agree.

28. White House colleague of Christina Romer, interview with the author, May 8, 2011.

29. See Scheiber, "The Escape Artist."

30. Scheiber, "Loose Change."

31. Top White House aide, interview with the author, September 3, 2011.

CHAPTER 15: SNOOKERED

1. Obama administration colleague of Bill Daley, interview with the author, September 28, 2011.
2. Obama administration official, interview with the author, September 28, 2011.
3. Obama economic official, interview with the author, August 10, 2011.
4. Ibid.
5. White House economic aide, interview with the author, July 29, 2011.
6. White House official, interview with the author, October 4, 2011.
7. White House aide, interview with the author, October 4, 2011.
8. White House official, interview with the author, October 24, 2011.
9. Carol Lee, "Key Obama Aide Relinquishes Some Duties," *Wall Street Journal*, November 8, 2011; available at http://online.wsj.com/article/SB10001424052970203733504577024443125874140.html.
10. Obama administration official, interview with the author, September 28, 2011.
11. For exit polls on the 1996 New Jersey Senate race, see "The Vote '96," AllPolitics, CNN-Time, November 6, 1996; available at www.cnn.com/ELECTION/NJSxp.html.
12. Regena Thomas, interview with the author, April 2008.
13. Obama campaign colleague of David Plouffe, interview with the author, September 13, 2010.
14. For a more detailed explanation of the behavior of independent voters, see Ruy Teixeira, "Obama's Unhealthy Obsession with Independents," *The New Republic*, August 2, 2011; available at www.tnr.com/article/politics/93041/obama-independent-voters. See also John B. Judis, "Trouble Ahead," *The New Republic*, April 22, 2011; available at www.tnr.com/print/article/john-judis/87202/obama-economy-unemployment-budget-paul-ryan. And John B. Judis, "You've Got Them All Wrong, Mr. President," *The New Republic*, November 18, 2010; available at www.tnr.com/print/article/politics/79246/independent-voters-barack-obama-midterms.
15. John Sides, "Do Democrats Understand Political Independents?" The Monkey Cage blog, Campaigns and Elections, November 16, 2010; available at http://themonkeycage.org/blog/2010/11/16/do_democrats_understand_politi/.
16. For evidence of this, see Pew Research Center, "Independents Oppose Party in Power . . . Again," September 23, 2010. Report avail-

able at www.people-press.org/2010/09/23/independents-oppose-party
-in-power-again/.

17. CBS News, "CBS News Poll, 11/11/10," published November 16, 2010;
results available at www.cbsnews.com/stories/2010/11/11/politics/
main7045964.shtml.

18. Participant in 2011 budget negotiations, interview with the author,
October 18, 2011.

19. Treasury Secretary Tim Geithner, interview with the author, August 8,
2011.

20. First reported in Carl Hulse, "Budget Impasse Increasing Risk of U.S.
Shutdown," *New York Times*, March 25, 2011; available at www
.nytimes.com/2011/03/26/us/politics/26fiscal.html?_r=1&ref=todays
paper&pagewanted=print.

21. White House aide, interview with the author, October 4, 2011.

22. Paul Kane, Philip Rucker, and David A. Fahrenthold, "Government
Shutdown Averted: Congress Agrees to Budget Deal, Stopgap Funding,"
Washington Post, April 8, 2011; available at www.washingtonpost
.com/politics/reid-says-impasse-based-on-abortion-funding-boehner
-denies-it/2011/04/08/AFO40U1C_story.html.

23. President Barack Obama, "Statement on the Bipartisan Agreement
on the Budget," April 9, 2011; available at www.whitehouse.gov/
blog/2011/04/09/president-obamas-statement-bipartisan-agreement
-budget.

24. Former Obama administration official, interview with the author, September 14, 2011.

25. White House colleague of David Plouffe, interview with the author,
September 3, 2011.

26. White House aide, interview with the author, October 4, 2011.

27. David M. Herszenhorn and Helene Cooper, "Concessions and Tension,
Then a Deal," *New York Times*, April 9, 2011; available at www.nytimes
.com/2011/04/10/us/politics/10reconstruct.html?pagewanted=all.

28. Representative Jim Jordan on 2011 budget deal, April 12, 2011. Statement available at http://blogs.wsj.com/washwire/2011/04/12/head-of
-conservative-caucus-opposes-budget-deal/.

CHAPTER 16: THE WRONG WAR

1. The White House, Office of the Press Secretary, "Fact Sheet: The
President's Framework for Shared Prosperity and Shared Fiscal Re-

sponsibility," April 13, 2011; available at www.whitehouse.gov/the-press-office/2011/04/13/fact-sheet-presidents-framework-shared-prosperity-and-shared-fiscal-resp.

2. See, e.g., Henry J. Aaron, "It's Taxes, Stupid!" *Kaiser Health News*, October 12, 2011; www.brookings.edu/opinions/2011/1012_taxes_health_costs_aaron.aspx.

3. Joseph Stiglitz interviewed in Ari Berman, "How the Austerity Class Rules Washington," *The Nation*, October 19, 2011; available at www.thenation.com/print/article/164073/how-austerity-class-rules-washington.

4. Kara Brandeisky, "How Clinton Handled His Debt Ceiling Crisis Better Than Obama," *The New Republic*, August 2, 2011; available at www.tnr.com/print/article/politics/93043/obama-clinton-debt-ceiling-crisis.

5. Treasury aide, interview with the author, September 28, 2011.

6. White House aide, interview with the author, October 4, 2011.

7. Treasury aide, interview with the author, September 28, 2011.

8. Second Treasury official, interview with the author, November 3, 2011.

9. White House official, interview with the author, October 26, 2011.

10. Damian Paletta and Carol E. Lee, "President Open to Deal on Debt Cap," *Wall Street Journal*, April 12, 2011. Available at http://online.wsj.com/article/SB10001424052748703841904576257263426340504.html.

11. White House economic aide, interview with the author, September 3, 2011.

12. Remarks by President Barack Obama at the George Washington University, Washington, DC, April 13, 2011. Transcript available at http://blogs.wsj.com/washwire/2011/04/13/text-of-obama-speech-on-the-deficit/.

13. White House colleague of Biden, Lew, Sperling, and Reed, interview with the author, September 29, 2011.

14. Former Citigroup colleague of Jack Lew, interview with the author, April 12, 2011.

15. Clinton White House veteran working in Obama White House, interview with the author, October 26, 2011.

16. Ibid.

17. For a good, pithy explanation of how the 1997 budget deal was a mirage, see Jonathan Chait, "The Balanced Budget Scam," *The New Republic*, August 31, 2011; available at www.tnr.com/blog/jonathan-chait/94371/the-balanced-budget-scam.

18. White House official, interview with the author, October 24, 2011.

19. Ibid.

20. Person in the room for Biden-Cantor talks, interview with the author, October 21, 2011.

21. White House official, interview with the author, October 24, 2011.

22. White House official, interview with the author, October 26, 2011.

23. Person in the room for Biden-Cantor talks, interview with the author, October 26, 2011.

24. Person involved in Biden-Cantor talks, interview with the author, October 21, 2011.

25. Jonathan Chait made this point repeatedly during the negotiations. See, e.g., "Obama Negotiates with Self, Loses," *The New Republic*, April 15, 2011; available at www.tnr.com/blog/jonathan-chait/86883/obama-negotiates-self-loses.

26. Remarks by President Barack Obama in the East Room of the White House, Washington, DC, July 25, 2011.

27. Jaime Guajardo, Daniel Leigh, and Andrea Pescatori, "Expansionary Austerity: New International Evidence," IMF Working Paper WP/11/158. Paper available at www.imf.org/external/pubs/ft/wp/2011/wp11158.pdf.

28. Paul Krugman, "The Downgrade Doom Loop," *New York Times*, August 8, 2011. Article available at http://krugman.blogs.nytimes.com/2011/08/08/the-downgrade-doom-loop/.

EPILOGUE

1. White House aide, interview with the author, October 24, 2011.

2. President Barack Obama, Remarks Before a Joint Session of Congress, September 8, 2011; available at www.whitehouse.gov/the-press-office/2011/09/08/address-president-joint-session-congress.

3. Jake Sherman and Carrie Budoff Brown, "Obama Stays Away from Deficit Panel," *Politico*, November 2, 2011; available at http://dyn.politico.com/printstory.cfm?uuid=728C1C16-B150-454A-AA0B-EC196F52A248.

4. Washington Post–ABC News poll, conducted October 31 through November 1, 2011; available at www.washingtonpost.com/wp-srv/politics/polls/postabcpoll_110311.html.

5. Carol E. Lee and Janet Hook, "GOP Balks at Taxes to Finance Jobs Plan," *Wall Street Journal*, September 13, 2011; available at http://online.wsj.com/article/SB10001424053111904353504576566802250477510.html?mod=WSJ_hp_LEFTTopStories#printMode.

6. White House official, interview with the author, October 24, 2011.

7. Ibid.

8. Clinton veteran who worked in Obama administration, interview with the author, March 15, 2011.

9. Alan S. Blinder and Mark Zandi, "How the Great Recession Was Brought to an End," July 27, 2010; available at www.economy.com/mark-zandi/documents/End-of-Great-Recession.pdf. See also Executive Office of the President Council of Economic Advisers, "The Economic Impact of the American Recovery and Reinvestment Act of 2009, Seventh Quarterly Report," July 1, 2011; available at www.whitehouse.gov/sites/default/files/cea_7th_arra_report.pdf.

10. President Barack Obama, Remarks to General Motors Plant Employees at Lordstown Assembly Plant, Warren, Ohio, September 15, 2009; available at www.whitehouse.gov/the-press-office/remarks-president-gm-lordstown-assembly-plant-employees-ohio-9152009.

11. Peter Orszag, interview with the author, August 10, 2011.

INDEX